The Social Worker's Guide to Children and Families Law

The Social Worker's Guide
to Children and
Families Law

Lynn Davis

Jessica Kingsley *Publishers*
London and Philadelphia

First published in 2009 by Jessica Kingsley Publishers

This second edition first published in 2014
by Jessica Kingsley Publishers
73 Collier Street
London N1 9BE, UK
and
400 Market Street, Suite 400
Philadelphia, PA 19106, USA

www.jkp.com

Library of Congress Cataloging in Publication Data
Davis, Lynn, 1962- author.
The social worker's guide to children and families law / Lynn Davis. -- Second Edition.
pages cm
Includes bibliographical references and index.
ISBN 978-1-84905-440-9
1. Children--Legal status, laws, etc.--England. 2. Parent and child (Law)--England. 3. Social workers--
England--Handbooks, manuals, etc. I. Title.
KD3305.D38 2014
346.4201'5--dc23

2013047020

British Library Cataloguing in Publication Data
A CIP catalogue record for this book is available from the British Library

ISBN 978 1 84905 440 9
eISBN 978 0 85700 814 5

Printed and bound in Great Britain

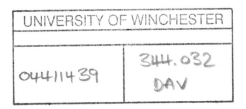
Contents

Part 5 Care Proceedings

Acknowledgements

I am grateful to my colleagues, clients, child care lawyers, social workers and foster carers for all they have taught me over the years.

I am indebted to my editor Steve Jones and the staff at Jessica Kingsley Publishers for their help in guiding me through the publishing process.

Thanks go to Mum, Mark and the pack for their support and encouragement.

This book is dedicated to my friends, especially Michelle, who actually reads my books!

Preface

This book is the product of my experience as a child care lawyer and trainer specialising in child care law since before the implementation of the Children Act 1989.

As for the first edition of this book, my aim is to make the essential principles of the law accessible and practical and I hope the book will be useful.

No book can be a substitute for legal advice on a particular case, but I hope that it will give readers an understanding of key legal issues and help them to ask their lawyers the right questions.

This second edition has been thoroughly revised to take account of many significant developments since the first edition and it is up to date as of April 2014. Law and practice in this area is evolving fast, so please be alert to the possibility of more changes since publication.

To avoid repetition of 'he/she' I have chosen one gender or the other throughout.

The book discusses the law of England and Wales. At times I have referred simply to English law, but intend no disrespect to Welsh colleagues.

Any opinions expressed are entirely my own, and I take full responsibility for, and apologise for, any mistakes.

Introduction

We live in interesting times. There is a momentum for change, with reform of the family court system, streamlining of child protection procedures, increased court focus on human rights and a government drive to reduce delay in children's cases and promote adoption, all in a challenging economic climate.

There is also a change in attitudes towards the social work profession. It is a moment of opportunity for social workers to step forward and claim their rightful role as expert professionals. For social work to become a confident, competent profession, practice must be based on sound foundations.

The law is the very bedrock of social work practice. A working knowledge of the key legal provisions is just as much a vital tool of the social worker's trade as an understanding of attachment theory or anti-discriminatory practice.

The law defines your role as a social worker. It empowers you to protect children and promote their welfare, and it defines the limits of your powers and the boundaries of your duties, striking the balance between state power and individual freedom. The law confers rights and responsibilities, powers and duties.

Embrace the law as part of your core knowledge base. Ensure that you understand the fundamental principles so you can apply them to your case work, identifying legal issues and asking the right questions.

This book aims to build your knowledge step by step, to help you to understand the key provisions and to enable you to use the law to enhance your practice.

Part 1

Fundamentals

Chapter 1

Human Rights

Why start here? Quite simply, because every aspect of the law and every action you take (or decide not to take) as a social worker is subject the Human Rights Act 1998 (HRA).[1] All the remaining chapters of the book must be read with this one in mind.

What are human rights?

There are many definitions of human rights but, for our purposes, the term 'human rights' means those contained in the European Convention on Human Rights and Fundamental Freedoms 1950 (the Convention) because those are the rights incorporated into UK law by the HRA. The Convention is not linked to the European Union, membership being much wider.[2]

The Articles

The full text of each of the Convention Articles is set out in the HRA, but they are commonly referred to by their shorthand titles. The most important are:

Article 2   Right to life

Article 3   Prohibition of torture and inhuman or degrading treatment or punishment

Article 4   Prohibition of slavery and forced labour

Article 5   Right to liberty and security of person

---

1   Human Rights Act 1998. London: Stationery Office. Available at www.legislation.gov.uk/ukpga/1998/42/contents, accessed on 30 March 2014.
2   47 countries are signatories at the time of writing.

Article 6   Right to a fair trial

Article 8   Right to respect for private and family life, home and correspondence

Article 9   Freedom of thought, conscience and religion

Article 10   Freedom of expression

Article 12   Right to marry and found a family

Article 13   Right to an effective remedy

Article 14   Freedom from discrimination in the delivery of rights under the Convention

First Protocol

Article 2   Right to education

Human rights in UK law

The HRA aims to ensure that UK law respects human rights. All new legislation must be drafted and all pre-existing law interpreted in a way which is compatible with the Convention; everything is viewed through the lens of human rights.

Courts try to make the existing law fit with the Convention; this sometimes demands some mental dexterity. For example, Article 5 guarantees the right to liberty, subject to exceptions when deprivation of liberty is justified (such as imprisoning criminals). The only exception specifically about children allows detention for 'educational supervision'. But s25 Children Act 1989 (CA89), dealing with secure accommodation, does not mention education at all – it is concerned with children who place themselves or others at serious risk. Is s25 compatible? This was considered by the Court of Appeal,[3] which focused on the word 'education'. If it just means schooling, s25 CA89 is incompatible. However, the court found that 'education' is a far broader concept, including social and emotional learning and development, and is sufficiently wide to allow s25 CA89 to fit with the HRA.

If, despite mental gymnastics and verbal contortions, a statute cannot fit with the HRA, the higher courts can declare the legislation 'incompatible'. This does not make the statute invalid; if it did, there

---

3   *Re K (A Child) (Secure Accommodation Order: Right to Liberty)* [2001] 1 FLR 256 (Court of Appeal).

would then simply be a gap in the law. Instead, it triggers an obligation to amend the law using a fast-track Parliamentary process.

Public authorities

All public authorities (including central government, the police, courts, health authorities and local authorities) have a duty not to infringe an individual's human rights.[4] Local authorities must therefore consider the human rights implications of every decision, including those taken by social workers. The HRA impacts on every aspect of your work.

Any UK court can hear human rights arguments. Someone whose human rights are breached or threatened by a public authority's actions can bring a free-standing human rights case[5] or plead human rights in a case which is primarily about something else; in care proceedings a mother might argue that a care order would breach her Article 8 right to a family life.

If rights are breached, the court can choose any remedy in its jurisdiction to suit the case, including awarding compensation or refusing an order. To prevent a breach occurring, the court can issue an injunction. This happened in a case[6] where a local authority proposed to remove a baby placed for adoption because the prospective adopter had gone blind following an emergency brain operation just after the baby was placed. The High Court found a breach of the prospective adopter's rights to a family life and to a fair procedure. It made an injunction to stop the baby being removed, allowing a properly considered decision to be made; fortunately so, given that ultimately, following further assessments and glowing reports, an adoption order was made with the local authority's support.[7]

When all domestic remedies are exhausted, there may be a further appeal to the European Court of Human Rights (ECtHR) in Strasbourg. The supervision of government action by a supra-national court can sometimes give rise to political antagonism but is an important safeguard.

---

4   s6 HRA.
5   s7 HRA.
6   *RCW* v. *A Local Authority* [2013] EWHC 235 (Fam) (High Court).
7   *RCW* v. *A Local Authority* [2013] EWHC 2129 (Fam) (High Court).

Human rights breaches by individuals

The HRA only protects against actions by public authorities, not individuals. However, sometimes authorities can in effect be held responsible for the actions of individuals. For example, in *A* v. *UK*,[8] a boy was beaten with a cane by his stepfather who was prosecuted but acquitted on the defence of 'reasonable chastisement'.[9] The ECtHR found that the UK system had failed the child. The court said that States must:

> ... take measures designed to ensure that individuals within their jurisdiction are not subjected to torture or inhuman or degrading treatment or punishment, including such ill-treatment administered by private individuals. Children and other vulnerable individuals, in particular, are entitled to State protection in the form of effective deterrence against such serious breaches of personal integrity.[10]

There are obvious and significant implications for child protection authorities. The abuser may be an individual, but a public authority has a positive duty to step in and protect. If it fails to do so, it is the public authority which is responsible for the breach of the child's human rights. This should be in the forefront of your mind in all child protection cases.

Understanding human rights – The 'living instrument'

To interpret human rights, we look to case law from the ECtHR as well as our own courts. The Convention is known as a 'living instrument'. Its meaning is not set in stone; instead its interpretation can vary over time to reflect society's changing understanding. *A* v. *UK* (above) is a case in point. When the Convention was drafted in 1950, beating children with canes was widely accepted, but by the time A's case came to court in 1998 it was adjudged to constitute 'torture or inhuman or degrading treatment or punishment'.

So the ECtHR can consider the same issue at different times and give different answers. In 1998 the ECtHR decided[11] that UK law did not breach a transsexual person's rights by refusing to recognise her

---

8   *A* v. *UK* [1998] ECHR 85 ECtHR case no. 100/1997/884/1096.
9   A defence which has since been abolished.
10 *A* v. *UK* [1998] ECHR 85 at paragraph 22.
11 *Sheffield and Horsham* v. *UK* [1998] 2FLR 928 ECtHR case no. 31 1332/1997/815 13816/1018 131019 at paragraph 90.

post-operative gender because each signatory State had the right to decide for itself.[12] Just four years later the ECtHR[13] declared that 'the right of transsexuals to personal development and to physical and moral security in the full sense enjoyed by others in society cannot be regarded as a matter of controversy' and that 'the very essence of the Convention was respect for human dignity and human freedom'. So transsexual people have the right to be recognised and be allowed to marry in their post-operative gender. The House of Lords then declared UK law to be incompatible and this in turn led to the Gender Recognition Act 2004.[14]

An issue undergoing the same process at the time of writing is the question of same sex marriage. In *Schalk* v. *Austria*[15] the ECtHR did not uphold a right to same sex marriage, saying each State must decide for itself. However, it noted in its judgment[16] that it could 'no longer consider that the right to marry enshrined in [the Convention] must in all circumstances be limited to marriage between two persons of the opposite sex', clearly signalling that this is an area of evolving rights. The UK took the step of allowing same sex marriage in the Marriage (Same Sex Couples) Act 2013.[17]

A system that is not set in stone but can move with the times may seem attractive but it can be unsettling to live on shifting sands, not knowing whether an answer will be the same from one year to the next. Arguably the law should set standards, not follow society's whims. What happens if the prevailing mood moves in an unsavoury direction – should the courts reflect society's views in their decisions? How do judges determine what the prevailing view is? In practical terms, however, it is simply important to remember that Convention jurisprudence is flexible and can move on.

---

12 This is an application of the doctrine of the 'margin of appreciation' which strikes a balance between the particularities of national laws and cultures on the one hand and universally applicable standards of human rights on the other.

13 *Goodwin* v. *UK* [2002] 2FLR 487 ECtHR case No 28957/95 and *I* v. *UK* [2002] 2FLR 519 ECtHR case no. 25680/94.

14 Gender Recognition Act 2004. London: Stationery Office. Available at www.legislation.gov.uk/ukpga/2004/7/contents, accessed on 30 March 2014.

15 *Schalk and Kopf* v. *Austria* [2010] ECtHr case no. 301414-04.

16 *Schalk and Kopf* at paragraph 61.

17 Marriage (Same Sex Couples) Act 2013. London: Stationery Office. Available at www.legislation.gov.uk/ukpga/2013/30/contents/enacted, accessed on 30 March 2014. The first same-sex marriages took place on 29 March 2014.

Approaching a human rights case

As always with the law, it is important to look at the exact words used. A close look at the various Articles shows that they may be:

- unqualified, or
- subject to specific exceptions, or
- subject to a general qualification.

Article 3 is an unqualified right. It outlaws torture and similar behaviour, full stop. There are no exceptions.

Article 5 (right to liberty of person) is subject to specific exceptions. People can legitimately be deprived of their liberty in certain listed circumstances such as imprisonment following criminal conviction or detention for mental health reasons.

Article 8 is the most important for social workers as it deals with family life. Instead of specific exceptions, it is subject to a general qualification which may justify interference with the right.

Article 8

1. Everyone has the right to respect for his private and family life, his home and his correspondence.

2. There shall be no interference by a public authority with the exercise of this right except such as is in accordance with the law and is necessary in a democratic society in the interests of national security, public safety or the economic well-being of the country, for the prevention of disorder or crime, for the protection of health or morals, or for the protection of the rights and freedoms of others.

In practice, courts analyse cases step by step as follows:

1. Does the complaint fall within the right claimed?
2. If so, has there been an interference with that right?
3. If so, is the interference lawful?
4. What are the aims of the interference?
5. Are those aims legitimate?

6.   Are there relevant and sufficient reasons for the interference?

7.   Are those reasons proportionate to the restrictions placed on the enjoyment of the right?

The last point raises the important doctrine of 'proportionality'. Essentially, this means that the interference with someone's right may only go as far as is necessary and no further.

Case Study: Article 8 in care proceedings

Andrew, aged two, is subject to care proceedings due to neglect. Since being in foster care he has caught up physically and developmentally. His mother Bianca has a learning disability and her lawyers argue that she received inadequate support. Bianca and Andrew both enjoy contact but the local authority plans to place Andrew for adoption with no ongoing direct contact. Bianca wants Andrew home. Her lawyers argue that Article 8 is breached.

1.   *Does the complaint fall within the right claimed?*
      Yes. All care, contact and adoption cases clearly fall within Article 8.

2.   *If so, has there been or will there be an interference with that right?*
      Yes. No-one can deny that taking a child from his mother and ending contact is an interference with family life.

3.   *If so, is the interference lawful?*
      Assuming the relevant laws, court rules and procedures have been followed, the authority's actions are lawful.

4.   *What are the aims of the interference?*
      The authority's objective is to protect Andrew.

5.   *Are those aims legitimate?*
      Yes. No-one can seriously argue that the protection of vulnerable children is not a legitimate aim.

6.   *Are there relevant and sufficient reasons for the interference?*
      At this point, the parties' cases diverge. The authority must produce evidence to justify its case. Bianca's lawyers might concede that the authority's reasons are relevant, but argue that they are not sufficient.

7. *Are those reasons proportionate to the restrictions placed on the enjoyment of the right?*

Here the parties sharply disagree. The authority argues that its plans are the only way to meet Andrew's needs: nothing less will do. Bianca's lawyers argue that, even if the authority establishes some of its case, its proposals go too far. Each further step down the line restricting Andrew and Bianca's relationship requires extra justification. So, even if the case is made for a care order, termination of contact does not automatically follow – that must be justified separately. The further step of adoption (the most radical order of all) requires the clearest justification. The authority must explicitly justify every step it asks the court to take. Depending on the evidence, the court may agree that Andrew cannot return home, but find that terminating contact (let alone adoption) would be a step too far. The court will go as far as necessary but no further; interference with family life must be proportionate.

Key Articles

The most important Articles for children and families workers are 2, 3, 5, 6, 8 and 14. They should be as familiar to you as the provisions of CA89 and you should be able to use them to analyse cases and present them to court.

Article 2

This protects the right to life, applicable at the extreme end of child protection. A sad list of children have had their Article 2 rights breached by failures in the child protection system.

Article 3

This Article prohibits torture and other similar treatment. The case of the boy beaten by his stepfather (as described previously) shows that it has a broader ambit than the word 'torture' might at first imply.

Article 3 clearly applies in cases of physical abuse, but it is also possible to degrade someone or treat them inhumanly without touching them. This Article therefore goes beyond physical abuse to include physical neglect, emotional abuse and even emotional neglect.

The local authority has a positive duty to protect children and can be pursued for failure to intervene when it knew (or should have known) that a child was being abused[18] (it can also be sued for taking unjustified action). The possibility of litigation heightens the need to keep careful records at every stage, noting decisions and the reasons for them. It is also worth remembering that people have a right to see their own records[19] which should show that decisions (whether in hindsight they were good or bad) were made carefully and in good faith, trying to respect and balance everyone's rights. Decisions not to take action are just as significant as decisions to act. Court cases often take place many years after the event; if the case concerns events during the applicant's childhood, the time clock for litigation does not even start running until he is an adult. By then, no-one in the department is likely to remember his case. Everyone is dependent on the quality of the records kept at the time.

Article 5

The right to liberty is directly relevant to cases where children are placed in secure accommodation by the local authority. This right is subject to specified exceptions, all of which refer to 'lawful' detention, so if the detention does not comply with the letter of the law, it cannot be justified. For example, under CA89, a child cannot be detained in secure accommodation for more than 72 hours without court authority. If by some miscalculation a child is locked up for 73 hours before going to court, that detention is no longer lawful and is an unjustified breach of Article 5.

Children are often deprived of elements of their liberty – we decide where they live and go to school, and impose rules and restrictions on them. Is this a breach of Article 5? In a case[20] concerning restrictions placed on a young person to stop her harming herself or others, the Court of Appeal said not; an adult in the exercise of parental responsibility may impose or authorise restrictions on a child, although these must not in their totality amount to a deprivation of liberty.

---

18   *Z and Others* v. *UK* [2001] 2FLR 612 ECtHR case no. 29392/95.
19   *Gaskin* v. *UK* [1990] 1FLR 167 ECtHR case no. 10454/83.
20   *RK* v. *BCC and others* [2011] EWCA Civ 1305 (Court of Appeal).

Article 6

The 'right to a fair trial' naturally applies to court cases. Article 6 is a critical consideration in emergency provisions whereby children can be removed into police protection with no trial at all or by a court which hears only one side of the story (via an Emergency Protection Order made without notice).[21]

Fairness 'is objective and not subjective to one of the parties'.[22] It includes ensuring that everyone can understand and participate in proceedings. In one case[23] where insufficient measures were taken in care proceedings to allow a vulnerable father to participate, findings that he injured his child were set aside because his Article 6 rights were breached. At the re-trial, following a comprehensive assessment, the father was provided with an intermediary, advocates asked questions the father could understand, and the court allowed regular breaks.[24]

However, Article 6 is not limited to court cases: it applies to any procedure which determines civil rights and obligations, including decision-making processes. Properly involving and consulting people affected by local authority actions is a legal requirement, not just good practice. Decisions must be taken properly. When a local authority decided to remove a baby placed for adoption without giving the prospective adopter a chance to address its concerns, this breached Article 6.[25] Another local authority's inadequate review procedures for two boys in care and failure to take their case back to court breached their Article 6 rights.[26] The Court of Appeal has decided that the court must consider the fairness of the procedure as a whole,[27] so failure to invite parents to just one meeting did not make the whole process invalid.

Another aspect of Article 6 is the right to a fair and public hearing, but family cases are held in private. Does this breach the Convention? The ECtHR rejected this argument and decided that a State can designate a whole class of case as an exception to the general rule where

---

21 See Chapter 10 for more information on emergency procedures.
22 *Thorpe LJ in R (A Child)* [2012] EWCA Civ 1783 (Court of Appeal) at paragraph 17.
23 *Re M (A Child)* [2012] EWCA Civ 1905 (Court of Appeal).
24 *Re A (A Child)* [2013] EWHC 3502 (Fam) (High Court).
25 *RCW v. A Local Authority* [2013] EWHC 235 (Fam) (High Court); see page 14.
26 *A and S v. Lancs CC* [2012] EWHC 1689 (Fam) (High Court).
27 *Re V (Care: Pre-birth Actions)* [2004] EWCA Civ 1575 [2005] 1FLR 627 and *Re J (Care: Assessment: Fair Trial)* [2006] EWCA Civ 545 (both Court of Appeal).

necessary to protect children's privacy.[28] Nevertheless, there is a trend for increasing media access to family courts.

Article 6 also requires decisions to be made within a reasonable time – as the old legal maxim says, 'justice delayed is justice denied'.[29] Currently, determined efforts are being made to reduce delays in children's cases.

Article 8 – Privacy

The tension between confidentiality and openness in children's cases can bring into conflict the privacy element of Article 8 and the right to freedom of expression (Article 10). Each case is different and depends on its own facts.

In one case during filming for a TV programme, a young mother with a mental disorder whose child was to be placed for adoption was filmed in distressing circumstances.[30] The court weighed up her Article 8 rights against the BBC's right to freedom of expression on a subject of genuine public interest. The court found that the interest in freedom of expression did not outweigh the massive invasion of the mother's privacy and dignity.

In another case, people who had been taken into care as children in an alleged ritual abuse case wanted to publicise their stories.[31] The proposed programme would reveal the identities of social workers involved. The court weighed up the competing rights of freedom of expression against privacy, and decided the breach of the social workers' rights was proportionate and pursued the legitimate aim of informed and open media discussion of matters of public interest.

Article 8 – Family life

This element of Article 8 is engaged in every case of local authority intervention in family life. It should be second nature to consider and address Article 8 in your analysis and presentation of cases. 'Family life' is not limited to the relationship between children and parents with parental

---

28   B v. UK; P v. UK [2001] 2FLR 261 ECtHR.
29   The origin of this maxim is unclear. Suggested attributions include Gladstone and Penn.
30   T (by her Litigation Friend the OS) v. BBC [2007] EWHC 1683 (QB) (High Court).
31   BBC v. Rochdale MBC [2005] EWHC 2863 (Fam) (High Court).

responsibility. It continues beyond childhood and into adulthood and can include unmarried families (gay or straight[32]), siblings, half-siblings and extended family. It can also include psychological (but biologically unrelated) parents, such as foster carers.[33] It incorporates the concept of identity and a child's right to know who his family members are.

In family court cases, different parties often have competing, mutually incompatible Article 8 rights, so these have to be balanced against one another. Where the rights of parent and child conflict, the ECtHR has determined that, if any balancing of interests is necessary, the child prevails.[34]

The court often has to balance the parents' Article 8 right to family life against the local authority's duty to protect the child from a breach of his Article 3 right not to be ill-treated. Another balancing act had to be performed[35] when a young woman alleged that a man had abused her when she was a child. This gave rise to concerns for his ten-year-old daughter. It would be impossible to investigate the child's case without revealing the identity of the woman, so her right to confidentiality and privacy on the one hand had to be weighed against the child and her parents' right to a family life and to a fair trial. There were also competing public interests. The Supreme Court decided: 'X's privacy rights are not a sufficient justification for the grave compromise of the fair trial and family life rights of the parties which non-disclosure would entail.'[36]

Article 14

Article 14 prohibits discrimination on 'any ground such as sex, race, colour, language, religion, political or other opinion, national or social origin, association with a national minority, property, birth or other status'. The wording is broad enough to include issues which are not explicitly mentioned, such as disability, age or sexual orientation, and in future will no doubt cover other types of discrimination which we currently unknowingly practise.

---

32 *Schalk and Kopf* v. *Austria* (see above); the ECtHR found that 'family life' applies to a cohabiting same sex couple just as it would to an opposite sex couple.
33 *O* v. *Coventry City Council* (Adoption).
34 *Yousef* v. *Netherlands* [2003] 1FLR 210 ECHR case no. 33711/96 at paragraph 73.
35 *In the Matter of A (A Child)* [2012] UKSC 60 (Supreme Court).
36 *Re A*; per Lady Hale.

At first glance it seems to go beyond all our discrimination legislation in one neat package, but in fact it outlaws discrimination only in the delivery of other Convention rights. In other words, 'free-standing' discrimination is not covered; the Article only applies if it can be allied to another Article. For example, the ECtHR considered a Portuguese court decision awarding residence to the child's mother on the grounds that the father's homosexuality was an 'abnormality' and the child should not grow up in an abnormal situation.[37] The father pleaded Article 14 allied with Article 8, saying effectively: 'I am being denied my right to a family life with my child because I am gay and that is unjustified discrimination.' The ECtHR found no reasonable and objective justification for the Portuguese court's position, no legitimate aim was being pursued and there was no proportionality between the means and the aim. The discrimination was unlawful.

Points for practice

1. Make human rights considerations explicit in every aspect of your practice.

2. Have a checklist on the front of every file noting human rights points to consider. Include the topic in all reviews, in supervision and in all court reports.

3. Consider the rights of everyone involved in every decision to act – or not to act – and record reasons clearly.

4. Human rights demand that the process, not just the decisions made, must be fair, reinforcing good social work practice of involving and consulting service users throughout.

5. Don't be defensive: use human rights creatively and positively.

---

37   *Salgueiro da Silva Mouta* v. *Portugal* [2005] 2FLR 596 ECtHR case no. 33290/96.

Chapter 2

Key Points in Children and Families Law

Sources of law

Finding the law is not a simple matter. There is no single point of reference: our law is a tapestry of primary legislation (statutes, or Acts of Parliament), secondary legislation (statutory instruments or regulations) and case law, together with guidance on how to apply it.

Statutes

Primary legislation is our starting point. A statute, such as the Children Act 1989 (CA89), starts life as a Bill which is then passed by Parliament, receives Royal Assent and comes into force in due course. The date is part of the Act's title and can be important to distinguish between different Acts with the same name such as the Children Acts 1975, 1989 and 2004.

The date records the year the Act was passed, not when it came into force – most of the Adoption and Children Act 2002 (ACA) only became law at the end of 2005. Some Acts are passed but never come into force, such as much of the Family Law Act 1996.

Statutes can be wide-ranging and complicated, for example the CA89 which re-wrote the law relating to children. To divide a large volume of material into manageable chunks, statutes are broken down into numbered sections. The letter 's' stands for the word 'section': s1 is the standard abbreviation for 'section 1'. Sections themselves can be subdivided into subsections numbered first with a figure, (1), then a letter, (1)(a), and finally a Roman numeral, each in brackets, (1)(a)(i).

Statutes can be amended by later legislation repealing or adding sections, so it is important always to ensure that you are consulting the up-to-date version. A section number followed by a capital letter shows that the section has been inserted by a later statute, for example s15A CA89 (dealing with special guardianship), which was added by the ACA. The added section has the same force as any other.

In major statutes such as CA89, related sections are grouped together in 'Parts', numbered using capital Roman numerals; for example, CA89 Part III deals with local authority support for children and families and Part IV with child protection.

Complicated detail is often found in Schedules at the end of a statute, instead of in the body of the Act. So s17 CA89 contains the essential principles of services to children in need, while the detailed services are listed in Schedule 2. Schedules have the same force as any other element of the statute.

Regulations

Secondary or 'delegated' legislation, often in the form of regulations, fleshes out the bones of a statute. Authorisation for a statutory instrument is found in the statute itself. For instance, s22C CA89 sets out where a looked-after child can be placed and that such placements are subject to regulations made by the relevant national authority. So to find the details, we must look to the Care Planning, Placement and Case Review (England) Regulations 2010. All statutory instruments have a SI number – SI showing the year of issue and number, in this case SI 2010/959.

Understanding statutes

Having found the relevant provision, the next challenge is to understand it. Each word must be separately considered. Some words are defined in the statute itself in an interpretation section, as in s105 CA89, or within an individual section, such as the definition of 'harm' in s31(9) CA89.

If no definition appears in the statute itself, we look to see if the meaning of a word or section has been defined in case law – if not, we use the normal plain English meaning.

Case law

However carefully statutes and regulations are drafted, questions arise as to their meaning or application to a particular situation. Argument is put to the court which decides the question in the context of that case. If this decision is appealed, it could become a 'test case', determining the issue for all cases thereafter. This is because of the 'precedent' system whereby decisions of the highest courts (Court of Appeal and Supreme Court[1]) are binding on all lower courts, so a case ostensibly concerning one child determines the law for every child in the land.

To illustrate: in s31 CA89, one of the grounds for a care order is that the child is 'likely' to suffer significant harm. What does 'likely' mean – almost inevitable, anything slightly more than a vague possibility or somewhere in between? The Supreme Court,[2] following earlier House of Lords cases, confirmed that it means 'a real possibility' that the harm will occur, based on facts established on the balance of probabilities. That has decided the question for all cases hereafter, as the Supreme Court is the highest court in the land. The Court of Appeal, one stage lower in the hierarchy, sets binding precedents for courts below it, whereas High Court decisions are persuasive rather than binding. Whenever you see a reference to a case, note which court decided it.

When children's cases are reported, initials are used to preserve confidentiality. The Supreme Court case mentioned above is *Re B (A Child)* [2013] UKSC 33, that is, the 33rd case decided by the Supreme Court in 2013. In case citations, UKSC is the Supreme Court, UKHL the House of Lords, EWCA is the Court of Appeal, and EWHC refers to the High Court, followed by an indication of which Division the case was heard in such as Family (Fam), Administrative court (Admin) or QBD (Queen's Bench Division).

When judges' names are reported, their status in the court hierarchy is also given: 'J' after a surname indicates a High Court judge, 'LJ' is a Lord or Lady Justice of Appeal in the Court of Appeal and the Justices of the Supreme Court have the title 'Lord' or 'Lady'. 'P' denotes the President of the Family Division.

---

1   The Supreme Court replaced the House of Lords as the highest court in the land in October 2009.

2   *Re B (A Child)* [2013] UKSC 33 (Supreme Court).

Guidance

Along with any legislation, the relevant government department often issues guidance on its implementation, such as *Working Together*.[3] s7 Local Authority Social Services Act 1970 (LASSA) imposes a legal duty on local authorities to 'act under the general guidance' of the relevant Secretary of State. So any guidance issued under that section (including many important documents in child protection) must be followed unless there is an exceptional, clearly documented reason to justify doing otherwise. The Court of Appeal[4] approved the following explanation:

> guidance does not have the binding effect of secondary legislation and a local authority is free to depart from it, even 'substantially'. But a departure from the guidance would be unlawful unless there is cogent reason for it, and the greater the departure, the more compelling must that reason be…except perhaps in the case of a minor departure, it is difficult to envisage circumstances in which mere disagreement with the guidance could amount to a cogent reason for departing from it.

Failure to comply can result in judicial review. For example, a local authority's policy on allowances for Special Guardians was struck down because it was inconsistent with guidance.[5] However, guidance itself never has the force of law so, if anything within it is inconsistent with statute or case law, it cannot prevail.

Key statutes
Children Act 1989 (CA89)

This is the starting point for all questions of children law and is the Act you need to know most intimately in your work. Its provisions are discussed in detail in the rest of the book, and key sections listed in Appendix 1.

---

3   DFE (March 2013) *Working Together to Safeguard Children – a guide to inter-agency working to safeguard and promote the welfare of children.* Available at www.education.gov.uk/ aboutdfe/statutory/g00213160/working-together-to-safeguard-children, accessed on 30 March 2014.

4   *R (X)* v. *London Borough of Tower Hamlets* [2013] EWCA Civ 904 approving the words of Males J.

5   *R (TT)* v. *LB Merton* [2012] EWHC 2055 (Admin).

Children Act 2004 (CA04)

This Act made structural and organisational changes to children's services and inter-agency working at national and local level. It established the Children's Commissioner, the post of Director of Children's Services and Local Safeguarding Children Boards. Its effects underlie your work, but you are unlikely to need to know its detailed provisions.

Adoption and Children Act 2002 (ACA)

This completely reformed adoption law and made changes to the CA89. It is the key statute for all adoption cases.[6]

Human Fertilisation and Embryology Act 2008 (HFEA08)

This Act made changes to the definition of the word 'parent' making it possible for a child to have two female parents and no father.[7]

Crime and Courts Act 2013

This establishes a new single family court (replacing the Family Proceedings, County and High Courts), from April 2014.

Children and Families Act 2014

This Act makes some significant changes to the Children Act including a modification of the welfare principle and the imposition of a statutory 26-week timescale for care proceedings.

Children Act 1989 – Fundamental provisions

The fundamental principles of CA89 should be engraved on your heart. They apply whenever a CA89 case comes to court.

s1(1) – Welfare principle

People often recite the phrase 'the child's welfare is paramount' without analysing what the subsection actually says.

---

6   See Chapters 15 and 16 for more information on adoption.
7   For more information see Chapter 3.

> s1(1) When a court determines any question with respect to –
>
>   (a) the upbringing of a child; or
>
>   (b) the administration of a child's property...
>
> the child's welfare shall be the court's paramount consideration.

The statutory duty applies only to courts considering children's cases, and only when the issue concerns the child's upbringing (or property). It does not apply, for example, to preliminary applications for leave, nor to applications to place a child in secure accommodation when the court simply determines whether the statutory grounds are met: the child's welfare is not paramount.[8]

The welfare principle is also subject to other statutory provisions, so a court cannot make a care order, for example, unless the statutory grounds are met, even if it would be in the child's best interests to do so.

To some it comes as a surprise to realise that the welfare principle applies only to courts – not to local authorities or other agencies. It may not be a bad objective to adopt, but it is not a statutory duty and cannot be used as a trite slogan. Local authorities have other statutory duties and wider considerations to take into account, including balancing the needs of everyone in their area and managing their budget. Unlike the courts, local authorities cannot treat the needs of each individual child as paramount.

What does 'paramount' mean? The child's welfare overrides that of others, but it is not the only consideration. Lord McDermott's 1969 analysis is still helpful today:

> ...it seems to me that [those words] must mean more than that the child's welfare is to be treated as the top item in a list of items relevant to the matter in question. I think they connote a process whereby, when all the relevant facts, relationships, claims and wishes of parents, risks, choices and other circumstances are taken into account and weighed, the course to be followed will be that which is most in the interests of the child's welfare... That is...the paramount consideration because it rules on and determines the course to be followed.[9]

---

8   *Re M (Secure Accommodation Order)* [1995] 1FLR 418 (Court of Appeal).

9   *J* v. *C* [1969] 1 All ER 788 (House of Lords) at pages 820–821. The case concerned an old legislation under which the child's welfare was 'first and paramount'.

But what happens when one child's needs conflict with those of another? If both children are the subject of applications, theoretically each is paramount but, in practice, the needs of one have to be weighed against the other.

Case Studies: Conflicting interests

Charlie and David are half-brothers. Their mother cannot look after them. Charlie's father, wants Charlie (but not David) to live with him. The maternal grandmother wants to care for both boys. Charlie wants to live with his dad. David wants to be with Charlie. Both adults apply to court and s1 CA89 applies to the applications. The court has a dilemma: for Charlie, the best solution is to go to his dad, albeit alone, but for David, it would be best for the brothers to stay together with their grandmother. Each child's welfare may be paramount but the court cannot make an order which is ideal for each; it has to compromise. Charlie goes to live with dad and David goes to live with grandmother with extensive contact between the boys.

George's mother, Hannah, is only 14. George and Hannah are both subject to care proceedings. Hannah will be deeply distressed if George is permanently removed. From her perspective it would be best for George to stay in foster care until she can care for him. But George needs competent care and security now. Each child's welfare is paramount, but there is a conflict between their interests. Although Hannah is herself a child subject to proceedings, she is also George's mother, so his needs are likely to be put above hers. As Orwell might have put it, some interests are more paramount than others.

Ian and Karen are siblings placed separately. Ian desperately wants to see Karen. If he applies to court for a contact order, he is the applicant, not the subject of the application: Karen's upbringing, not his, is in question. The court is not concerned with Ian's welfare, even though he is a child in some distress: Karen's welfare is paramount.

Involvement of both parents

A new provision s1(2A)[10] adds a statutory presumption applied in applications for parental responsibility or private law orders that a

---

10 Added to CA89 by the Children and Families Act 2014, in force from 22 April 2014.

child's welfare is served by the involvement of both parents in his life, unless the contrary is shown.

s1(3) Welfare checklist

Declaring that the child's welfare is paramount is one thing; deciding what it means for a particular child is another. Munby LJ said:[11]

> Evaluating a child's best interests involves a welfare appraisal in the widest sense, taking into account, where appropriate, a wide range of ethical, social, moral, religious, cultural, emotional and welfare considerations. Everything that conduces to a child's welfare and happiness or relates to the child's development and present and future life as a human being, including the child's familial, educational and social environment, and the child's social, cultural, ethnic and religious community, is potentially relevant and has, where appropriate, to be taken into account. The judge must adopt a holistic approach.

To guide the court on the factors to take into account, s1(3) CA89 gives a list of considerations, commonly known as 'the welfare checklist'. These apply whenever the court considers an application for an order under s8 CA89 (orders for residence or contact, specific issue or prohibited steps orders), for a special guardianship order or care order. They do not apply to emergency protection or child assessment applications when information is likely to be limited, although it is good practice to inform the court of any available details whether the subsection is obligatory or not. The list is not exclusive, so other relevant factors should also be considered.

---

11   *Re G* [2012] EWCA 1233 (Court of Appeal) at paragraph 27.

s1(3) …a court shall have regard in particular to –

(a) the ascertainable wishes and feelings of the child concerned (considered in the light of his age and understanding);

(b) his physical, emotional and educational needs;

(c) the likely effect on him of any change in his circumstances;

(d) his age, sex, background and any characteristics of his which the court considers relevant;

(e) any harm which he has suffered or is at risk of suffering;

(f) how capable each of his parents, and any other person in relation to whom the court considers the question to be relevant, is of meeting his needs;

(g) the range of powers available to the court under this Act in the proceedings in question.

CHILD'S WISHES AND FEELINGS

The list is not in order of priority, but it is of symbolic significance that the child's views appear first. Children rarely give evidence, so family courts depend on professionals to state and explain the child's views. Social workers can help the court to understand what the child is really saying, through his words and behaviour. Is the child free to express his true views or is he under pressure to say the 'right thing'? How much weight should be given to his views? What a child wants and what is best for him are not always the same, and sometimes the contents of item (a) on the checklist will be different from your recommendation to the court.

PHYSICAL, EMOTIONAL AND EDUCATIONAL NEEDS

This heading falls squarely within social work competence. It is always important to identify the needs of the individual child, not simply the needs of any typical child of the same age.

EFFECT OF CHANGE

This is sometimes called the 'status quo' principle but that overstates its purpose. This heading reminds us that no intervention in a child's life is neutral; change itself has an impact which must be considered. Unnecessary change should be avoided, but clearly a status quo which is harmful should not be preserved; for example, Pauffley J found 'both startling and alarming' the use of the 'status quo' argument to refuse to return a child to his mother.[12] The court may need to weigh short-term adverse effects against long-term benefits.

AGE, SEX, BACKGROUND AND CHARACTERISTICS

This heading includes such important factors as racial, cultural and linguistic heritage and any special needs. All of the child's characteristics need to be put into their proper perspective in the case; one element does not have greater importance than another. In one case,[13] the child of orthodox Jewish parents was living with non-practising Catholics. When the parents wanted the child back, religion and culture were obviously important issues. However, in the context of the child's welfare overall, the court said 'religious and cultural heritage cannot be the overwhelming factor in this case…nor can it displace other weighty welfare factors.'[14]

HARM

This word is defined by s31(9) CA89 and refers to abuse or neglect which impairs a child's health or development.[15]

CAPABILITY OF PARENTS AND OTHERS TO MEET THE CHILD'S NEEDS

This subheading assesses how the resources available within the child's network fit the child's needs already established in item (b). The child's parents are the first port of call but the court may also look to the extended family, friends or anyone else connected with the child.

---

12 *Re NL (A Child) (Appeal; Interim Care Order; Facts and Reasons)* [2014] EWHC 270 (Fam) (High Court).
13 *Re P (s91(14) Guidelines) (Residence and Religious Heritage)* [1999] 2FLR 573 (Court of Appeal).
14 Butler-Sloss LJ in *Re P* at page 586E.
15 See Chapter 9 for more details.

COURT'S POWERS

A key feature of the Act's design is the court's ability to use some of its powers creatively to do what is best for the child. It is not limited to making or refusing the order sought and it can make some orders without any application if that is in the child's interests. Never limit your thinking to the application before the court – consider all available options.

Case Study: Care order or family placement

The local authority applies for a care order in respect of Oliver with a plan to place him for adoption. The court decides that it would be in his best interests to live with Patricia, his grandmother. The court declines the care order and instead makes a package of orders no-one applied for – an order for residence to Patricia, supervision order to the local authority, an order for contact to Oliver's mother and prohibited steps order preventing father from contacting Oliver.

s1(2) – 'No delay' principle

> s1(2) In any proceedings in which any question with respect to the upbringing of a child arises, the court shall have regard to the general principle that any delay in determining the question is likely to prejudice the welfare of the child.

Long delays in a child's case can have a serious impact. For example, in a contact dispute the longer the child goes without seeing someone, the harder it becomes to re-introduce contact; the longer siblings are separated, the harder it becomes to place them together; and child protection procedures can take so long that a child becomes unadoptable. For this reason there is a considerable drive to speed up all processes concerning children.

However, there can be a tension between speed and making the right decision. Delay can be constructive, even essential, and the court may need social work advice on how to strike the right balance. It is better to take time to make the right decision than to make the wrong one quickly. As Pauffley J put it, 'justice must never be sacrificed upon the altar of speed.'[16]

s1(5) – 'No order' principle

> s1(5) Where a court is considering whether or not to make one or more orders under this Act with respect to a child, it shall not make the order or any of the orders unless it considers that doing so would be better for the child than making no order at all.

This subsection has been widely misunderstood. Some thought it meant that every single alternative had to be explored before taking the matter to court, and that no order should be made if agreement could be reached. Others thought there should be no order unless there was a specific justification. In fact, it is much simpler than that. As Ward LJ[17] explained:

> … in my view this section is perfectly clear. It does not, in my judgment, create a presumption one way or the other. All it demands is that before the court makes any order it must ask the question: will it be better for the child to make the order than make no order at all? The section itself gives the test to be applied and the question to be asked. If judges in each case do just that they cannot go wrong, it being axiomatic that every case is different, and each case will depend on its own peculiar facts.[18]

s91(14) – Preventing applications
Unlike s1 CA89, this is not a fundamental principle underlying all CA89 applications but it is a provision which can be used in any appropriate case under CA89. It gives the court dealing with one application power to exercise some control over future applications. It has been used for instance to put a stop to repeated applications which make the court

---

16   *Re NL (A Child) (Appeal; Interim Care Order; Facts and Reasons)* [2014] EWHC 270 (Fam) (High Court).

17   *Re G (Children)* [2005] EWCA Civ 1283 (Court of Appeal) at paragraph 10.

18   *Re G* at paragraph 10.

process itself harmful to a child[19] and to provide extra security for special guardianship orders.

> s91(14) On disposing of any application for an order under this Act, the court may (whether or not it makes any other order in response to the application) order that no application for an order under this Act of any specified kind may be made with respect to the child concerned by any person named in the order without leave of the court.

The person named in a s91(14) CA89 order cannot apply for a specified type of order without first obtaining the court's permission, allowing the court to filter out unmeritorious applications. It adds an extra hurdle, but even if this is crossed it does not necessarily mean that the application itself will be successful.

What about the human rights of the person subject to this restriction? The right to a fair trial is clearly relevant, but s91(14) CA89 does not deny access to the court, it simply adds another stage to the proceedings. Nonetheless, it is a power to be used sparingly and with great care. As a matter of justice, no such restriction should be imposed without giving the person concerned the opportunity to comment first,[20] and any order should be proportionate to the need – the court must carefully consider what kind of applications should be restricted and for how long. The Court of Appeal confirmed that in exceptional cases a s91(14) order can be made without any time limit or until the child turns 16, but the court must clearly spell out its reasons for its order.[21] The order cannot include any other conditions, such as specifying what needs to change before the court will consider a further application, but the judge can make this clear to the person concerned,[22] and any later court will expect to see the issues addressed before allowing an application to proceed.

---

19 Such as *N (A Child)* [2009] EWHC 3055 (Fam) (High Court) described by the judge as 'the most plain and obvious case for a s91(14) order it is possible to imagine'.
20 *C (A Child)* [2009] EWCA Civ 674 (Court of Appeal).
21 *Re S (Permission to Seek Relief)* [2006] EWCA Civ 1190 (Court of Appeal).
22 *Stringer* v. *Stringer* [2006] EWCA Civ 1617 (Court of Appeal).

Points for practice

1. Always be aware of the legal context of your actions, powers and duties. Regularly reflect on the statutory basis for your actions and remind yourself of the applicable legal principles.

2. Have a copy of s1 CA89 to hand to ensure you are considering relevant factors.

3. Use the law creatively. Embrace it as a tool of your trade, not something to be wary of or intimidated by. Having a command of legal principles and available options can help you to analyse cases clearly.

Chapter 3

Parents, Parental Responsibility and Children's Autonomy

Parents

In the past, life was simple. The law had no trouble coping with the conventional family model of a man and woman who married, had children and brought them up together. But as society becomes increasingly complex and families become ever more varied, the law struggles to keep up. Everyday words like 'parent' become more difficult to define.

In normal life we rarely consider the legal relationships between children and the adults around them, but as a social worker you often have to deal with families in difficulty where quick decisions have to be made. You need to know who has the right to make those decisions and who needs to be consulted.

You need to be clear about who is (and who is not) a child's 'parent' as well as who has parental responsibility (PR). These are not necessarily the same: a biological parent may not be a 'parent' in law; a 'parent' may not have PR and someone can have PR despite being neither biologically nor legally a 'parent'. There are legal consequences to a person's status. For example, a legal 'parent' has a presumption of reasonable contact to a child in care,[1] whereas only a parent with PR is automatically a party to care proceedings or has the right to consent to adoption.

---

1   s34 Children Act 1989.

39

It is possible to be neither a parent nor have PR but nonetheless have a 'family life' with a child, which is protected under the Human Rights Act. Such people must not be overlooked in consultations and planning for the child.

Who is a 'parent'?

The word 'parent' is no longer simply a question of biology. The Human Fertilisation and Embryology Act 2008 (HFEA08) made important changes to the legal concept of parenthood.

How many parents can a child have?

The HFEA08 provides that a child cannot have more than two parents. If he has two female parents, he cannot have a legal father as well (even if the biological father is acknowledged and involved in the child's life).

There is, however, no legal limit to the number of people who can have PR for a child.

Who is the child's mother?

Generally, the 'mother' is the woman who carries and gives birth to the child, whether or not she is also the biological mother. Thus, an egg donor is not the child's 'mother'; that status belongs to the woman who gives birth.

The birth mother can only lose her status as 'mother' in two exceptional cases: surrogacy (on the making of a parental order) and adoption (on the making of an adoption order). In each case, the birth mother's relationship with the child is extinguished and a new parental relationship is created.

A child can have no legal mother at all, for example if he is adopted by a male couple as the adoption order terminates the birth mother's role.

Who is the child's father?

Generally, the term 'father' refers simply to the biological father, who is treated as a 'parent' in law (subject to some exceptions). He does not necessarily have PR (see following) but does usually have some automatic rights such as applying for PR or an order for contact.

If the mother is married, the law assumes that her husband is the child's father unless the contrary is proven. Even if another man is shown to be the biological father, he does not automatically gain a right to a family life with the child under Article 8 HRA:

> biological kinship between a natural parent and a child alone without any further legal or factual element indicating the existence of a close personal relationship is insufficient to attract the protection of Article 8.[2]

Biological fathers are inevitable; legal fathers are not – a child may have no legal father at all. Many children of single mothers have no acknowledged father. Children can also be adopted by female couples who then have exclusive status, eliminating any former father. Sperm donors are a particular case. Men who donate sperm through a registered clinic have long been exempted from acquiring any legal relationship with or responsibility for any resulting child.[3] If the mother is married, her husband is the legal father unless he was opposed to the artificial insemination. If she lives with a man, her unmarried partner is recognised as the legal father provided the insemination is done via a licensed clinic (subject to various conditions).

What about private 'DIY' arrangements, often between lesbian couples and male friends? Previously, these situations were treated no differently than any other child born out of wedlock and the mother's partner had no automatic recognition.

With the advent of the HFEA08, everything changed. If a lesbian couple in a civil partnership arrange to conceive a child, when that child is born the woman who carries the child is the mother, her partner is a 'female parent' and the law provides that 'no man shall be treated as the father'.[4] As Black J said:

> It is manifestly clear that, by passing the 2008 Act, Parliament changed the law on donation to recognise lesbian parents as joint legal parents. Those provisions not only confer parenthood but also expressly eliminate the legal status of the man who is the biological father in such circumstances.[5]

---

2 *Anayo* v. *Germany* [2010] ECHR case no. 20578/07 at paragraph 56.
3 Note, however, that for donations made since 1 April 2005, the child when adult is entitled to know the donor's identity, date and place of birth and last known address.
4 s45 HFEA08.
5 *Re G (a minor); Re Z (a minor)* [2013] EWHC 134 (Fam) (High Court) at paragraph 70.

Just to be doubly clear, HFEA08 also explicitly states that where a person is the mother, father or parent, then they have that status for all legal purposes and if they are not a parent, they are not a parent for any legal purpose.[6]

As Baker J said:

> the policy underpinning these reforms is an acknowledgement that alternative family forms without fathers are sufficient to meet a child's needs...the policy underpinning...the 2008 Act is simply to put lesbian couples and their children in exactly the same legal position as other types of parents and children.[7]

Case Study: Lesbian civil partners

Anne and Beth are lesbian civil partners who want to start a family. They approach their friends David and Evan. They decide that David will provide sperm for Anne to have a baby. It is a private arrangement, not involving a licensed clinic. All works well and Flora is born.

A few years later, the couples decide to repeat the experience and Greg is born. Relationships become strained; the men feel that the women are trying to exclude them from the children's lives, while the women feel that the men are interfering too much. David decides to go to court for contact. He discovers that, between the two births, the law changed when the HFEA08 came into force.

For Flora, Anne is the mother, Beth has no automatic legal status (although she is eligible to apply for a step-parent PR order) and David is the father without PR. He has an automatic right to apply for an order for contact or to seek PR.

However, for Greg, Anne is the mother, Beth is the second female parent and David has no legal relationship to Greg; Greg has no father. David has no right to apply for contact (he has to ask the court for permission to apply) and he cannot apply for PR.[8]

This is new territory for the courts, which are trying hard to develop a principled approach. It is difficult to devise general guidance and each case must be considered on its own facts.

---

6   s48(1) HFEA08.

7   *Re G (a minor); Re Z (a minor)* [2013] EWHC 134 (Fam) (High Court) at paragraphs 113 and 114.

8   This illustration is a simplified version of the even more complicated facts of *Re G (a minor); Re Z (a minor)* [2013] EWHC 134 (Fam) (High Court).

Parental responsibility

PR is a key legal concept. We might instinctively know what PR entails but defining it is a surprisingly difficult task. s3(1) CA89 does not even make an attempt: it simply tells us that PR consists of 'all the rights, duties, powers, responsibilities and authority which by law a parent of a child has in relation to the child and his property'. It includes:

- naming the child
- feeding, housing and maintaining him
- educating him
- arranging and consenting to health care
- choosing his religious upbringing.

PR diminishes as a child's autonomy grows. Parents decide everything for a newborn baby, whereas 17 years later they are doing well if he still listens to them.

Who has PR?

Being a parent and having PR are not the same. It is possible to be a parent without PR and to have PR without being a parent.

MOTHERS

The easiest starting point lies with a child's mother, who automatically has PR[9] except in the case of adoption or surrogacy. This applies even if she herself is still under 18.

MARRIED COUPLES

Married parents both have PR,[10] whether they married before or after the child's birth.[11] A husband is presumed to be the father of his wife's child unless proved to the contrary, so if a child has married parents, you can generally safely assume that both have PR.

Marriage refers only to a formal marriage – there is no such thing as 'common law marriage'.

---

9   s2(1) and 2(2)(a) CA89.
10   s2(1) CA89.
11   s2 Legitimacy Act 1976.

CIVIL PARTNERS

Assuming one of the partners in a same sex relationship is the child's birth parent, the normal rules apply to determine his/her PR. As for heterosexual couples, just being in a relationship with a child's parent confers no automatic status, so the partner has to take positive steps to acquire PR (see step-parent provisions section below).

As seen above, both partners in a lesbian civil partnership can have PR for a child born by assisted conception.[12] The second female parent can acquire PR by being registered on the birth certificate, by an agreement with the child's mother or by a court order.

UNMARRIED PARENTS

Many couples living together wrongly assume that they each have equal status. In fact, the law draws a distinction between couples in formalised and informal relationships – perhaps inevitable if you consider that unmarried fathers range from committed, involved fathers at one end of the spectrum to one-night stands, sperm donors and even rapists at the other.

Unmarried fathers are usually 'parents' but they do not have PR[13] automatically; they have to take positive action to acquire it. Essentially there are three options,[14] each of which can be easily substantiated by documentary evidence:

1.   *Registration.* The father's name registered on the birth certificate on or after 1 December 2003 confers PR (before that date, a father's name on a certificate has no legal effect).

2.   *Agreement.* An agreement between mother and father confers PR provided it is in a prescribed form, signed and witnessed at court and registered at the Principal Registry of the Family Division.

3.   *Court order.* The biological father can seek a PR order from the court. Only he can apply; neither the mother nor child can force him to take on responsibility. If paternity is disputed, the court can require DNA testing. The court then considers the

---

12   s4ZA CA89.
13   s2(2) CA89.
14   s4 CA89.

evidence given by both parties applying the s1 CA89[15] welfare principle and the following factors:

- commitment – for example, financial support, contact and involvement in the child's education
- attachment – the relationship between father and child
- reasons for application – does he genuinely want to take responsibility for his child or is the application more about his relationship with the mother, be it a desire to get back together with her or to make her life difficult?

Courts generally consider that a father who shows enough interest in his child to want PR usually merits it:

it is important that, wherever possible, the law should confer on a concerned father that stamp of approval because he has shown himself willing and anxious to pick up the responsibility of fatherhood and not to deny or avoid it.[16]

PR puts him in the same position as a married father and the mother herself. As McFarlane LJ put it:

The granting of equal status, namely that of parental responsibility to this father, is not simply a matter of ticking a box; it is to do with status. He now has the status of a father with parental responsibility but the word, I would stress to both him and the mother, is not the word 'rights' which they will read into the lines of that phrase, but the word 'responsibility', which is plainly written on the label.[17]

However, PR is not an automatic entitlement and will be refused if the father poses a risk to the child, if his reasons for applying are 'demonstrably wrong' or if he is likely to misuse PR.[18]

The granting or otherwise of PR is a question of status and is not the same as whether he should see the child: a father can be granted PR but refused contact,[19] they are 'wholly separate applications'.

---

15 See Chapter 2 for more information.
16 Ward LJ in *Re C & V* [1998] 1FLR 392 (Court of Appeal) cited with approval by Thorpe LJ in *W (Children)* [2013] EWCA Civ 335 (Court of Appeal).
17 *Re W* at paragraph 16.
18 *PM* v. *MB & Anor* [2013] EWCA Civ 969 (Court of Appeal).
19 *Re W* above, per Thorpe LJ.

STEP-PARENTS

A 'step-parent' means a parent's spouse or civil partner, not an informal cohabitant. Marrying or entering a civil partnership does not confer PR of itself – active steps have to be taken. Many re-constituted families live together blissfully unaware that only one of the people playing a parental role in fact has PR.

The three options[20] for step-parents wishing to acquire PR closely mirror those for unmarried fathers:

1. *PR agreement.* Entered into by the step-parent and the birth parent(s) who already have PR (i.e. always the mother, and sometimes the father). The agreement gives PR to the step-parent, shared with those who already had it. Similar formalities apply as for an unmarried father's PR agreement.

2. *Court order.* An option if an agreement is not possible, because a parent with PR opposes or cannot be found. s1 CA89 applies and courts will probably consider the same factors as for unmarried fathers. Just as for PR agreements, an order adds another person with PR without eliminating anyone else.

3. *Adoption.* This is the only way for a step-parent actually to become the child's 'parent', rather than just obtaining PR. The Adoption and Children Act 2002 (ACA) allows the 'step' half of the couple to adopt the child.[21] Exceptionally, such adoptions are available to the birth parent's cohabitant,[22] not just to his/her spouse or civil partner. Adoption is a drastic order as it terminates previous PR (except that of the birth parent half of the 'step' couple). So, where a stepmother adopts a child, in law she becomes the child's mother, replacing the birth mother who loses her PR and all legal relationship with the child. Clearly, adoption is a drastic step with profound human rights implications.

---

20 s4A (1) CA89.
21 Under the previous legislation only single people or married couples could adopt so that, bizarrely, the birth parent had to adopt his/her own child at the same time as his/her spouse!
22 s51(2) ACA.

Step-parents also have available the other provisions for 'non-parents' set out below, but where possible are more likely to use the provisions specifically designed for their situation.

NON-PARENTS

Children often live with grandparents, relatives or family friends under informal arrangements, the parties involved giving no real thought to the legal situation. Legally, the carers are acting on behalf of the person with PR who, consciously or otherwise, has delegated that responsibility.[23]

However, such people can acquire PR in their own right through a court order, a sensible step where the arrangement is long-term, there are tensions between the parties or the person with PR is unreliable or cannot always be found. Which type of order is appropriate depends on the circumstances of each case. The orders are discussed in detail later in the book,[24] but in terms of PR their effects are as follows:

- *Order for residence.*[25] Confers PR on the person the child is to live with for the duration of the order. PR is shared equally with others who have it.

- *Special guardianship order.*[26] Grants PR to the special guardian (who cannot be a birth parent) for the duration of the order. PR is shared, but the special guardian can act without reference to others with PR.

- *Adoption order (ACA).* Grants exclusive PR to the adopters, extinguishing other people's PR.

LOCAL AUTHORITY

'Looked after' children may be:

- 'in care', subject to a care order made by the court[27]

- 'accommodated' under a voluntary arrangement.[28]

---

23   s2(9) CA89.
24   See Chapter 5 for residence and special guardianship and Chapter 15 for adoption.
25   s8 CA89 – child arrangements order concerning residence for orders after implementation of the Children and Families Act 2014, residence orders for earlier cases.
26   s14A CA89.
27   s31CA89 – for more information see Chapters 11–13.
28   s20 CA89 – for more information see Chapter 8.

When a child is in care, the local authority (but not the social worker or foster carer) has PR. Birth parents do not lose their PR but their power to exercise it can be restricted, if necessary for the child's welfare.

Accommodated children are looked after under a purely voluntary arrangement by which a parent delegates PR to the local authority to the extent and for so long as s/he chooses. Neither the local authority nor the carer has PR.

ORPHANS

An orphan's position depends on whether any advance provision has been made.[29] Parents can appoint a 'testamentary guardian' to have PR for their children in the event of their death, but if they die without making such provision, someone wishing to become the child's guardian can apply to court. The s1 CA89 principles apply to the application and the court's order gives the guardian PR for the child.

If there is no guardian, the local authority must accommodate and maintain the orphaned child,[30] but it does not acquire PR: local authorities can only acquire PR through a care order and simply having no-one with PR does not of itself give grounds for a care order. Some children therefore have no-one at all with PR for them, a small but important gap in the law.

SURROGACY

The complicated details of the law relating to surrogacy are beyond the scope of this book, but it is useful to know that in surrogacy cases a 'parental order' means that the child is treated in law as the child of the commissioning couple (at least one of whom has provided sperm/eggs), not of the surrogate mother. The commissioning couple gain exclusive PR for the child and the woman who actually gave birth has no legal relationship with the child.

---

29   s5 CA89.
30   s20 CA89.

Case Study: Who has PR?

These children are in the same class. Who can sign consent for a school trip?

Their home situations are as follows:

Abdul – married parents – *both parents have PR.*

Britney – unmarried parents – *her mother inevitably has PR. Her father has PR if his name is on the birth certificate, he has a formal PR agreement or court order but not otherwise.*

Colin – single mother – *his mother has PR. If his parents were married, the father has PR even if they are now separated or divorced. If not, his father's position is the same as Britney's father.*

Daisy – mother and stepfather – *her mother has PR. Her father's situation is the same as Colin's father. If her stepfather has a step-parent PR agreement or order, he also has PR which could be shared three ways. If he has adopted Daisy, only he and Daisy's mother have PR. If he is just living with Daisy's mother without being married, only an order for residence or adoption will give him PR.*

Ellie – father and father's male partner – *her mother has PR even if she is no longer on the scene unless Ellie has been adopted. Ellie's father may or may not have PR depending on his status – the fact that he cares for her full-time determines nothing. If the couple are in a civil partnership, father's partner is in the same position as Daisy's married stepfather; if not, he is like Daisy's unmarried stepfather.*

Finn – mother and mother's female partner – *Finn's mother has PR. If Finn was born as a result of a planned assisted conception in a clinic (or informally if the couple are in a civil partnership), he has a mother and a female parent but no father. Mother's partner has PR if she is on the birth certificate, or has a formal agreement or a court order. If it was not an assisted conception, mother's partner is in the same position as Ellie's father's partner.*

Georgio – grandparents – *unless his grandparents have adopted him, Georgio's mother still has PR as may his father. The grandparents may be acting under the parents' delegated PR or they may have PR in their own right through an order for residence (PR shared with the parent(s)) or a special guardianship order (PR shared but can be exercised to the exclusion of the parents).*

Hassan – foster parents – *if he is accommodated, his parent(s) retain full PR and delegate elements to the local authority. If he is in care, the local authority has PR and can limit the parents' exercise of their PR if necessary in Hassan's best interests.*

Ian – adoptive parents – the adoption order terminated Ian's birth parents' PR. His adoptive parents have exclusive PR.

Joshua – an orphan who lives with family friends – his carers only have PR if they were appointed as guardians in his parents' wills or by the court.

How does PR end?

Once acquired, PR is not easily lost. It is not ended by divorce or dissolution of a civil partnership, nor by abandonment. The only way a parent can relinquish PR is by consenting to an adoption order.

PR can end as follows:

- child attains 18

- child or parent dies

- child is adopted (ending birth parents' PR)

- a parental order is made in a surrogacy case (ending the surrogate mother's PR)

- the court revokes or discharges the court order or agreement by which PR was acquired

- a care order is revoked by the court (ending the local authority's PR).

PR acquired by agreement or court order can be removed by the court. In the case of an order for residence, this could be due to a simple change in circumstances – the child no longer needs to live with the people who had the order so the order is discharged and the PR disappears. However, in other cases it is a more unusual decision taken only in serious cases, such as cases of sexual abuse or domestic violence witnessed by the child, where the father's continuing role threatens the child's security or stability. In one such case, Wood J said, 'if the father did not have parental responsibility it is inconceivable it would now be granted to him…there is no element of the bundle of responsibilities that make up parental responsibility which this father could, in present or foreseeable circumstances, exercise in a way which would be beneficial for [the child]'.[31] There is no equivalent provision for people who have automatic PR (such as mothers or married fathers) whose PR cannot be removed, no matter how appallingly they behave.

Exercising PR

You may not be aware of it, but every time you consent to a school trip or take your child to the GP, you are exercising PR. In day-to-day life, most PR is exercised almost unconsciously.

DELEGATING PR

PR cannot be surrendered or transferred, but some or all of it can be delegated.[32] Every time your child has a babysitter, you are temporarily delegating aspects of your PR. When a child is voluntarily accommodated, the parent(s) delegate the day-to-day exercise of PR to the local authority.

SHARING PR

As we have seen, many children have more than one person with PR at the same time. If everyone with PR had to agree on every single decision it would be unwieldy even in the most harmonious family, and no decisions at all could be taken for a child whose parents had lost contact with each other. The law therefore sensibly allows PR to be exercised in almost all cases by any one person who has it.

> s2(7) CA89 Where more than one person has PR for a child, each of them may act alone and without the other (or others) in meeting that responsibility...

As a social worker, you can usually act on the basis of consent from one person with PR. Others with PR should of course still be consulted and involved in the process, but if one parent is more accessible and/or co-operative than another, that parent's consent suffices.

---

31   *A v. D (Parental Responsibility)* [2013] EWHC 2963 (Fam) (High Court) at paragraph 59.
32   s2(9) CA89.

However, there are some exceptions to the general rule. Where there is an order for residence, the consent of everyone with PR or court leave is needed for the child to leave the UK for more than a month or to change the child's surname.[33] The courts have applied the same rule to surname change even where there is no residence order.[34] Case law decisions also mean that consent of everyone with PR is required for potentially momentous decisions such as ritual circumcision,[35] and for immunisations.[36]

As most decisions can be made by one parent without the other, there is the potential for conflict. Resident parents often effectively make all the decisions and take all the responsibility for the child, but even having an order for residence does not give that right in law. Except where there is a special guardianship order or care order, those with PR have equal status, regardless of who takes day-to-day care of the child. Where people with equal rights and responsibilities cannot agree, ultimately the matter can go to court for decision, using the private law provisions of CA89.[37]

People without PR

You might think that someone who is not a parent and has no PR cannot have any responsibility for or authority over a child, but this is not always so. A little-known subsection can be important in practice (see box below).

---

s3(5) CA89 A person who –

(a) does not have parental responsibility for a particular child; but

(b) has care of the child,

(c) may (subject to the provisions of this Act) do what is reasonable in all the circumstances of the case for the purpose of safeguarding or promoting the child's welfare.

---

33   s13(1) CA89.
34   Re PC (Change of Surname) [1997] 2FLR 730 (High Court).
35   Re J (Specific Issue Orders: Child's Religious Upbringing and Circumcision) [2000] 1FLR 571 (Court of Appeal).
36   Re C (Welfare of Child: Immunisation) [2003] 2FLR 1054 (High Court) and 1095 (Court of Appeal).
37   See Chapters 4–6.

This subsection does not go into detail about what action is or is not permitted – it is specifically designed to cover a myriad of unpredictable circumstances, so the wording deliberately leaves a lot to common sense.

Case Study: Foster carer's actions

Kayla fosters Lily, who is accommodated. The plan is for Lily to stay in foster care for three months while her mother Molly resolves her drug problems. Molly arrives unexpectedly, demanding to take Lily home immediately. Neither Kayla nor the local authority have PR but Kayla refuses simply to hand Lily over and insists that Molly waits while she telephones the social worker. She is using her common sense and unwittingly relying on s3(5) CA89, which is sufficient to buy some time. It is clearly better than the alternative of handing Lily over and trying to retrieve the situation later.

Children's autonomy

Childhood ends at 18. At the dawn of the 18th birthday, a child is transformed into a fully competent adult. But in the years leading up to that point the situation is not so cut and dried. The United Nations Convention on the Rights of the Child provides that:

> Parties shall assure to the child who is capable of forming his or her own views the right to express those views freely in all matters affecting the child, the views of the child being given due weight in accordance with the age and maturity of the child.[38]

In some cases, the law prescribes an age at which a person can do a particular thing[39] or take decisions or responsibility for himself, regardless of his individual characteristics or circumstances. There is little apparent logic or consistency in these provisions: a child is criminally responsible for his actions from age 10, he can consent in his own right to medical, surgical or dental treatment at the age of 16,[40] he

---

38   Article 12.1.
39   See Children's Legal Centre (2008) *At What Age Can I...? A Guide to Age-based Legislation*, updated by Joanne Claridge.
40   s8 Family Law Reform Act 1969.

can have a driving licence from the age of 17, he can consent to sex at 16 but he cannot watch explicit sex at the cinema until he is 18.

But if there is no age limit prescribed by law, we have to look at the more flexible (and therefore less clear) concept of competence, which depends on the individual person and the particular circumstances. The key case to help us understand this concept is the landmark decision of Gillick.[41]

The case itself centred on contraceptive advice for under-16s without their parents' knowledge or consent, but, reasoning by analogy, the principles established have been applied in many other situations. Lord Templeman said:

> It is, in my view, contrary to the ordinary experience of mankind…to say that a child or a young person remains in fact under the complete control of his parents until he attains the definite age of majority, now 18 in the United Kingdom, and that on attaining that age he suddenly acquires independence. In practice, most wise parents relax their control gradually as the child develops and encourage him or her to become increasingly independent. Moreover, the degree of parental control actually exercised over a particular child does in practice vary considerably according to his understanding and intelligence and it would, in my opinion, be unrealistic for the courts not to recognise these facts.[42]

He described a parent's legal right as 'a dwindling right which the courts will hesitate to enforce against the wishes of the child, and the more so the older he is'.

If you believe a child needs a medical examination or an interview as part of a child protection investigation, can the child herself give consent? The problem is that there is no simple rule: the answer can be different for different children in the same situation, or for the same child in different situations.

Case Studies: Capacity to consent

Karen and Lily are both 14 years old. They both allege sexual abuse. An intimate medical examination is proposed. Although Karen is

---

41   *Gillick v. West Norfolk and Wisbech Area Health Authority and Another* [1986] 1 AC 112. [1986] 1FLR 224 (House of Lords).

42   Gillick case at page 9B.

distressed by the prospect, she understands what the examination will entail and the reasons for it. She can give her consent. Lily has a significant learning disability. When things are explained to her in an appropriate way, she understands in general terms but she cannot really grasp the implications. She must of course be consulted but she is not able give informed consent.

Marc is 15. He is bright, intellectually able and generally emotionally stable. He has never been ill until a virus suddenly affects his heart. He needs a heart transplant, without which he will die. Marc does not want the operation. His doctors judge that, for most things, Marc is competent. But they are reluctant to let him die, so they take the case to court. The court decides that the decision is too far-reaching and too far beyond Marc's experience to accept his refusal and it finds he is not competent to refuse consent. However, no-one would have questioned his competence if he had agreed.

Noelene is 10. She has a chronic medical condition and has been in and out of hospital her whole life. She is familiar with all the treatments, side-effects and long-term implications. When it comes to her medical treatment, she has a competence beyond her years.

Olly is 14, articulate and able. In a normal situation he would be generally competent. He becomes involved in care proceedings. He is in emotional turmoil, torn between loyalty to his abusive parents and his wish for safety. He agrees with whoever is speaking to him at the time. His decision-making is impaired by his situation. His solicitor cannot take direct instructions from Olly. Instead, she consults him but takes instructions from the Children's Guardian.

Competence involves:

- the child's age – generally, the older the child the more likely she is to be competent
- the child's intellectual, cognitive and emotional functioning affecting her ability to understand the issues
- the nature and implications of the decision in question – how complicated are the issues involved, and how far-reaching or long-lasting its effects
- the information available to the child
- her freedom of choice and pressure or sense of loyalty affecting her capacity to make a truly voluntary decision.

The question of competence is separate from the assessment of the decision made. A competent person has the right to make a bad decision; making a bad choice does not make us incompetent. However, for young people, there is a tension between their right to self-determination and the State's duty to protect. So the courts are reluctant to allow young people the freedom to make life-threatening mistakes; for example, the court refused to allow an anorexic teenager to starve herself to death.[43] A poignant example involved a 15-year-old Jehovah's Witness.[44] He refused a blood transfusion and his parents refused to consent on his behalf. The High Court overruled his refusal and he was given a transfusion. A few years later his condition returned, and he again refused a transfusion. By this time he was an adult and his competence was not questioned. He was allowed to refuse despite the fatal consequences of that decision.

Lord Donaldson said that young people should have:

> … the maximum degree of decision-making which is prudent. Prudence does not involve avoiding all risk, but it does involve avoiding taking risks which, if they eventuate, may have irreparable consequences or which are disproportionate to the benefits which could accrue from taking them.

He continued that adolescence is:

> a period of progressive transition from childhood to adulthood and as experience of life is acquired and intelligence and understanding grow, so will the scope of the decision-making which should be left to the minor, for it is only by making decisions and experiencing the consequences that decision-making skills will be acquired. As I put it in the course of the argument, and as I sincerely believe, 'good parenting involves giving minors as much rope as they can handle without an unacceptable risk that they will hang themselves'.[45]

There is a tension between autonomy and welfare. There are some 'lifestyle choices' that agencies cannot allow young people to make. Case files in Rochdale, for example, referred to young people as 'making their own choices' or 'engaging in consensual sexual activity' when in

---

43   *Re W (A Minor) (Medical Treatment: Court's Jurisdiction)* [1992] 3WLR 758 (High Court).
44   *Re E (A Minor) (Wardship: Medical Treatment)* [1993] 1FLR 386 (High Court).
45   *Re W (A Minor) (Medical Treatment: Court's Jurisdiction)* [1993] 3WLR 758 (House of Lords) per Lord Donaldson MR at page 770.

fact they were groomed and sexually abused by paedophile gangs.[46] As the Chief Executive of the Children's Society said, agencies 'need urgently to change their attitude to vulnerable, exploited teenage girls, who are being routinely dismissed as "troublesome" or "promiscuous" or as having made lifestyle choices.'[47]

Points for practice
PR

1. As soon as you start work with a new family, establish who are the child's parents and who has PR (remembering that they may not be the same). Note it clearly on the file where you can find it at short notice.

2. Remember that the answer may be different for each child of the family.

3. Remember that the answer may change over time (for example if people marry or enter civil partnerships or if the law changes) – keep the note up to date.

4. Ask to see relevant certificates and court orders – take copies for your file.

Competence

1. Whenever you work with a child, note any factors relevant to competence. This will stand you in good stead if an issue arises at short notice.

2. Whenever you decide whether to act on a child's consent, record your assessment of competence and your reasons for it.

---

46   See Rochdale Safeguarding Children Board (September 2012) *Review of Multi-agency Responses to the Sexual Exploitation of Children*. Available at http://democracy.york.gov.uk/documents/s78816/Annex%20A.pdf, accessed on 2 April 2014.
47   Children's Society response to the sentencing of a gang convicted of systematic grooming and abuse of teenage girls in Oxford, 27 June 2013.

Part 2

Private Law

Chapter 4

Section 8 Orders, Specific Issues and Prohibited Steps

Private law

Children Act 1989 (CA89) cases are often divided into 'private law' (disputes between individuals) and 'public law' (those involving the local authority, typically care proceedings).

Private law orders are found in Part II CA89. They allow the court to make decisions in disputes between individuals about any aspect of parental responsibility (PR), such as where a child lives, who he sees, where he goes to school, what medical treatment he has or what religion he follows.

The court can make one or more of the orders set out in s8:

1. Child arrangements order[1] – deciding who the child lives with, sees or otherwise has contact with (replacing the original residence and contact orders).

2. Specific issue order (SIO) – directing a particular exercise of PR.

3. Prohibited steps order (PSO) – forbidding a particular exercise of PR.

---

1 Amendments introduced by s12 of the Children and Families Act 2014. In this book the terms 'order for residence' and 'order for contact' include both old-style residence and contact orders and new child arrangements order determining with whom a child lives or who a child sees (respectively).

Another option is a special guardianship order (SGO) conferring PR which is shared but can be exercised exclusively.[2]

Local authorities and private law cases

Private law proceedings involve individuals; local authorities operate in the public law sphere. Public and private law orders do not mix; s8 orders and care orders are incompatible. A care order discharges previous s8 orders and an order for residence discharges a care order. Contact is dealt with under different sections: s34 for children in care and s8 for private law cases.

So why does a social worker need to understand private law orders? This is because:

- the authority may have to provide a welfare report to court[3]

- a local authority report is mandatory in a SGO application

- public law proceedings could result in private law orders. All options must be considered when analysing paragraph (g) of the welfare checklist[4] (the range of powers available to the court) and making recommendations to the court

- the court can make a family assistance order[5] requiring the local authority to assist a child or family involved in private law proceedings

- children in private law disputes may be 'children in need' requiring support services from the local authority

- they may be in need of protection – there can be an overlap between private and public law. The court can direct the local authority to prepare a report if it suspects actual or likely significant harm.[6]

---

2   s14A CA89, added to the CA89 by the Adoption and Children Act 2002. For more information see Chapter 5.
3   s7 CA89.
4   s1(3)(g) CA89.
5   s16 CA89.
6   s37 CA89 – see pages 69–70 for more information.

Grounds

CA89 does not prescribe specific grounds for s8 orders or SGOs, so s1CA89[7] applies. The child's welfare is paramount and the welfare checklist is considered.

Who can apply?

Some people have a right to apply for s8 orders or SGOs; others need court permission first. The court can also make these orders of its own motion with no application if it is in the child's best interests to do so.[8]

APPLICATION AS OF RIGHT

The people entitled to apply for any s8 order[9] are:

- a parent (including a father without PR)
- a guardian or special guardian
- a step-parent with PR
- anyone who already has an order for residence for the child.

Orders for residence or contact (but not SIOs or PSOs) can be applied for by:

- a parent's spouse or civil partner (current or ex) where the child is treated as a child of the family
- anyone with whom the child has lived for at least three years
- anyone who has the consent of:
  - anyone with an order for residence
  - or the local authority if the child is in care
  - or, in any other case, everyone with PR.

Local authority foster carers or relatives ('relative' means a grandparent, sibling or uncle/aunt) who have had a child living with them for a least a year can apply for an order for residence or SGO for that child.

---

7   See Chapter 2 for more details.
8   s10(1)(b) and s14A(6)(b) CA89.
9   Except an order for residence if a SGO is in force, in which case leave is always required no matter who the applicant is.

One of the key differences between orders for residence and SGOs is that parents cannot apply for SGOs.[10]

Case Studies: Who can apply?

Yasmin and Annie are civil partners. They jointly parented Yasmin's son Zack although Annie never obtained step-parent PR for him. When they separate acrimoniously, Yasmin refuses to allow Zack to see Annie. Annie has the automatic right to apply for an order for contact because Zack was a child of the family. However, she cannot seek a SIO or PSO to control Yasmin's exercise of PR without court leave. If Annie had obtained step-parent PR, she could have applied for any s8 order.

Brigitte's unmarried parents are separated. Her father, who is French, has no PR. He wants Brigitte to go to a bilingual school. Her mother wants her to go to the local school with her friends. As a parent, even without PR, Christophe has the right to apply for a SIO to determine where Brigitte should go to school.

APPLICATION WITH COURT LEAVE

For those who do not have an automatic right to apply, there is a two-stage process. Grandparents fall into this category: they do not have any privileged status in respect of their grandchildren. First, they must seek court leave; only if that is granted can they make their application. Granting leave is not a question of the child's upbringing, so the welfare principle does not apply. Instead, the court considers the factors listed in s10(9) CA89:

- the nature of the proposed application
- the applicant's connection with the child
- any risk that the application itself (regardless of the outcome) might cause harmful disruption to the child's life
- if the child is looked after by a local authority (in care or accommodated), the authority's plans for the child and the parents' wishes and feelings.

---

10   For more detail on SGOs see Chapter 5.

The merits of the proposed application are also relevant (without pre-judging the issue); leave will not be granted if there is no realistic prospect of success. Obtaining leave does not mean that the application itself will succeed – the court could allow the application to proceed but then refuse the order.

CHILD APPLICANTS

Children have no automatic right to apply for s8 orders. They have to seek the court's permission and there are specific provisions to apply. First, the court must be satisfied that the child has sufficient understanding to make the proposed application.[11] If so, the court still has a discretion. It will consider whether the application has any realistic chance of success, and why the child, rather than someone else, is applying.

Case Study: Child's application for leave

Estranged from her parents, 14-year-old Georgia lives with her friend's parents. She wants them to have PR so she wants them to have an order for residence. She cannot apply without court leave. Even assuming she is competent to make the application, the court may consider it more appropriate for the carers to make their own application. Unless they have Georgia's parents' agreement, or she has been there for at least three years, they too will need to seek leave to apply for an order for residence

---

A child who wants an order in respect of another child is treated as any other applicant for court permission to apply. When the court looks at the prospects of success, the court considers the welfare of the child subject to the application, not the child applicant.

---

11   s10(8) CA89.

Case Study: Child's application in respect of another child

Holly is in foster care. Her sister Ivy has been adopted. Holly wants to see Ivy, but the adopters refuse because Holly is still in contact with the girls' birth mother. Holly needs leave to apply for an order. The court considers the factors in s10(9) CA89. The very application itself (let alone any order) may disrupt Ivy directly as her wishes and feelings would be sought and indirectly because of its effect on her adopters. The prospects of success of an application are limited as Ivy's welfare, not Holly's, would be paramount and the court is unlikely to do anything to destabilise the adoption. Leave is unlikely to be granted.

FOSTER CARERS

Foster carers without an automatic right to apply have an extra hurdle to overcome. They cannot even ask the court for leave in respect of a child fostered currently or in the last six months unless:

- they have the local authority's consent

- they are the child's relatives, or

- the child has been living with them for a year.[12]

This is to stop carers inappropriately impeding plans for a fostered child.

Case Study: Foster carer's application

Jane is a local authority foster carer caring for baby Kevin until an adoptive placement is found. She is not considered a suitable long-term carer for Kevin. Eight months into the placement, carers are identified, but Jane wants to keep him. Can she apply to court for an order for Kevin to live with her to stop the local authority's plans?

Without the authority's support, as the placement has been for less than a year, she has no automatic right to apply for an order, nor the right even to apply for leave. This is unless Kevin is accommodated (not in care) and she has the support of all those with PR.

---

12 s9(3) CA89.

For a SGO she would have to give three months' notice of her intention even to apply for leave, giving the authority plenty of time to move Kevin.

The authority must be keenly aware of the passage of time. Once the magic one year mark is reached, Jane has an automatic right to apply, delaying plans for Kevin.

If Kevin's case is already before the court, for example in care proceedings, the court could, of its own motion, make an order in Jane's favour even if she is not entitled to apply for one.

BIRTH RELATIVES OF ADOPTED CHILDREN

An adoption order terminates all previous legal relationships, so birth parents are no longer 'parents' and have no automatic right to apply for a s8 order or a s51A ACA order. No-one in the birth family can apply for an order without court leave first. Except in unusual cases, they are likely to have an uphill struggle even to obtain court leave, let alone an order.[13]

Court applications
Before going to court

Wherever possible, safe and appropriate, it is best to avoid going to court at all and to try to resolve issues by agreement. For this reason pre-proceedings requirements have been introduced to try to divert cases from court.[14] This involves both the prospective applicant and respondent attending a Mediation Information and Assessment Meeting (MIAM) (together if possible, but separately if not) with a family mediator to find out about mediation and other forms of alternative dispute resolution.

Exceptions are made if, for example:

- the mediator decides it is inappropriate

- there is actual or feared domestic violence

- the case is urgent or brought without notice

- there is child protection social work involvement.

---

13   See Chapter 16 for more on post-adoption contact.
14   Originally the Pre-Application Protocol under Practice Direction 3A issued under the Family Procedure Rules 2010, made a statutory requirement by s10(1) of the Children and Families Act 2014.

The court process

Cases which cannot be diverted from court are governed by the Family Procedure Rules 2010 (FPR),[15] supplemented by Practice Directions. The rules start with a statement of the overriding objective[16] to deal with cases justly having regard to any welfare issues. This involves:

- dealing with cases expeditiously and fairly
- acting proportionately to the nature, importance and complexity of the issues involved
- ensuring the parties are on an equal footing
- and, in a sign of the times, saving expense and allocating an appropriate share of the court's resources (bearing in mind demands of other cases).

The court must always consider whether alternative dispute resolution is appropriate,[17] and it can adjourn proceedings to enable parties to explore alternative options or to go for mediation.

Early on in a case, usually within four weeks, a First Hearing Dispute Resolution Appointment (FHDRA)[18] is held with the assistance of a CAFCASS (Children and Family Court Advisory Support Service) officer and any available mediator. The court considers:

- the possibility of resolving some or all of the issues with the assistance of the CAFCASS officer or mediator
- further dispute resolution
- any risks in the case (particularly in terms of domestic violence)
- timetabling the case
- ensuring judicial continuity
- the child's role in the proceedings, including whether he knows about the case, how his wishes and feelings are to be ascertained, whether he should be a party and who will tell him the outcome

---

15 Family Procedure Rules 2010. Available at www.legislation.gov.uk/uksi/2010/2955/contents/made, accessed on 30 March 2014.
16 FPR 2010 r1.1.
17 FPR Rules 2010 r3.2.
18 Set out in the Child Arrangements Programme (replacing the Revised Private Law Programme), Practice Direction 12B.

- narrowing issues, reaching agreement where possible and identifying outstanding issues in dispute.

Any agreements are subject to court scrutiny and approval, which may be deferred pending outstanding safeguarding checks or risk assessment.

The child's role

Children are not automatically parties to proceedings in private law cases as they are in care proceedings. There is no obvious logic to this; private law cases can be just as bitter, complex and protracted as care proceedings and the issues for the child (who he lives with, who he sees) are just as profound. In care proceedings the court has professional input from both the local authority and Children's Guardian; in private law cases it may have neither. The court can make a child a party to private law proceedings if it is in the child's best interests.[19] However, the Practice Direction[20] makes it clear that this is exceptional and the court must first consider whether there is an alternative such as asking the family court reporter to do more work, seeking expert advice or involving social services.

Each case is decided on its own merits but the Practice Direction gives illustrative examples, all from the serious end of the spectrum, such as situations where:

- the CAFCASS officer recommends it
- the child's position is inconsistent with and cannot be represented by any of the adult parties
- an older child is proposing a course of action
- more than one child is involved and their interests conflict or one is in a particularly disadvantaged position
- disputes are intractable or in cases of implacable hostility
- there may be significant harm associated with the dispute
- there are serious allegations of abuse of the child or domestic violence
- complex medical or mental health issues need to be resolved

19   Family Procedure Rules 2010 r16.2(1).
20   Practice Direction 16A.

- there are international issues
- there is a contested issue about scientific testing.

A child party is represented by a solicitor and a CAFCASS Guardian (unless he is competent to instruct the solicitor), rather than simply having his interests reflected in a welfare report. If you are involved in a complex case, raise the issue of whether the child should be made a party and separately represented.

Reports to court
S7 REPORTS
Courts in private law cases are often faced with warring parties and high emotions. Parties are often unrepresented, appearing in person. The court may find itself short of objective information and in need of professional advice on the child's welfare. For that reason, s7(1) CA89 gives the court power when 'considering any question with respect to a child under this Act' to ask CAFCASS or the local authority for a report 'on such matters relating to the welfare of the child as are required...' The court usually asks the local authority rather than CAFCASS to report if it has current or recent involvement with the family. The court can request an oral or written report.[21] Once a direction is made, there is a statutory duty to provide a report.[22]

The order usually specifies the topics to be addressed in each case. However, if other relevant matters come to light during the course of enquiries, it may be appropriate to seek further directions to broaden the scope of the report or to direct parties to file further evidence.

Welfare reports can include hearsay (second-hand information) and opinion evidence which the court can take into account provided it is relevant.[23] Indeed, courts are often grateful for a well-informed professional opinion to assist it in determining the child's best interests.

S37 REPORTS
Reports under s7 and s37 are completely different. The court can only direct a s37 report when 'it appears that it may be appropriate for a care

---

21 s7(3) CA89.
22 s7(5) CA89.
23 s7(4) CA89.

or supervision order to be made'. This is therefore a way for the court to refer possible abuse or neglect to the local authority for investigation; it is, in the words of McFarlane LJ a 'jurisdictional bridge' between private and public law proceedings.[24]

The report must state whether the local authority intends to apply for a care or supervision order, provide services or assistance or take other action. s37 orders are not made lightly, so if the local authority decides not to take proceedings, the report must give reasons for the decision and details of what the authority proposes to do instead.[25]

If it is really concerned about the child's welfare, the court can even make an interim care order and appoint a Children's Guardian when it issues the s37 direction. Ultimately, however, the court cannot force the authority to commence care proceedings; that decision lies with the local authority alone.

A direction to report to court must be taken very seriously and given proper priority. Failure to do so can have serious consequences. In one case[26] the local authority had to pay costs because their first report was five weeks late and failed to consider important government and case law guidance, the social workers attended court late and then decided they needed to hold a legal planning meeting (eight months after the direction was made). A second report was filed four weeks late. The judge said:

> ...the failures in this case are not 'minor'; they are extensive, and have had a profound effect on the conduct of the proceedings. The Local Authority has in my judgment failed fundamentally to investigate, address, or analyse the serious issues in the case...[27]

Unfortunately, often the least experienced social workers are asked to compile reports and, as the authority is not a party to the proceedings, they are not entitled to legal representation. However, they should have legal advice and should never go to court unsupported.

STATUS OF REPORTS TO COURT

The court must take reports into account but it does not have to follow recommendations – the court decides the case, no-one else. However,

---

24   Re K (Children) [2012] EWCA Civ 1549 (Court of Appeal) at paragraph 23.
25   s37(3) CA89.
26   HB v. PB [2013] EWHC 1956 (Fam) (High Court).
27   HB v. PB at paragraph 52.

if the court reaches a different conclusion from the report it gives its reasons for doing so.[28]

Family assistance orders

In family proceedings, the court has power to make a family assistance order (FAO) whether or not it makes any other sort of order.[29]

The order directs the local authority or CAFCASS to provide a worker to advise, assist and befriend anyone named in the order, who may be:

- a parent, guardian or special guardian of the child
- anyone the child is living with
- anyone who has an order for contact with the child
- the child.

Adults named in the order must consent to it being made. FAOs last for 12 months unless a shorter duration is specified.

FAOs can be allied to orders for contact to help in establishing, improving or maintaining contact, for example to secure supervision of contact. FAOs can also require the officer to report to the court on any matters relating to any s8 order in force, including whether the order should be varied or discharged.

CAFCASS role

If a CAFCASS officer involved in private law proceedings suspects that a child is at risk of harm, she should make a risk assessment and provide it to the court so the court can consider what action to take.[30] This applies only to CAFCASS officers because local authority social workers do not need a special provision: they can simply invoke the local authority's child protection powers.[31]

---

28   *W (Children)* [2012] EWCA Civ 1788 (Court of Appeal).
29   s16 CA89.
30   s16A CA89.
31   See Chapter 9 on child protection.

Duration of s8 orders

Other than orders for residence, s8 orders do not last beyond the age of 16 unless the circumstances of the case are exceptional.[32]

Variation and discharge

s8 orders can be varied or discharged by the court. The application is made under s8(2) CA89 and s1 CA89 applies, so the question is whether it is in the child's best interests to alter or end the arrangements made by the original order. Generally speaking, the same people can apply for variation or discharge as can apply for a s8 order in the first place, with the addition of anyone on whose application the original order was made and anyone named in an order for contact.[33]

This means that s8 orders are not permanent so children's cases can return to court, sometimes repeatedly. Where this becomes extreme, the court can make an order under s91(14) CA89 to prevent further applications as in one case[34] where residence and contact proceedings started when the child was two and a half years old and continued for six years, by which time he was pleading with the guardian, the independent social worker and his school to make the fighting stop. The parents' (especially the father's) focus on their own agendas was such that they were apparently oblivious to the emotional harm caused to their son. The court made a s91(14) order for four years.

The fact that an order for residence can be returned to court for variation or discharge, unlike a SGO, makes it inherently less secure than a SGO (still less an adoption order).[35]

Prohibited steps and specific issue orders

These orders are mirror images of each other. Their names are self-explanatory: a prohibited steps order (PSO) prevents a particular step whereas a specific issue order (SIO) directs one.

These orders cover the whole spectrum of decisions taken in a child's life (apart from residence and contact), including education, health and religion. Increasingly, reported cases reveal the c ourts struggling to find the right way forward where there is a clash of cultures or beliefs

---

32   s9(6) CA89.
33   s10(6).
34   N (A Child) [2009] EWHC 3055 (Fam) (High Court).
35   For a comparison of ROs, SGOs and adoption orders see Appendix 2.

between the child's parents. This can put the court in a difficult position, choosing between sincere and heartfelt principles, but if individuals cannot agree then it is the court's job to decide.

As always under s8 the court's concern is the child's welfare, which is paramount. It considers the welfare checklist to help determine where the child's best interests lie.[36]

Prohibited steps orders

s8(1) CA89 ...'a prohibited steps order' means an order that no step which could be taken by a parent in meeting his parental responsibility for a child, and which is of a kind specified in the order, shall be taken by any person without the consent of the court.

Although PSOs regulate steps which are an exercise of PR, they are not limited to parents and can be addressed to anyone.

PSOs have been used to address many and varied issues including:

- preventing a child being taken out of the country or moving to a distant part of the UK[37]

- preventing a person from seeking contact with a child

- preventing a person arranging for a child to appear in a TV programme

- stopping a parent from changing a child's school

- preventing a change of surname

- barring certain elective surgery.

However, PSOs must relate to some sort of exercise of PR and cannot deal with aspects of an adult's own life rather than an action towards a child. So a PSO cannot be used to exclude someone from the family home;[38] instead, an application should be made for a Family Law Act 1996 injunction.

---

36 See Chapter 2 for more information on the welfare principle and welfare checklist.
37 For example, *F (Children)* [2010] EWCA Civ 1428 (Court of Appeal), which involved a proposed move of four children to the Orkneys.
38 *D* v. *D* [1996] 2FLR 273 (Court of Appeal).

Specific issue orders

> s8(1) CA89 ...'a specific issue order' means an order giving directions
> for the purpose of determining a specific question which has arisen,
> or which may arise, in connection with any aspect of parental
> responsibility for a child.

Like PSOs, SIOs cover the whole range of issues and can see the courts
grappling with complex and delicate matters, trying to find where the
child's best interests lie.

RELIGION

When the marriage of a Jewish couple from the orthodox Chareidi
community broke down, the father wanted the children to follow a
strictly observant way of life, including a Chareidi education in single-
sex schools following a narrow Talmudic syllabus. Their mother (with
whom the children lived) wanted them to go to a co-educational
modern Orthodox school with a wider education and thus greater career
options. As the children had lived with their mother since the parents
split up, they had already experienced a less strictly observant way of
life. Munby LJ[39] explained that the law takes 'an essentially neutral view
of religious beliefs and a benevolent tolerance of cultural and religious
diversity'. He continued:

> It is not for a judge to weigh one religion against another. The court
> recognises no religious distinctions and generally speaking passes no
> judgment on religious beliefs or on the tenets, doctrines or rules of any
> particular section of society. All are entitled to equal respect, so long
> as they are 'legally and socially acceptable'.[40]

But the court had to choose between the parents' beliefs, deciding
the children's best interests by acting as a 'judicial reasonable parent'.
For Munby LJ, that involved considering society's values of equality
of opportunity, fostering aspiration and putting the child in the best
position to make his own decisions in the future. The court decided

---

39   *Re G* [2012] EWCA Civ 1233 (Court of Appeal).
40   *Re G* at paragraph 36.

that the children should go to the more liberal school proposed by the mother.

As the choice of religion is an exercise of PR, courts can determine the religion in which a child is brought up. It could even be a different religion from that of the resident parent, although that would be highly unusual. These propositions were confirmed in Re J,[41] which arose from the separation of a Muslim father and non-Muslim mother. The couple's five-year-old son lived a secular lifestyle with his mother. The father wanted an order for his son to be brought up as a Muslim. The order was declined because the child did not live in a Muslim environment, and the father himself did not actively practise his religion or mix in Muslim circles. The court decided that the father could provide knowledge of his religion on contact visits.

Another case concerned the children of a Muslim mother and Hindu father.[42] After their separation, the mother wanted to bring the children up as Muslims, saying that they would otherwise be excluded from their community. These children knew about their dual heritage and until their parents' separation had been involved in the practice of both religions. Baron J said that children of mixed heritage should be able to choose for themselves which religion to follow and should be allowed to have the best of both worlds. To present these children to the world as anything other than children of mixed heritage would be to practise an 'impermissible deception'.

In another case,[43] the Anglican father took his four-year-old son to church and Sunday school while the Jehovah's Witness mother took him regularly to the Kingdom Hall and did not want him to take part in any other religious practice, school assemblies or nativity plays. The judge confirmed that PR is joint and equal; neither parent has a predominant right to choose a child's religion. Where parents follow different religions, both of which are socially acceptable, the child should learn about and experience both. The court can restrict practices which conflict with the other parent's lifestyle where that conflict impacts on the child's welfare. The judge held that there was no reason why

---

41 Re J (Specific Issue Order: Muslim Upbringing & Circumcision) [1999] 2FLR 678 (High Court) and Re J (Specific Issue Orders: Child's Religious Upbringing and Circumcision) [2000] 1FLR 571 (Court of Appeal).

42 Re S (SIO: Religion) [2005] EWHC 2769 (Fam) (High Court).

43 Re N (A Child – Religion – Jehovah's Witness) [2011] EWHC B26 (Fam) (High Court).

the child should not continue to attend both church and the Kingdom Hall. Neither parent was to restrict the child's participation in school activities. Further, in case a blood transfusion was ever recommended, the mother was ordered to inform the medical authorities immediately of the father's contact details and his right to give consent.

CIRCUMCISION

The father in the Re J case (above) also applied for an order for the boy to be circumcised. This was normal practice in the father's culture, but was vigorously opposed by the mother. This was the first case ever to examine whether ritual (as opposed to medical) circumcision of boys was lawful at all.[44] The High Court – later backed by the Court of Appeal – found that ritual circumcision with parental consent is lawful, but if parents disagree, in spite of s2(7) CA89, one parent alone cannot proceed and disputes should be referred to the High Court.

Carefully balancing all of the arguments and the facts of the case, the judge decided not to make a SIO because the child was experiencing a secular upbringing in England, not mixing in circles where circumcision was the norm, the intervention was irreversible, painful and involved some physical and psychological risk and, importantly, the mother would be unable to present it positively to the child. Wall J said: 'it is a strong thing to impose a medically unnecessary surgical intervention on a resident parent who is opposed to it.'[45]

IMMUNISATIONS

In Re C the court again confirmed that separated parents have equal rights before the court.[46] Two fathers applied for orders that their children should have the MMR immunisation. Both mothers, who had residence orders, opposed the applications. The High Court (later upheld by the Court of Appeal) decided that the benefits outweighed the risks, including the mothers' emotional distress, and immunisations were in the children's best interests. The court stressed this was not a general approval of immunisation; refusing to have a child immunised

---

44   Female circumcision is illegal under the Prohibition of Female Circumcision Act 1985.

45   Re J, page 700C at paragraph 4.

46   Re C (Welfare of Child: Immunisation) [2003] 2FLR 1054 (High Court) and 1095 (Court of Appeal).

is a legitimate exercise of PR but if parents disagree then the court must decide.

TELLING CHILDREN THEIR ORIGINS

The mother of eight-year-old twins and her partner (who the twins thought was their father) did not want the children to be told about their true paternity.[47] The Court of Appeal confirmed that the family courts can take responsibility for this decision and directed that the children should be told the truth. In a similar case, DNA testing was ordered to determine whether twins were the product of an extra-marital affair or the children of the mother's husband.[48] The Court of Appeal said that there are few cases where the interests of children are served by the suppression of the truth.

POLICE INTERVIEWS OF CHILD WITNESSES

If police want to interview witnesses who are too young to consent for themselves, they usually need parental agreement. What if consent is refused? In one case seven-year-old twins were the only eye-witnesses when their 16-year-old brother shot dead their 12-year-old sister.[49] Their mother, the only person with PR, declined consent for the police to interview the twins. The police applied to court.

Ryder J decided that giving or withholding permission for a police interview is an aspect of PR so it can be controlled by the court by a SIO (or by using the High Court's inherent jurisdiction). Interestingly, he decided that in this case the child's welfare was not paramount because giving evidence to the police is not just a question of upbringing but part of the role of a citizen, bringing into play considerations of the rights of others, including the general public interest in the investigation of possible crimes. This was a case in which a balancing exercise had to be undertaken, weighing up the children's welfare against wider considerations. In the event, there was no conflict – the public interest required an interview but it was also the best thing for the children,

---

47   Re F (Children: Declaration of Paternity) [2007] EWCA Civ 873 (Court of Appeal).
48   Re H and A (Paternity: Blood Tests) [2002] EWCA Civ 383 (Court of Appeal).
49   Chief Constable of Greater Manchester v. KI and KW (by their Children's Guardian, CAFCASS Legal) and PN [2007] EWHC 1837 (Fam) (High Court).

who needed to talk. In the event, no order was needed as the mother backed down and gave her consent.

NAMES

The issue of children's names is an emotive one. Names indicate family connections and can be an integral part of a child's identity, reflecting aspects of the child's heritage, religion or ethnic background. Changing the name by which a child is known (the name on the Register of Births cannot be changed) can give rise to bitter disputes which find their way into the courts.

If there is an order for residence in force, a child's surname cannot be changed without written consent of everyone with PR or a court order.[50]

The High Court decided that, even where there is no order for residence, this is such a significant decision that all those with PR must agree[51] and if there is a dispute then the court can decide. As a father without PR has the right to apply for any s8 CA89 order, somewhat paradoxically he can go to court about a change of name even though his lack of PR means he has no right to choose the child's name in the first place.

The House of Lords was clear that a child's name is a very serious and profound issue, whatever the child's age.[52] The child's welfare is the court's paramount consideration, looking not just at the present situation but also future implications. Each case must be decided on its own facts and circumstances.

Courts are not generally impressed by arguments that a child's name should be changed to be the same as his carer or as siblings, or by any emotional or proprietorial claiming of parental rights. The length of time a child has used a particular name and practical difficulties of change may be significant factors.

A change was permitted was where a Bangladeshi Muslim mother had married the Indian Sikh father against her family's wishes.[53] When the marriage broke down, the mother was allowed to change her son's name from a Sikh name to a Muslim one so that she and her son would be accepted back into her Bangladeshi community.

---

50   s13(1) CA89.
51   *Re PC (Change of Surname)* [1997] 2FLR 730 (High Court).
52   *Dawson v. Wearmouth* [1999] 1FLR 1167 (House of Lords).
53   *Re S (Change of Names: Cultural Factors)* [2001] 2FLR 1005 (High Court).

s8 and human rights

When the court overrides parents' wishes, is this not a breach of their human rights? In the immunisation case, the High Court recognised that ordering an exercise of PR against a parent's wishes is indeed a breach but, because Article 8 is a qualified right, breaches can be justified.

Points for practice

1. s8 orders should be used flexibly (singly or in combination) to meet the needs of any case. Consider all the options in any court case (private or public law).

2. Work through the welfare checklist step by step to keep your focus on the child's welfare, not the adults' emotions and demands.

3. Never overlook human rights issues. Always address Article 8.

Chapter 5

Arrangements for Children (Residence) and Special Guardianship Orders

s8 orders

The most contentious private law disputes usually follow relationship breakdown and centre on where children live and who they see. Under the Children Act 1989 (CA89), these disputes fall within s8.

Before the Children and Families Act 2014 (CFA) there were two self-explanatory separate orders, 'residence' (RO) and 'contact' orders. After the implementation of CFA these are combined into a single 'child arrangements order' (CAO) which can specify when and with whom a child is to live, spend time or otherwise have contact.[1]

What is the difference? At first glance, CAOs look very much like ROs and contact orders rolled into one. The policy behind the change is to try to reduce the sense of winners and losers. Imagine if both parents want residence. Under the original version, one could 'win' a RO and the other have 'only' contact. Under the revised version, both have the same order, a CAO, albeit in different terms. The focus is supposed to be on the practical care arrangements which meet a child's needs, rather than the name of the order or a sense of entitlement.

---

1   For ease of reference ROs and CAOs regulating residence are jointly referred to as 'an order for residence' and contact orders and CAOs regulating contact are referred to as 'an order for contact'.

Whether warring parties will actually feel or behave differently if the CAO specifies that the child lives with one and sees the other remains to be seen.[2]

Another more subtle change is that the original contact order is addressed to the person the child lives with, who is to 'allow' contact, suggesting that contact is in that person's gift, whereas under the revised version contact is simply ordered by the court.

Grounds

There are no specific grounds to be proven for any s8 orders. Where a child lives and with whom he has contact are clearly questions concerning his upbringing, so s1 CA89 applies. Everything comes down to the child's welfare.

Parliament resisted pressure to introduce a presumption that parents should have equal involvement in a child's life. Instead, a new provision s1(2A)[3] adds a statutory presumption that a child's welfare is served by the involvement of both parents in his life, unless the contrary is shown. Involvement may be direct or indirect but expressly does not imply any particular division of a child's time. A new subsection s1(6) makes it clear that the presumption applies only if the parent's involvement does not put the child at risk of harm. These additions to the welfare principle apply to applications for s8 orders, special guardianship orders and applications for PR.[4]

Who the child lives with

Courts usually decide who the child lives with, not where; restrictions on where people can live clearly have human rights implications. However, in exceptional cases, courts can add a condition to an order for residence, or can use a PSO or SIO to prevent a move even within the UK. The move could be inappropriate because it would make contact with the other parent impractical, whether the motivation is genuine,[5]

---

2   This is particularly the case given that in reality many parents still refer 'custody' and 'access' orders, which is old terminology pre-dating the Children Act 1989.
3   Added to CA89 by the Children and Families Act 2014, in force from 22 April 2014.
4   Amendments to s1 CA89 made by s11 of the Children and Families Act 2014.
5   *F (Children)* [2010] EWCA Civ 1428 (Court of Appeal), which involved a proposed move of four children to the Orkneys.

or deliberately planned to thwart contact, as in a case where a mother planned to move from London to Newcastle to make life difficult for the father.[6] In another case involving a girl with Down's syndrome and heart problems, the court prevented a move from London to Cornwall because of the child's medical needs, her limited understanding and the difficulties the move would pose for contact.

Parental responsibility (PR)

It makes sense that the person looking after a child should have PR so this is automatically conferred by an order for residence.

FATHER OR FEMALE PARENT

If a father or female parent without PR obtains an order for residence, the court must also make a PR order at the same time. This PR lasts until the child is 18 even if the order for residence is later discharged.

PR is not automatically granted with an order for contact. However, if a CAO specifies that the child is to spend time with a father or female parent without PR, the court must grant PR if it is appropriate to do so.[7]

NON-PARENTS

Non-parents who obtain an order for residence automatically acquire PR, but only for the duration of the order. The court has the power to grant PR to non-parents when making a CAO for contact. It is important to note that these people acquire PR but they do not become a 'parent'.[8]

Case Study: PR for grandparents

April's married parents cannot care for her, so she lives with her grandparents Brenda and Colin. The parents have delegated their PR to the grandparents but Brenda and Colin feel insecure and sometimes it is difficult to contact the parents when they need them. They want PR

---

6   *B v. B (Residence: Condition Limiting Geographic Area)* [2004] 2FLR 979 (High Court).
7   Amendment to s12 CA89 made by the Children and Families Act 2014, Schedule 2, in force from 22 April 2014.
8   See Chapter 3 for more on parents and PR.

in their own right. If April has been with them for a year or more, or if both parents agree, they can apply to court by right; otherwise they need court leave first. For leave, the court considers the nature of the application, their connection with April, the risk that the application will disrupt April and the prospects of success. In the application itself, April's welfare is paramount and s1 CA89 applies. This includes the 'no order' principle in s1(5) CA89. Is an order necessary? There is no dispute about where April lives, but an order will confer PR on the grandparents and that itself justifies an order.[9] April now has two parents but four people with PR: her parents and her grandparents. There is no need for an order for contact because agreement is working well.

Sharing PR

PR under an order for residence is shared equally. As we saw in Chapter 4, the person the child lives with has no greater power, rights or responsibilities than anyone else with PR for that child. This is very different from a special guardianship order (SGO), where the special guardian can act alone to exercise PR to the exclusion of other holders of PR.[10]

While an order for residence is in force, the child's name cannot be changed and she cannot be taken out of the UK for more than a month without either the consent of everyone with PR or court permission.[11]

Shared orders

The court can make orders for residence to more than one person at a time. This is of course appropriate where the child is to live with a couple together, so both partners have equal status. It can also be appropriate for separated couples. Under the original s8, joint ROs could reflect the real situation better than a RO to one and contact to the other and convey an important message to child and parents. Under the new version of s8, both parties can have a CAO which can specify if necessary the division of time between two households.

---

9   This was the situation in *B* v. *B (A Minor) (Residence Order)* [1992] 2FLR 327 (High Court).

10   See later section for more information about special guardianship.

11   s13 CA89.

Case Study: Same sex partners

Uta and her husband Victor have a daughter, Wendy. When the couple divorced, a joint RO was made reflecting the extensive involvement Victor has in Wendy's life. Wendy's main home is with Uta and her partner Xanthe, who bring Wendy up together. Although the arrangement works well in practice, Uta and Xanthe are concerned about Xanthe's status. Delegating PR does not reflect the true nature of their situation and they are worried about what would happen should Uta die (when Victor could in theory demand Wendy's immediate move to him). Uta and Xanthe are not civil partners, so Xanthe cannot seek a step-parent PR agreement or order; and as Wendy was not born by assisted conception, the HFEA08 does not apply. A three-way RO or CAO is the appropriate order.[12] This gives Xanthe PR which she would not otherwise have. Only Uta and Victor are Wendy's parents.

Do parents have priority?

It is sometimes argued that children have a right to be brought up by their natural parents. Clearly, having a relationship with his natural parents is a relevant factor in a child's welfare. Lord Nicholls said:

> [The children's] welfare is the court's paramount consideration. In reaching its decision the court should always have in mind that in the ordinary way the rearing of a child by his or her biological parent can be expected to be in the child's best interests, both in the short term and also, and importantly, in the longer term. I decry any tendency to diminish the significance of this factor. A child should not be removed from the primary care of his or her biological parents without compelling reason. Where such a reason exists the judge should spell this out explicitly.[13]

However, the Supreme Court[14] confirmed that the question is one of welfare, not rights. Lord Nicholls was simply reflecting common experience but the fact is that many of the cases which appear before the courts are out of 'the ordinary way'. The correct approach was as follows:

> All consideration of the importance of parenthood in private law disputes about residence must be firmly rooted in an examination of

---

12   This was the solution in *T* v. *T* [2010] EWCA Civ 1366 (Court of Appeal).

13   *In re G (Children) (Residence: Same-sex Partner)* [2006] UKHL 43 (House of Lords) at paragraph 2.

14   *B (A Child)* [2009] UKSC 5 (Supreme Court).

what is in the child's best interests. This is the paramount consideration. It is only as a contributor to the child's welfare that parenthood assumes any significance. In common with all other factors bearing on what is in the best interests of the child, it must be examined for its potential to fulfil that aim.[15]

The case involved four-year-old 'Harry' who had lived since birth with his maternal grandmother, his parents being unable to care for him. When he was about 18 months old, the grandmother obtained a RO by consent. She promoted contact to both parents and Harry was settled and thriving. The father's circumstances changed and, supported by the mother, he applied for a RO for Harry to live with him and his new wife. The evidence was that they would be capable of providing competent care. Should Harry stay with his grandmother or go to his father? The magistrates decided for the grandmother. On appeal, the judge decided for father on a presumption in favour of a biological parent. The Court of Appeal agreed but the Supreme Court returned Harry to his grandmother, saying that the magistrates had been right to weigh up all the factors in Harry's life, including the stability and security of his grandmother's home as against the biological link with his father.

Unconventional families

The Court of Appeal[16] has made it clear that, whatever the family structure, the key issue is always the child's welfare, and each case must be decided on its own facts without any assumptions or presumptions. The case involved a two-year-old boy born to a lesbian mother and a gay father. Although the mother was in a long-term same-sex relationship, she was from a religious family so she and the father married to give an appearance of a conventional family. The father therefore had PR. The parties agreed that the child would live with the mother and her partner, with the father playing a role in the child's life. The relationship broke down when the father sought staying contact. He applied for a contact order, and the mother and her partner applied for ROs and SIO to limit the father's contact. The judge at first instance held that the father's role was secondary and that he should have no staying contact for three to

---

15   Lord Kerr in *Re B* at paragraph 37.
16   *A v. B and C* [2012] EWCA Civ 285 (Court of Appeal).

four years. The Court of Appeal sent the case back for further hearing, and took the opportunity to set out some guidance:

- All cases are fact-specific and are to be decided on the welfare principle alone.
- A parent's role in a child's life depends on the child's best interests.
- There are no general rules to be applied to 'alternative' family structures.
- The concept of 'principal' and 'secondary' parent was disapproved (even if in practice one is the primary carer and the other plays a secondary role).
- Contact is to promote the child's welfare, not to reflect roles agreed by the parents.
- Courts should be cautious in attaching much weight to pre-birth agreements.

The Court of Appeal also indicated that courts may need expert advice on the particular case (not the non-specific research relied on by the judge). The child may need to be joined as a party to proceedings to ensure that adult concerns are not allowed to dominate.

Local authority role

Local authorities do not have a duty to support anyone with an order for residence. For those other than parents or a parent's spouse or civil partner, there is a discretionary power to give financial support towards the cost of the child's accommodation and maintenance.[17] In reality, this is only likely to happen if the order is a way of taking or keeping the child out of the care system. There are no specific provisions for other types of service or support for people with orders for residence; they fall within the authority's general duties under s17 CA89 towards children in need.[18] This is in contrast to SGOs and adoption where the local authorities have a positive duty to provide financial and other support.

---

17   CA89 Schedule 1 paragraph 15.
18   For more information see Chapter 7.

Special guardianship orders

Special guardianship orders (SGOs) appear in s14A–G CA89. They were added into the CA89 by the Adoption and Children Act 2002[19] to provide another weapon in the court's armoury, stronger than an order for residence, but not as drastic as adoption. SGOs only apply to non-parents so are not apt for separating couples, but they can be ideal for extended family placements and foster carers who want to keep a child long-term.

Why so special?

Two key features make SGOs stronger than orders for residence: greater autonomy in exercising PR and greater security.

However, SGOs are not as far-reaching as adoption orders. Adoption is life-long and changes the child's whole identity, terminating all pre-existing legal relationships, terminating birth parents' PR and making the child in all respects a member of the adoptive family, including a change of name. SGOs do none of these things: they simply add another person with a powerful version of PR.

Autonomy

A special guardian (SG) obtains PR, shared with others who already have it, but it is not an equal partnership. The SG can act totally independently to the exclusion of others with PR; effectively he has autonomy. This includes deciding who the child should live with as the SGO does not dictate a child's residence. In fact, the SG has more power than a local authority with a care order as the SG does not have to show that it is necessary for the child's welfare for him to overrule the parents.

There are some limits on the SG's powers. He cannot change the child's surname or take her out of the UK for more than three months without either the consent of all those with PR or court permission, nor is he a 'parent', so he cannot agree to the child's adoption or appoint a guardian.

> s14C(1)(b) CA89 Subject to any other order in force with respect to the child under this Act, a special guardian is entitled to exercise parental responsibility to the exclusion of any other person with parental responsibility for the child (apart from another special guardian).

---

19   In force since 2005.

Security

SGOs have an element of security built in. They are not irrevocable like adoption orders but neither are they subject to parents' automatic right to apply for variation or discharge like s8 orders. When a SGO is in force, no-one can apply for an order for residence without court leave[20] and the child's parents cannot apply to revoke the order without first showing the court at a preliminary hearing that there has been a significant change in circumstances.[21] Such a change is necessary but not sufficient – it gives the court a discretion, not an obligation, to grant leave to apply. The court will also consider the child's welfare and the prospects of the application succeeding.[22] However, a local authority which had a care order prior to the SGO does have the right to apply for variation or discharge of a SGO.

So SGs and the children they care for are freed from the prospect of repeated court applications to change the child's residence. However, there is no restriction on other applications under s8 CA89, although this could be added if appropriate by making an order under s91(14) CA89.

Case Study: SGO for foster carer

Fourteen-year-old Nicola has been with her foster carer Meera for four years. Nicola wants to stay with Meera but hates being in care and wants to be rid of social workers. Meera would like to have PR in her own right. Nicola's mother Odette wants Nicola to stay permanently with Meera, who she likes. Odette has intermittent mental health problems and at times is difficult to work with so Meera does not feel comfortable about sharing PR equally, so an order for residence would not be enough. However, adoption would be artificial and inappropriate – Nicola has a clear sense of her own identity and has no wish to cut all legal connections with her mother and entire family. A SGO could be the perfect solution.

---

20 s10(7A) CA89.
21 s14D CA89.
22 *G (A Child)* [2010] EWCA Civ 300 (Court of Appeal), Wilson LJ giving guidance, reasoning by analogy from similar wording in the ACA and the case of *M* v. *Warwickshire County Council* [2007] EWCA Civ 1084 (Court of Appeal).

Who can apply?

Parents cannot apply for a SGO;[23] much as one parent might like to be able to exercise PR to the exclusion of the other, they cannot do so and must find a way to share PR.

People with an automatic right to apply for a SGO (excluding a parent in each case) are:

- a child's guardian
- anyone with an order for residence
- anyone with whom the child has lived for at least three years
- anyone with the consent of either:
    - anyone with an order for residence
    - the local authority if the child is in care
    - everyone with PR
- a local authority foster carer or a relative (grandparent, sibling or aunt/uncle) with whom the child has lived for at least a year.

Other people can only apply with court leave. The court can also make a SGO if it thinks it appropriate even if no-one has applied.[24] The court could therefore make a SGO in an application for a s8 order, care order or adoption order so you should consider this possibility when reporting to the court under s1(3)(g) of the welfare checklist (the range of powers available to the court).

Grounds

There are no specific grounds so s1 CA89 applies. The child's welfare is paramount, and the welfare checklist set out in s1(3) CA89 must be considered.

The local authority's role

SGOs are not a local authority placement, so the authority does not assess and approve applicants or match children with carers as it does in fostering or adoption. Nonetheless, SGOs are often used to achieve

---

23   s14A CA89.
24   s14A(6)(b) CA89.

permanence for children in care and many local authorities encourage long-term foster carers to consider SGOs.

Anyone seeking a SGO must obtain court leave (if necessary) and then give the local authority three months' written notice of his intention to apply. The notice triggers the authority's duty to investigate the application and prepare a thorough report for the court. The court cannot make a SGO without this report,[25] but if most of the information is already before the court (for example, in reports for care proceedings) there is no need to file a whole new report; instead, the information can be cross-referenced.[26]

Regulations set out the required contents of the report, including:[27]

- full details of the child and his family
- wishes and feelings of the child and his family
- full details of the proposed SG including:
    o health
    o capacity as a carer
    o a report of interviews with three referees
- an analysis of the implications of a SGO for:
    o the child
    o his parent(s)
    o the prospective SG
    o any other relevant person
- an assessment of the relative merits of a SGO and any other relevant order
- a recommendation as to whether:
    o a SGO or any other order should be made
    o there should be contact arrangements.

---

25   s14A(11) CA89.
26   *Re S (Adoption or Special Guardianship Order) (No. 2)* [2007] EWCA Civ 90 (Court of Appeal).
27   Special Guardianship Regulations 2005 SI 2005/1109. Available at www.legislation. gov.uk/uksi/2005/1109/contents/made, accessed on 30 March 2014.

Other orders

Before making a SGO, the court must consider whether to make an order for contact under s8 CA89 at the same time and whether to discharge or vary any existing CA89 order. The court can also give leave for the child to be known by a new surname[28] and consideration may be given to adding extra security by means of a s91(14) order.

Local authority support

Local authorities have a duty to provide support services for SGs.[29] The long-term nature of SGOs is reflected in the fact that these provisions closely resemble those for adopters and are considerably stronger than provisions for those with orders for residence.

On request, the authority must assess the need for services, report on the outcome of the assessment and draw up a package of support which may include counselling, advice and information, respite care and therapeutic provision.

Guidance says that financial support should be based on the fostering allowance. As Black J said: 'some children who are placed with special guardians are in situations which have derived from former fostering arrangements…and the cost of bringing up these children may not be significantly less than the cost of bringing up fostered children.'[30] Authorities cannot deviate from guidance without clear, rational justification[31] or they risk judicial review.

The court can ensure that a support package is devised in accordance with guidance, but the precise detail of the support package is for the local authority to decide. Hedley J explained:

> Section 14F imposes duties on a local authority but it does not empower the family court to direct how or (in some aspects) even whether such duties are to be performed. Moreover, the statute gives the court no power to make directions as to payment of money or provision of services. Of course judges may properly express views to local authorities and are entitled no doubt to expect that they will

---

28   s14B(2)(a) CA89.
29   Details are set out in the Special Guardianship Regulations 2005 SI 2005/1109.
30   B v. LB Lewisham [2008] EWHC 738 (Admin) (High Court).
31   There have been several cases of judicial review, for example R (TT) v. LB Merton [2012] EWHC 2055 (Admin) (High Court).

receive serious consideration…and of course it is only the judge who in the end can make the special guardianship order.[32]

The choice of orders

First you must be clear which orders are available (on application or of the court's own motion) and understand the legal characteristics of each option. Then consider the needs of the child against possible orders to find which best serves the child's interests. The child's welfare is paramount and each case must be considered on its own facts, with no presumptions.

Where does the principle of minimum intervention or proportionality fit in? An order for residence is less intrusive than a SGO, which in turn is far less intrusive than an adoption order. However, this does not mean that an order for residence should necessarily be preferred; the key point to remember is that the child's welfare comes first. If there is a choice of orders which might be equally applicable, choose the less interventionist option.

Messages from case law

Cases illustrate some of the factors the courts take into account particularly in choosing between SGOs and adoption.

Re S[33] concerned a long-term foster placement. The mother had turned her life around since the care proceedings, and she and the carer had a good relationship, each recognising the other's importance to S. Contact worked well. S herself wanted to live with the carer and see her mother regularly. A SGO with the added security of a s91(14) CA89 matched S's needs.

AJ[34] was a boy who had been living with his aunt and uncle since he was six months old. The care plan was for him to remain there permanently. His parents were unreliable and had not maintained regular contact, although the carers were committed to contact and ensuring AJ knew his real identity. The carers saw the parents as unpredictable and difficult and there was a real risk that the mother would ask for

---

32   *Suffolk County Council* v. *Nottinghamshire County Council* [2012] EWCA Civ 1640 (Court of Appeal).

33   *Re S (Special Guardianship Order)* [2007] EWCA Civ 54 (Court of Appeal).

34   *Re AJ (Special Guardianship Order)* [2007] EWCA Civ 55 (Court of Appeal).

AJ back at some stage. The court made an adoption order in spite of arguments about the distortion of family relationships (aunt becomes mother; mother becomes aunt). The Court of Appeal did not consider this to be a major problem as there was no intention to use the change in legal relationships to conceal AJ's true origins.

Psychological factors can be important. In *Re M-J*,[35] the mother's half-sister cared for the child and wanted to adopt him. The mother wanted the child back and never accepted the placement was permanent, making the carer anxious and insecure. The need for total security of the placement was a key factor in the court's decision to make an adoption order.

E[36] had lived with her grandparents since she was a small baby due to her parents' drug problems and domestic violence. The grandparents wanted to adopt but the local authority was concerned about their reluctance to be open about E's true origins. The grandparents accepted a SGO but applied to change E's surname. The application was refused. Ward LJ said:

> Sympathetic though I am to their predicament, their concerns overlook the value of the lesson we are all taught at our mother's knee: honesty is the best policy. This family must honestly face up to its fractured constitution. E must learn to live with the fact that she is being brought up by her grandparents.[37]

In another case involving grandparents, Hedley J explained the benefit of a SGO:

> ...it permits familial carers, who are not parents, to have all the practical authority and standing of parents, whilst leaving intact real and readily comprehensible relationships within the family. It avoids K...having to learn that apparent relationships are not the real ones, without in any way restricting the role of the maternal grandparents effectively to parent K as the sole exercisers of parental responsibility.[38]

---

35   *Re M-J (Special Guardianship Order)* [2007] FWCA Civ 56 (Court of Appeal).
36   *Re L (Special Guardianship: Surname)* [2007] EWCA Civ 196 (Court of Appeal).
37   *Re L* at paragraph 39.
38   *S v. B and Newport City Council; Re K* [2007] 1FLR 1116 (High Court) paragraphs 21–23.

However, in another extreme case[39] where the father had murdered the mother and raped her sister, it would not have been appropriate for the grandmother to have to share PR even with the extra power of a SGO. An adoption order was made.

Points for practice

1.   In any court case, make a list of the possible orders available to the court. Keep the key characteristics of each order clearly in mind.

2.   Start with an analysis of the child's needs and find the order which best fits the case.

3.   List advantages and disadvantages for each possibility to help find the most suitable option.

4.   Remember other s8 CA89 orders and/or a s91(14) CA89 order can be added – a package of orders might be appropriate.

5.   Keep the child's welfare to the forefront of your mind; do not get distracted by the agendas of the adults.

---

39   *N* v. *B and ors* [2013] EWHC 820 (High Court).

Chapter 6

Arrangements for Children (Contact)

Contact cases are among the most long-running, bitter and harmful disputes before the court. Although they can concern contact between children and their grandparents, siblings, extended family members or others, most cases arise from parental relationship breakdown. According to government figures, some 40,000 children a year are subject to contact applications.[1]

Many people consider that an adversarial court system is not the best way to resolve such disputes. Wall J said:

> the court process is stressful for both parents and for children, it is expensive for those who are not publicly funded, it is slow and adversarial. It tends to entrench parental attitudes rather than encouraging them to change. It is ill adapted to dealing with the difficult human dilemmas involved notably when it comes to the enforcement of orders... Contact in my experience works best when parents respect each other and are able to co-operate; where the children's loyalties are not torn and where they can move between their parents without tension, unhappiness or fear of offending one parent or another.[2]

McFarlane LJ expressed the hope that, by stressing the 'responsibility' part of PR, '...some parents may be encouraged more readily to engage with the difficulties that undoubtedly arise when contemplating post-separation contact than may have hitherto been the case.'[3]

---

1   Government briefing paper on the Children and Families Bill 2013.
2   Re O (Contact: Withdrawal of Application) [2003] EWHC 3031 (High Court).
3   Re W (Children) [2012] EWCA Civ 999 at paragraph 80 (Court of Appeal).

These sentiments may express the triumph of hope over experience, but to try to divert cases from court, parties must consider mediation in an appropriate case before launching a court application.[4]

Once proceedings have been started, the court can try again to encourage parents to see things from the child's point of view by making a contact activity direction[5] at an interim stage. This requires a parent party to the proceedings to take part in an activity to promote contact with the child. The scope of such directions is widened under the Children and Families Act 2014,[6] to extend beyond the promotion of court-ordered contact ordered to improve the quality of involvement in the child's life generally.

One such activity is the Separated Parents Information Programme (PIP),[7] a four-hour group programme for parents (the couple in dispute each attend a different group but all groups are mixed gender) intended to focus on the child's needs and perspectives. A research study commissioned by the DfE[8] found that parental feedback was generally positive but there seemed to be little impact on the court process or the likelihood of reaching agreement.

Orders

If the case proceeds, the order is sought under s8 CA89. The original contact order required the person with whom the child lived to 'allow' the child to visit, stay or otherwise have contact with a named person.

Under the revised s8 CA89 following implementation of the Children and Families Act 2014, a child arrangements order (CAO) can regulate arrangements for the child including deciding with whom and when she is to spend time or otherwise have contact. The order is not addressed to the person with whom the child lives. For ease of

---

4   See Chapter 4 for more information.
5   s11A CA89 introduced by the Children and Adoption Act 2006.
6   Amendments made to s11A–E CA89 by Schedule 2 of the Children and Families Act 2014.
7   Attended by over 18,000 parents in 2011–12.
8   DFE (June 2011) *Building Bridges? An Evaluation of the Costs and Effectiveness of the Separated Parents Information Programme*, DfE-RR140. Available at www.gov.uk/government/publications/an-evaluation-of-the-costs-and-effectiveness-of-the-separated-parents-information-programme-pip, accessed on 30 March 2014.

reference, in this book contact orders and CAOs concerning contact are both referred to as 'orders for contact'.

These orders can be made in combination with other private law orders – orders for residence, prohibited steps orders, specific issue orders, special guardianship orders or (very rarely) adoption orders. However, s8 orders for contact are not compatible with care orders: contact for children in care is governed by s34 CA89.

What is contact?

Contact is a wider concept than the old idea of 'access'. Not limited to face-to-face visits (supervised or otherwise), it can include staying contact, telephone calls, video calls, text messages, letters, emails, contact via social networking sites, sending and receiving cards, presents or photographs as well as the provision of information through school and other reports. It can be as direct, open and flexible or as indirect, controlled and limited as circumstances require. Workers advising the court need to be alert to all the possible and appropriate options, including being aware of ever-changing technologies and social media.

Orders can be expressed in broad terms leaving the parties to make their own arrangements or, if necessary, can be prescriptive, even setting out the precise day, time, length and venue of visits, dictating arrangements for handing the child over or setting pre-conditions before contact can occur. An order can provide for contact to build up gradually over time, or an interim contact order can be made, allowing the situation to be reviewed and revised as necessary. The court can use its power under s11(7) CA89 to attach whatever conditions to the order as are necessary to make it work.

Case Studies: Contact

Anna and Ben separate. At first they are extremely antagonistic and both apply for residence. After mediation, they agree that the children should live with Anna with extensive contact to Ben. Although they are in agreement, an order is needed (in spite of the 'no order principle') to formalise arrangements but there is no need for the court to become involved in practical details, so the court approves a broadly expressed order, giving Ben contact to include weekly visits, an overnight stay once a month and staying contact for a week each school holiday.

Connie and Diana separate acrimoniously. They argue over every detail of arrangements and court attempts to encourage mediation fail. After a contested hearing, the court decides on the appropriate arrangements for the children, ordering the exact dates, times, duration, venue and conditions for contact visits, including a condition that visits will only proceed if Diana is sober at the time.

Eric's visiting contact with his children has gone well and he wants them to stay overnight. The children are happy about this but their mother, who they live with, is not. The court makes an interim order allowing for two overnight stays followed by a further hearing to review progress.

Is there a presumption of contact?

There is no express statutory presumption of contact for parents in private law cases; in contrast, parents whose children are in care have a statutory presumption of 'reasonable contact'.[9] However, in practice the courts work on the basis succinctly expressed by Ward LJ: 'every child is entitled to know its parents and to have contact with them unless there are cogent reasons to refuse it.'[10]

Clearly the human rights of parents and children alike are engaged in contact disputes, which fall squarely within Article 8 (the right to respect for private and family life). These rights are not limited to parents and children – they can also apply to extended family and psychological family members (such as foster or other non-related carers). Restrictions on these rights can only be justified if they are in accordance with the law, necessary and proportionate to the need. This means that contact should be restricted only to the extent that is necessary, but no further. So, if you are advising the court, start by considering whether flexible, unrestricted direct contact is in the child's best interests, and ensure that no greater restrictions are placed on contact than are necessary, looking at the situation as a whole. The checklist in Appendix 3 might help.

---

9   s34 CA89 – for more information see Chapter 14.
10   *Re L (Special Guardianship: surname)* [2007] EWCA Civ 196 (Court of Appeal) at paragraph 58.

Is there a presumption of equal contact?

In recent years, campaigners have argued strenuously for a presumption of equal contact. Allegations have been made that the system favours mothers over fathers. This is refuted by judges, who are always keen to stress that parents have equal rights before the court. But the fact remains that as more children reside with mothers than fathers, when the system fails it fails fathers and their children disproportionately, and sometimes spectacularly. One such case[11] clocked up 43 hearings conducted by 16 different judges over five years and amassed 950 pages of evidence. In terms unusually heartfelt for a High Court judge, Munby J[12] said that the previous two years of litigation were 'an exercise in absolute futility... The system has failed him (the father)... I feel desperately, desperately sorry for him.' It could of course be added that the system had also failed the child concerned. Everyone involved in the court system, including social workers advising the court or working with children and their parents, must do everything possible to ensure that such situations are not repeated.

However, both courts and Parliament are clear that a presumption of equal contact is not the appropriate solution. As Butler-Sloss P said:

> this would not be in the best interest of children whose welfare is the issue before the courts. The court is not and should not be tied to a certain number of days which would automatically be ordered to be spent by the absent parent with the child... It is, in my judgment, crucial that the court has the greatest flexibility in deciding on the type and quantum of contact according to the circumstances of each individual case.

Parliament decided against a presumption of equality in the Children and Families Act 2014. Although both parents' involvement in a child's life is generally presumed to be beneficial, 'involvement' may be direct or indirect: there is no presumption as to the division of the child's time. Furthermore, the child must not be put at risk of harm.[13]

This reminds us that the key issue is the child's welfare, not a parental sense of entitlement or injustice.

---

11   *Re D (Intractable Contact Dispute: Publicity)* [2004] 1FLR 1226 (High Court).
12   As he then was – he is now the President of the Family Division of the High Court.
13   Amendments to s1 CA89 made by s11 of the Children and Families Act 2014.

Determining contact cases

As with all s8 cases, there are no specific grounds to be proven in a contact application. The court therefore bases its decision on the child's welfare, which is paramount, and it considers the welfare checklist. It may also request a welfare report from CAFCASS or the local authority.

Aspects of the welfare checklist

CHILDREN'S WISHES AND FEELINGS

Ascertaining the child's true wishes and feelings may require skilled social work, including understanding unspoken messages. Children caught up in contact disputes may not speak readily, they may be acutely aware of parental emotions and animosity, experience torn loyalties, try to say the 'right thing' or they may even be coached as to what to say.

Under the checklist, children's wishes and feelings must be considered 'in the light of their age and understanding'.[14] Parental influence can impact on the weight to be given to the children's expressed wishes. For example, in one case[15] 15- and 13-year-old children who lived with their father and had not seen their mother for over eight years said they did not want contact. But the Court of Appeal found that their views had to be seen in the context of a case of irrational and implacable hostility. As Ward LJ said, teenagers' views:

> ordinarily carry great weight, but we have to bear in mind not only their age, but their understanding. Their understanding in this case is corrupted by the malignancy of the views, with which they have been force-fed over many years of their life, until so blinded by them that they cannot see the truth either of their mother's good qualities or of the good it will do them to have some contact with her.[16]

EFFECT OF CHANGE OF CIRCUMSTANCES

In a contact case, this subsection should not be seen as a presumption in favour of the status quo; the fact that one parent might have successfully blocked contact between the child and the other parent is not a good reason to maintain that situation. The court may need advice on how to balance short-term difficulty or distress against long-term benefits.

---

14   s1(3)(a) CA89.
15   *Re M (Contact: Long-term Best Interests)* [2005] EWCA Civ 1090 (Court of Appeal).
16   *Re M* at paragraph 26.

NO DELAY
This takes on particular significance in contact cases. The longer a child goes without having contact, the harder it is to re-establish a relationship. If you are involved in a contact case, it is part of your responsibility to ensure that the case does not drift.

Adjudicating allegations
Sometimes in private law cases one party makes allegations (perhaps of child abuse or domestic violence) against the other. Clearly, the mere fact that an allegation is made cannot determine matters; sadly people sometimes make false allegations and even coach their children to do likewise. On the other hand, if the allegations are true they can have a significant bearing on the decision in the case. So the court must decide whether the allegations are substantiated and this is often done as a preliminary issue in a fact-finding hearing. Provision needs to be made for what happens in terms of contact or residence in the meantime, ensuring the safety of the child and the adults.

If you are the social worker compiling a report in a case where allegations are made and denied, it is not for you to decide who is telling the truth; that is the court's job. You may have to make alternative recommendations, depending on the findings the court makes.

Even if an allegation is true, it does not necessarily constitute a bar to contact; it is a factor (albeit perhaps an important one) to be weighed in the court's decision about the child's welfare.

Domestic violence and contact
Domestic violence is not limited to physical abuse; it includes threatening and intimidating behaviour or other abuse which may cause or risk causing harm to the child or other party. The meaning of the word 'harm'[17] under CA89 specifically includes harm caused to a child by him seeing or hearing someone else being ill-treated. So a child who hears from his upstairs bedroom what is going on downstairs can be harmed, without being directly involved in an incident of domestic violence.

---

17 For more information on the definition of 'harm' see Chapter 9.

Where there are allegations of domestic violence in any residence or contact application, the Court of Appeal[18] has confirmed that the court must follow the relevant Practice Direction, 12J. As soon as the court is aware of domestic violence allegations in a case, it must identify the factual and welfare issues, consider what impact the allegations (if true) could have on an eventual order and give directions to decide the issues.

Agreement

At a time when the court and everyone involved in proceedings is urged to promote conciliation and avoid conflict, it goes against the grain to question parties who agree the terms of an order, or agree to the withdrawal of an application. But agreements must be carefully scrutinised because of the risk that they may have been reached following intimidation, or because the victim wants to appease the perpetrator, lacks the self-esteem to pursue the allegations or has once again been assured of the perpetrator's undying love. If you are involved in a private law case, make sure that what is presented as an agreement is freely entered into and that, in your efforts to reduce conflict, you do not unwittingly add to pressure already felt by a vulnerable party.

Fact-finding hearings

If the allegations are disputed, the court may arrange a fact-finding hearing, ordering evidence from the parties and other relevant sources such as the police and health services. A s7 report will almost certainly be ordered and, in a complex case, the child may be made a party to the proceedings. The court must also consider how to secure the physical safety of anyone attending court.

The court must decide what will happen in the interim, minimising risk and ensuring the safety of the child and adults alike while awaiting a decision on the issue. This may involve supervision of contact or even suspension of direct contact, in which case indirect contact must be considered.

At a fact-finding hearing, the court makes findings as to the truth of allegations, the nature and degree of any domestic violence and its effect on the child, his parents and any other relevant person.

---

18   *Re W (Children)* [2012] EWCA Civ 528 (Court of Appeal).

Thereafter, the court may order a further welfare report or order social work, psychiatric, psychological or other assessments. If domestic violence is established, the court should provide information about local resources to assist the child or any adult party. It should also consider whether to impose a pre-condition of seeking advice or treatment on any party before it makes an order.

The court then goes on to decide the application itself in the light of the findings made. The final decision should be made by the same judge or magistrates (or at least the same Chair of the Bench).

Contact where domestic violence has occurred

Domestic violence is not an automatic bar to contact. However, the court should only order contact if it can be satisfied that the physical and emotional safety of the child and resident parent can be secured before, during and after contact.

The court must consider and correctly apply the following factors set out in the Practice Direction:[19]

- any harm the child has suffered as a consequence of the violence
- any harm he is at risk of suffering if an order is made for residence or contact
- the conduct of both parents towards each other and the child
- the effect of the domestic violence on the child and the resident parent
- the motivation of the applicant for contact, in particular whether it is a genuine desire to promote the child's best interests, or a way to continue violence, intimidation or harassment against the other
- the applicant's likely behaviour during contact and its effect on the child
- the applicant's capacity to appreciate the effect on the child and the resident parent of past violence and the potential for future violence

---

19 In *Re W (Children)* [2012] EWCA Civ 528 the Court of Appeal overturned a judge's decision because he failed properly to address the factors in the Practice Direction.

- the perpetrator's attitude to the past violence and capacity to change and behave appropriately.

Where the court nonetheless decides that direct contact is in the child's best interests, it must consider whether any conditions or directions are needed to make contact work. In particular, it should look at:

- supervision, if so, where and by whom

- conditions for the perpetrator to comply with, such as a requirement to seek treatment or advice

- whether contact or any provisions regarding contact should be for a specified period

- whether the order should be reviewed.

If direct contact is not in the child's interests, the court should consider whether indirect contact is appropriate. The court must of course always give reasons to explain its decision.

If the case returns to court on a review, care should be taken before removing safeguards put in place to make contact safe. As the Family Justice Council[20] pointed out, the fact that there are no incidents may not mean that the safeguards are unnecessary: it may mean that they are working.

Can the court order no contact?

It is possible for an order to specify that there is to be no contact of a particular kind or even no contact at all between the child and a named person.

Courts do not lightly stop contact between a parent and child. As Ward LJ[21] said: 'contact should not be stopped unless it is the last resort for the judge', so all other avenues should be exhausted first[22] and it may be appropriate for the child to be made a party to the proceedings. Even in a

---

20   Family Justice Council (2006) *Report to the President of the Family Division on the approach to be adopted by the Court when asked to make a contact order by consent where domestic violence has been an issue in the case.* Available at www.womensaid.org.uk/core/core_picker/download.asp?/id=1678&filetitle=Family+Justice+Council+report+on+contact, accessed on 30 March 2014.

21   *Re P (Children)* [2008] EWCA Civ 1431 (Court of Appeal).

22   Confirmed by the Court of Appeal in *Re C (A Child)* [2011] EWCA Civ 261 (Court of Appeal).

case where one parent has murdered the other, the courts do not start with a presumption that the offending parent should have no contact.[23]

However, there are cases when ending contact is the best thing for the child. One father[24] who had numerous convictions from a long history of domestic violence sought contact to his four young children. Their mother asked for an order for no contact along with an order to permit her to change the children's surnames to prevent the father from locating them, as he had vowed to do. The judge reminded herself of the draconian nature of the order sought and the Article 8 rights of parents and children. She focused on the children's welfare, finding they had suffered harm from the violence in the home and there was a risk of future harm. The mother's genuine fear of what the father might do would have an impact on the children's stability. The judge ordered no contact, direct or indirect, except for twice yearly letter box contact via CAFCASS to be accessed by the mother in accordance with the children's best interests. The court also allowed the children's surname to be changed to secure their safety.

Is contact compulsory?

The person with the benefit of an order for contact is not obliged to take it up so parents cannot be compelled to keep in touch with their children. Nor is an order for contact addressed to the child, so a child who refuses to co-operate is not in breach of any order. The older he is, the more he is able to vote with his feet and in any event orders regulating contact do not last beyond the age of 16.

What about the 'resident' parent? The original wording of s8 compelled the resident parent to 'allow' contact, so the Act did not contemplate a carer having to force a kicking and screaming child to attend. But neither did it imagine that a carer would actively thwart contact by tearing up letters, arranging for the child to be out at contact times or, more insidiously, poisoning the child's mind against the other

---

23   A principle confirmed in *Re T (A child) (murdered parent)* [2011] EWHC B4 – in fact, in that case the court ordered that there should be no contact of any kind, supported by a s91(14) order and an injunction to protect the maternal grandparent special guardians.

24   *AB v. BB and Others* [2013] EWHC 227 (Fam) (High Court).

parent so that she refuses to go. Such cases were described by Coleridge J as 'the scourge of the family justice system'.[25]

Making contact work

Making a contact order is one thing; making recalcitrant parents co-operate with the order is another. Various provisions have been introduced to try to make contact orders work

CONTACT ACTIVITY CONDITIONS

These can be attached to contact orders.[26] They require a parent to take part in a specified activity such as attending counselling or information sessions, parenting skills programmes or work to address violent behaviour. They cannot, however, include medical or psychiatric examination, assessment or treatment. Under CFA, 'activity conditions' are wider in scope and extend beyond the promotion simply of the contact ordered by the court, to improve the quality of involvement in the child's life generally.

MONITORING CONTACT

When a court makes or varies a contact order, it can order[27] a CAFCASS officer to monitor and report to court on compliance with contact or activity condition by the person granted contact or by the resident parent for a specified period of up to 12 months.

WARNING NOTICES

There must be no doubt that a contact order is an order of the court and compliance is compulsory. This is made explicit by attaching a notice[28] to the order warning the parties of the consequences of failing to comply with the order.

---

25   *A (Children)* [2009] EWCA Civ 1141.
26   s11C CA89 introduced by the Children and Adoption Act 2006 (CAA).
27   s11H CA89 added by the Children and Adoption Act 2006.
28   s11I CA89 added by the CAA.

ENFORCEMENT ORDERS[29]

These impose a requirement of unpaid work on anyone proven beyond reasonable doubt to have breached a contact order. This allows the court to punish the defaulting party without also effectively punishing the child.

COMPENSATION

A further option is an order[30] making the defaulting party compensate the other for any financial loss (such as wasted travel costs, lost wages or the cost of a cancelled holiday).

CONTEMPT OF COURT

Breaching a contact order, like any other court order, is contempt of court which can be punished by a fine or even imprisonment. Imprisoning a parent inevitably has an adverse impact on the child, so this power is rarely used but it can happen as in a case when the court imprisoned a mother who repeatedly flouted a contact order.[31]

Case Study: Enforcing a contact order

Bob has a drink problem. The children love him and want to see him as long as he has not been drinking. His contact order is supplemented by an activity condition for him to attend counselling sessions to help him control his drinking. The court asks CAFCASS to report on whether Bob attends his counselling and contact sessions.

The children's mother Cally openly refuses to comply with contact. She persistently ensures that the children are absent for planned contact sessions. Bob has to take unpaid leave for contact and pays his train fare for a wasted trip each time.

Cally risks an enforcement order for unpaid work, a compensation order to repay Bob's lost wages and travel costs. If she persists in her behaviour, Cally risks being held in contempt of court and could ultimately be sent to prison.

---

29   s11J CA89 added by the CAA. Government figures indicate that there are around 1300 applications each year for enforcement or compensation orders but only around 30 orders are made.
30   s11O CA89 added by the CAA.
31   *A v. N (Committal: Refusal of Contact)* [1997] 1FLR 533 (Court of Appeal).

Changing residence

If the person the child lives with repeatedly and deliberately thwarts contact, one option is to change the child's residence. This is absolutely not to be used to punish the recalcitrant parent – the child's welfare is paramount and changing residence of course has profound implications. Obviously, it is only available as an option where another suitable carer is available and is not to be used lightly. As Thorpe LJ said: 'the transfer of residence from the obdurate primary carer to the parent frustrated in pursuit of contact is a judicial weapon of last resort.'[32]

In one case[33] two boys aged ten and eight lived with their mother, her new partner and her two other children. The parents had separated three years earlier. The father had contact every Sunday for a whole day, but the mother stopped this for several months. She also encouraged the boys to speak negatively about their father, obtained new passports for them with her surname, not the father's, and she moved from Blackpool to Devon without notice to anyone. She clearly did not want the children to have a relationship with their father. However, the Guardian observed a positive contact session. Unusually, the judge met the boys and arranged a meeting between them and their father at court. The judge found that the boys loved their father and wanted to see him but were being prevented from expressing their feelings. Although changing residence would cause the children disruption and would separate them from their mother and half-siblings, the judge found on balance that this would be better than living with mother with no contact to father. He effectively gave the mother one last chance. He ordered two periods of staying contact with the provision that if these did not take place, the children's residence would be transferred to the father without further hearing. The sword of Damocles was thus suspended over the mother.

s91(14) orders

Repeated court applications can be harmful. In appropriate cases, courts can impose an order under s91(14) CA89[34] to limit further applications to court, as in the case of *Re N* where Munby J said:

---

32 *A (Children)* [2009] EWCA Civ 1141 (Court of Appeal).
33 *M (Children)* [2012] EWHC 1948 (Fam) (High Court).
34 See Chapter 2 for more details on s91(14) CA89.

Examination of the papers reveals a wholly deplorable situation. N is a young boy who has two parents who love him but who have demonstrated an unwillingness or inability to put his needs first and who as a result of their relentless pursuit of their own agendas have caused him emotional harm and arguably that emotional harm is significant. This situation cannot be permitted to continue. The parents need to stop trying to score points against each other and examine instead their own actions to ensure that N and his needs are put first.[35]

In that case, the s91(14) order limited further court applications in order to try to make the parents exercise their responsibility to resolve issues between themselves and not to apply to court for the most trivial matters.

Contact with others

Although most cases involve separated parents, it is important to remember that children have relationships with other people too and these may also become subject of contact applications, although non-parents usually need court leave to launch an application.

Sibling relationships can be particularly important in children's lives. An example of a case involving separated siblings[36] concerned a girl who lived with her mother who wanted contact with her half-siblings (aged nine and ten) who lived with their father. The mother had no involvement with the younger children. The father feared that the sister's application was a back-door attempt to re-introduce the mother into the children's lives. The CAFCASS officer believed that it was important for them to know about their background, heritage and family relationships and that communication with their sister would enlarge their knowledge of this aspect of their lives and so recommended letter contact. At first instance, the judge rejected the application, but the Court of Appeal ordered letter contact initially for six months managed by CAFCASS. Thorpe LJ found that the judge had elevated the father's anxiety above the potential real benefit for the children. As always in s8 cases, the court's key focus must be on the child's welfare.

---

35 *N (A Child)* [2009] EWHC 3055 (Fam) (High Court).
36 *H (Children)* [2010] EWCA Civ 1200 (Court of Appeal).

Child protection

Contact disputes can harm children. This can even reach the level of significant harm. It is important to be aware that private law cases have the potential to cross over into child protection.

Points for practice

1. Remain clear-headed and focused on the child. Constantly refer back to the welfare principle and welfare checklist.

2. Be mindful of the adults' agendas and relationships and the effect they have on the child. Take extra care in establishing the child's true wishes and feelings. Consider whether the child should be separately represented.

3. Do not give up. Contact disputes can be intractable. Dogged determination is required, as well as the imagination to consider new ways forward or options not yet attempted.

4. Try to encourage conciliation, but make sure any apparent agreement is freely entered into and is in the child's best interests.

5. Do not overlook relationships other than those between the child and the parent – grandparents, siblings and others can be very important for children.

Part 3

The Local Authority's Support Role

Chapter 7

Children in Need

One mother is struggling to cope: she needs advice and guidance. Another has no money for food or nappies until she receives her benefits: she needs help to get by. Another family needs a break from caring for their seriously disabled child: they need respite care. All come to the local authority for help.

Under the Children Act 1989 (CA89), the local authority's first role is to support children and their families, helping them stay together thus preventing the need for compulsory action. Child protection provisions are a safety net when the family and support services have failed; prevention is the first priority.

Statutory duties

The relevant sections, including the key s17, are grouped together in Part III CA89, supplemented by Schedule 2.

Preventive duty

Schedule 2 CA89 provides that a local authority must take 'reasonable steps' to:

- prevent children suffering ill-treatment or neglect, through the provision of Part III services[1]

- reduce the need for care proceedings or criminal proceedings against children[2]

---

1   CA89 Schedule 2 paragraph 4.
2   CA89 Schedule 2 paragraph 7(a).

- avoid the need to place children in secure accommodation[3]
- discourage children in their area from committing criminal offences.[4]

The statutory duties in Schedule 2 are striking in their breadth and vagueness, leaving the authority considerable discretion to decide how to achieve them.

It is important to look at the precise wording of the provisions. The duty imposed by Schedule 2 is not actually to prevent children from suffering ill-treatment or neglect but a duty to 'take reasonable steps through the provision of services' to do so. 'Reasonable' is the lawyer's favourite word. It blurs the edges, allowing room for judgment, argument and justification. A local authority must do something to stop children being ill-treated or neglected – doing nothing is unlikely to be 'reasonable' – but beyond that it is up to the authority's discretion, bounded only by the requirement to act lawfully and rationally. This allows each authority to manage its own budget and respond to local needs but it also means that provision can be remarkably different on either side of a local authority boundary.

Partner agencies

Local authorities are not alone in working with children and families. Authorities have a statutory duty under s10 Children Act 2004 (CA04) to make arrangements to promote co-operation with other partner agencies (such as health, education, police and offender services) to improve children's well-being in the widest sense of the word.

Agencies other than the local authority (education, health, police) may provide early help to try to prevent a family's situation reaching the stage of needing local authority involvement and a statutory assessment. *Working Together*[5] says that where a child and family would benefit from support from more than one agency, there should be an inter-agency assessment, using the Common Assessment Framework or other early help assessment. But if early help is not sufficient, or the other agencies feel that the child is 'in need' or at risk, a referral should be made to the local authority for a statutory assessment. When a child is referred to the

---

3 CA89 Schedule 2 paragraph 7(c).
4 CA89 Schedule 2 paragraph 7(b).
5 At paragraph 8.

local authority, a decision should be made within one working day about the type of response required, which may include a decision to undertake a s17 assessment.[6]

Children in need

How do these broad strategic duties relate to real children and their families who need help and support? The keystone in the statutory structure is s17 CA89.

---

s17 (1) CA89 It shall be the general duty of every local authority (in addition to the other duties imposed on them by this Part

   (a)   to safeguard and promote the welfare of children within their area who are in need; and

   (b)   so far as is consistent with that duty, to promote the upbringing of such children by their families, by providing a range and level of services appropriate to those children's needs.

Section 17 in practice
1. IS THIS CHILD IN NEED?

The duty under s17 CA89 only applies to children 'who are in need', a term defined in s17(10) CA89.

For the purposes of this Part a child shall be taken to be in need if –

   (a)   he is unlikely to achieve or have the opportunity of achieving or maintaining a reasonable standard of health or development without the provision for him of services by a local authority under this Part;

   (b)   his health or development is likely to be significantly impaired, or further impaired without the provision for him of such services; or

   (c)   he is disabled.

---

6   *Working Together* (2013) at page 26.

The definition signals the section's preventive intention – it looks ahead to what is likely to happen if nothing is done. Children do not have to already be falling behind to qualify – it is enough if it is clear they are likely to do so unless services are provided. As with any statutory definition, it gives rise to further questions.

What do 'health' and 'development' mean?

s17(11) CA89 defines 'health' and 'development' broadly to include physical and mental health and physical, intellectual, emotional, social and behavioural development.

What does 'disabled' mean?

'Disabled' is defined in terms matching those of the National Assistance Act 1948 for adult services. The reasoning behind this was to provide a seamless transition from childhood to adulthood services. Unfortunately the outmoded terminology seems less than sensitive today.

s17(11) CA89 For the purposes of this Part, a child is disabled if he is blind, deaf or dumb or suffers from mental disorder of any kind or is substantially and permanently handicapped by illness, injury or congenital deformity...

A child with disabilities is always a 'child in need', even if he is happy, healthy and thriving in the care of excellent parents.

Authorities also have a duty to maintain a register of disabled children in their area.[7] This is intended to be helpful, not stigmatising, and must not be confused with the register of children with a child protection plan. Registration is neither compulsory nor a pre-condition to receiving services.

Authorities must provide services for disabled children designed to 'minimise the effect'[8] of their disabilities and enable them to 'lead lives which are as normal as possible'.[9] Authorities can make direct payments

---

7   CA89 Schedule 2 paragraph 2.
8   CA89 Schedule 2 paragraph 6(a).
9   CA89 Schedule 2 paragraph 6(b).

to disabled children's parents for them to buy their own services instead of receiving services from the local authority.[10]

What is a 'reasonable standard' and what does 'significantly impaired' mean?

These words are not defined in CA89 so they must be given their ordinary and natural meaning. Clearly the section was deliberately drafted in broad terms, so each case can be judged in its own context.

How does the authority know which children are in need?

The authority must take reasonable steps to identify the extent to which there are children in need in its area and to publish information about available services, doing its best to ensure that the publicity reaches the people who need the services.[11]

The breadth of the definition of children in need means that it covers a wide range of situations from homeless teenagers to unaccompanied asylum seekers, from young carers to children leaving custody, from pregnant teenagers to young people with mental health problems. However there are concerns that, in challenging economic times, ever-tightening criteria mean that priority is given to those who are at risk or on the verge of child protection intervention who are only a subgroup of the much wider category of 'children in need'. Some argue[12] that this tendency could be compounded by the fact that the previous guidance specifically for children in need (the *Framework for Assessment of Children in Need and Their Families*) has been subsumed into the 2013 version of *Working Together*, which focuses primarily on child protection.

2. IS THE CHILD WITHIN OUR AREA?

This is a simple question of fact. If a child is physically present in the area, whether he lives there, goes to school there or arrives there as an unaccompanied minor seeking asylum, he is the responsibility of the local authority for that area.

---

10   s17(11) CA89.

11   CA89 Schedule 2 paragraph 1.

12   See for example the response of the campaign group Every Child in Need to the consultation about the 2013 *Working Together* and the cancellation of the *Framework* document. Available at www.everychildinneed.org.uk, accessed on 30 March 2014.

3. WHAT SERVICES SHOULD WE PROVIDE?

The objective is to safeguard and promote children's welfare by providing appropriate services set out in Schedule 2[13] including:

- advice, guidance and counselling
- occupational, social, cultural or recreational activities
- home help
- family centres.

Although there is a statutory duty, it is to provide such services or family centres 'as they consider appropriate', so once again there is a large measure of discretion for each authority to decide on its own nature and level of services.

These services are provided for children in general. The Act does not specify what should be provided in each individual case: that depends on an assessment of each child's needs and the proper exercise of discretion to decide what services to provide, if any.

Authorities should assess the child's needs and entitlements under other relevant legislation[14] (such as education and/or disability legislation) at the same time, to avoid duplication of assessment and to encourage a co-ordinated response.

Working Together is issued under s7 Local Authority Social Services Act 1970 so it must be followed unless there is a clear justification. Assessments should cover the three domains:

- the child's developmental needs
- parenting capacity
- family and environmental factors.

Assessments should draw together information from all relevant individuals and agencies, and must be seen as a process, not an event. 'Every assessment should be focused on outcomes, deciding which services and support to provide to deliver improved welfare for the child.'[15] Assessments should take a maximum of 45 days, although of course, if required, services should be provided pending the completion of the process.

---

13   CA89 Schedule 2 paragraphs 8 and 9.
14   CA89 Schedule 2 paragraph 3.
15   *Working Together* (2013) at paragraph 49.

There is a statutory duty under s17(4A) to consult the child:

> Before determining what (if any) services to provide for a particular child in need in the exercise of functions conferred on them by this section, a local authority shall, so far as is reasonably practicable and consistent with the child's welfare –
>
> (a) ascertain the child's wishes and feelings regarding the provision of those services; and
>
> (b) give due consideration (having regard to his age and understanding) to such wishes and feelings of the child as they have been able to ascertain.

4. WHO RECEIVES THE SERVICES?

Services can be given direct to the child in need himself, for example he can attend a playgroup. But often it is not the child, but a parent, who needs help such as advice on parenting. As long as this is provided with a view to safeguarding or promoting the child's welfare, it still falls within s17 – services can be given to the family or any family member.[16]

5. WHO PROVIDES THE SERVICES?

It is the local authority's job to secure the requisite services whether by delivering them itself or by delegating the task to others.[17] Authorities can and frequently do contract with other bodies, especially the voluntary sector, to provide s17 services.

6. CAN WE ASK OTHER AGENCIES TO HELP?

Often meeting a child's needs involves other agencies – a child might have special educational needs, or the family's difficulties might be exacerbated by housing or health problems. These issues require inter-agency co-operation.

As we have seen, s10 CA04 requires local authorities to promote children's well-being through co-operation with relevant bodies and partner agencies. Other agencies with responsibilities towards children

---

16   s17(3) CA89.
17   s17(5) CA89.

have their own statutory duty under s11(2) CA04 to ensure that 'their functions are discharged having regard to the need to safeguard and promote the welfare of children'.

There is also a duty to assist imposed by s27 CA89 on:

- other departments of the local authority
- other local authorities (including those without children's services functions)
- education authorities
- housing authorities
- health authorities in their various forms.

> s27(2) CA89 An authority whose help is…requested shall comply with the request if it is compatible with their own statutory or other duties and obligations and does not unduly prejudice the discharge of any of their functions.

If you need help from another agency which is not forthcoming despite the spirit of mutual co-operation, make a formal request for help under s27 CA89. A formal letter citing a statutory duty can often unblock channels and secure assistance when a polite request fails.

The duty to assist is not unconditional; it is qualified by reference to the other agency's own functions. So where a housing authority had already rejected a family's homelessness application after quite properly applying its own statutory criteria, the House of Lords found that it was not obliged to house the family at the request of Social Services under s27 CA89.[18]

Information sharing

Working Together says: 'effective sharing of information between professionals and local agencies is essential for effective identification, assessment and service provision'.[19] Fears about information sharing are often unfounded and based on legal misconceptions. *Working Together* indicates that all agencies should have arrangements in place which set

---

18   *R v. Northavon District Council ex parte Smith* [1994] 2FLR 671 (House of Lords).
19   *Working Together* (2013) at paragraph 22.

out clearly principles and processes for sharing information with other agencies. If in doubt, helpful government guidance is available to assist.[20]

7. CAN WE GIVE MONEY INSTEAD OF SERVICES?

s17 CA89 is primarily about services, 'assistance in kind' in the words of CA89, but it is also possible for the authority to provide financial support instead or in addition, including regular payments where appropriate. Previously, cash could only be provided in 'exceptional circumstances'[21] but this qualification was removed in an amendment to CA89.

8. CAN WE PROVIDE ACCOMMODATION UNDER S17 CA89?

At one stage, the answer to this question was unclear, so s17(6) CA89 was amended to state explicitly that services can include providing accommodation, not just helping a family find accommodation by providing a deposit or the first month's rent.

A child provided with accommodation under s17 is not 'looked after' (unlike a child accommodated under s20 CA89). However, an authority cannot escape its duties to looked after children simply by declaring that accommodation is provided under s17 CA89, not s20 CA89.[22]

Imagine a homeless family. The Housing Department tells them that they have exhausted their rights to housing under homelessness legislation and it is no longer obliged to house them. They have young children so they go to Children's Social Care for help. They refuse the offer of foster care for the children; they want the family to stay together. Does the authority have the power to house the whole family? Does it have a duty to do so?

Like any other s17 service, accommodation can be provided to the child's family, so the authority can use s17 CA89 to house the whole family. But must it do so? This question came to the House of Lords[23] where it was decided (by the narrowest of margins, a 3:2 majority) that

---

20   Available at www.education.gov.uk/childrenandyoungpeople/strategy/integrated working/a0072915/information-sharing, accessed on 30 March 2014.

21   These words were removed from s17(6) CA89 by the Children and Young Persons Act 2008.

22   For more details on s20 CA89 see Chapter 8.

23   *R (G) v. Barnet LBC; R (W) v. Lambeth LBC; R (A) v. Lambeth LBC* [2003] UKHL 57 (House of Lords).

Social Services are not legally obliged to accommodate families so that children can be housed with their parents. s17 CA89 imposes a general duty. Providing accommodation is not its primary function but just one service which might be provided, subject to the local authority's discretion. In our example, the authority can choose to accommodate the Smith family but it is not obliged to do so and neither parents nor children can claim this as a right. Otherwise, Children's Social Care would turn into a substitute housing department.

Accommodating abusers

The local authority also has a power (not a duty) to assist a person to obtain alternative accommodation if he is living in the family home and causing or likely to cause a child significant harm.[24] In principle the idea of removing the abuser, not the child, seems attractive, but in practice the provision is little used; it is difficult to police (how do you know s/he has really left?) and it may not safeguard the child (s/he could continue to abuse the child in spite of living elsewhere).

9. CAN WE CHARGE FOR SERVICES?

Assistance under s17 CA89 can be given unconditionally or subject to repayment or other conditions[25] (for example, providing day care as long as the mother uses the time to attend for drug counselling). But before providing a service or imposing conditions the authority must consider the family's means; it cannot demand repayment from anyone on income support or certain other benefits.[26]

10. CAN THE FAMILY SUE IF WE DO NOT PROVIDE THE SERVICES THEY WANT?

The House of Lords[27] decided that s17 CA89 imposes a 'general duty' owed by the authority to children in need overall, not a specific statutory duty towards individuals. This means that a particular family has no

---

24   CA89 Schedule 2 paragraph 5.
25   s17(7) CA89.
26   s17(8) and (9) CA89.
27   *R (G)* v. *Barnet LBC*; *R (W)* v. *Lambeth LBC*; *R (A)* v. *Lambeth LBC* [2003] UKHL 57 (House of Lords).

statutory right to any specified service and cannot sue for a breach of statutory duty if it is not provided.

One possible remedy in such cases is a complaint to the Local Authority Ombudsman where maladministration causes injustice.

The only court application realistically available for those with complaints under s17 CA89 is judicial review, a procedure under which the High Court regulates the exercise of administrative powers. This is not an appeal; the court does not actually judge the merits of the decision in question but instead looks at the procedures adopted and considerations taken into account. It can quash decisions which are:

- taken improperly
- unlawful or beyond the authority's legal powers
- taken considering the wrong factors
- plain unreasonable.

The 'unreasonableness' test is a high hurdle to surmount – the decision made must not only be wrong but so wrong that no reasonable authority could ever have come to that conclusion.

If an application is successful, the court can quash the decision and direct the authority to reconsider the matter, doing it properly this time. It is, however, possible for the authority to reach the very same decision but in a manner which is not open to further challenge.

Judicial review is not a simple remedy, but cases can succeed. For example,[28] a homeless mother who had unsuccessfully claimed asylum sought judicial review of the local authority's refusal to assess her son's needs under s17. The authority argued that s17 did not apply to asylum seekers. It had quite simply got the law wrong. It had a duty under s17 to assess a child's needs whenever it appeared necessary to do so; the government's duties under asylum and immigration legislation did not negate the authority's duties. The authority was ordered to assess the child's needs.

Although the court cannot direct the details of the services to be provided, it can intervene if decision-making processes are seriously

---

28   *R (on the application of ES)* v. *LB of Barking & Dagenham* [2013] EWHC 691 (Admin) (High Court).

flawed. One case, *Re T*,[29] concerned a seriously troubled 14-year-old boy with issues of sexual abuse (as both victim and abuser), violence, criminal activity and substance abuse. A risk assessment recommended a specialist residential placement. The local authority decided instead that his needs could be met by mainstream educational provision and placement in a children's home previously rejected as unsuitable.

On judicial review the court found that the authority was not bound to follow the assessment, but the decision was based on inadequate information and was fundamentally flawed. Inter-agency working had failed, and no reference was made to the boy's own wishes and feelings. The whole process was irrational and unreasonable, so the decision was quashed and the local authority was directed to reconsider.

Another case[30] concerned a 15-year-old girl with quadriplegic cerebral palsy and who was registered blind. For ten years a support package included regular respite care (up to five nights a week) with foster carers. Despite adaptations, the foster home was not and could not be made suitable. The carers wanted to move to a more suitable property but needed a loan from the housing association and needed the local authority's support. Instead, the local authority planned for the child to board at school four nights a week and spend one weekend a month at a residential facility. The child and her mother strongly opposed the end of her ten-year relationship with the carers.

On judicial review, the judge held that the care plan was unlawful. The authority had failed to consider the child's clear and consistent wishes, the mother's physical and emotional inability to provide the care needed, as well as the very strong links between carers and child. Having encouraged the child to make a second home with the carers the authority could not de-register them because their accommodation did not meet the child's needs. The court urged the authority to reconsider supporting the carers' application to the housing association but it would not order it to do so – the authority had to make its own decision, but it had to do so properly.

In another case,[31] an authority's eligibility criteria were challenged. These set the threshold for services so high that two autistic children had

---

29 *Re T (Judicial Review: Local Authority Decisions Concerning Child in Need)* [2003] EWHC (Admin) (High Court).
30 *R (CD)* v. *Isle of Anglesey County Council* [2005] 1 FLR 59 (High Court).
31 *R* v. *Lambeth LBC* [2012] EWHC (Admin) (High Court).

their services withdrawn. The families challenged the criteria themselves, the manner of their introduction (no consultation and no consideration of equality duties) as well as the application to the individual cases. The case was settled so no findings were made, but the authority agreed to withdraw the criteria.

Prevention and protection

Services under Part III of CA89 are voluntary and supportive, aiming to enhance the family's role, and are quite different from the interventionist child protection provisions which appear later in the Act. However, the boundary can become blurred.

At the most serious end of the s17 CA89 spectrum, children can be 'in need' because of abuse or neglect. Some cases start with a child protection referral but are resolved by registering the child as a child in need and providing services; other cases start with a request for services but, on assessment, child protection issues become apparent.

In the past, some abuse or neglect of disabled children was missed because they were seen only as children in need, provided with support by a specialist team whose mindset was not one of child protection.

It is important to remain alert to the need to move from one set of legal provisions to another when appropriate.

Points for practice

1. The children in need provisions are the bedrock of the statutory scheme. Support services should be given proper priority and funding.

2. Inter-agency co-operation is essential to prevent both gaps and duplication in services. Build links with other agencies and call on their help, reminding them of their legal duties if necessary.

3. Always ensure that s17 CA89 decisions are made properly, fairly, with appropriate consultation, and are carefully recorded.

Chapter 8

Accommodation

Accommodation – not care

Aaron and Barry are both in foster care. Their day-to-day care is the same. They are both 'looked after children', their placements made and maintained by the local authority. Each has a social worker and regular reviews, and they will have the same rights when they leave the foster home. However, legally speaking, their cases are profoundly different.

Aaron is 'in care': the local authority has parental responsibility (PR) for him because he is subject to a care order, made by a court under s31 Children Act 1989 (CA89) on the basis that he has suffered or is likely to suffer significant harm.

Barry is 'accommodated' under s20 CA89: his parents retain full PR, some of which they have delegated to the authority under a voluntary arrangement. No court has been involved and there is no need for findings of actual or likely significant harm. The local authority is providing a service to help Barry and his family. A summary of the similarities and differences between care and accommodation appears in Appendix 4.

Accommodation as a support service

Accommodation appears in s20 CA89, in the same Part of the Act as s17 as it is one of the local authority's support services for children and families. Requesting accommodation for a child should not be stigmatised as parental failure but seen as a responsible action, seeking help when it is needed.

The local authority does not obtain PR for an accommodated child. Consistent with the notion that accommodation is a support service, parents retain full PR and simply delegate aspects to the authority. Any existing court orders, such as an order for contact under s8 CA89, remain in force.

The duty to accommodate

When parents request accommodation for their child, does the local authority have a duty to provide it? The answer lies in the precise wording of s20 CA89.

---

s20(1) CA89 Every local authority shall provide accommodation for any child in need within their area who appears to them to require accommodation as a result of –

(a) there being no person who has parental responsibility for him;

(b) his being lost or having been abandoned; or

(c) the person who has been caring for him being prevented (whether or not permanently, and for whatever reason) from providing him with suitable accommodation or care.

A step-by-step approach must be followed, first to establish whether the child's situation falls within the section, and then to decide whether offering accommodation is the most appropriate response or whether other options (such as providing services to the child and family or calling on support from the wider family or social network) might be better.

As the duty to accommodate only arises in respect of a 'child in need', the first step is to determine whether a particular child falls within s17 CA89.[1] If so, the next question is whether his circumstances fit any of the definitions in s20(1) CA89.

Case Study: Unaccompanied minor

David arrives alone in the UK claiming asylum. He claims to be under 18. He may or may not have parents elsewhere in the world but he

---

1   See Chapter 7 for more information on children in need.

has none in the UK. He therefore falls within s20(1)(a) CA89 if he is indeed a child.

If there is a doubt about whether someone claiming to be a child is in fact under 18, an age assessment must be carried out. As Lady Hale put it,[2] whether someone is a child is a question of fact to which there is 'a right or a wrong answer. It may be difficult to determine what that answer is. The decision-makers may have to do their best on the basis of less than perfect or conclusive evidence.'

Ultimately if there is disagreement, the court may have to decide the question of age. This is a question of fact, whereas deciding what services to provide is a question of professional judgment and there are often no 'right' or 'wrong' answers. The courts are unlikely to intervene with such decisions unless they are not properly made.

Case Study: Orphan

Ethan's parents die in an accident, so there is no-one with PR for him. The local authority steps in and places him in foster care under s20(1)(a) CA89. If Ethan's parents appointed testamentary guardians or if anyone is willing to apply to court to become his guardian, he will swiftly move out of accommodation. If not, he may remain accommodated long term.

s20 CA89 never gives the local authority PR, so an orphan accommodated under s20(1)(a) CA89 could remain a child for whom nobody has PR for the rest of his childhood.

Case Study: A lost child

Felicity, aged three, is found wandering alone. As she is 'lost or abandoned', the local authority takes her in under s20(1)(b) CA89

2   *R (on the application of A)* v. *London Borough of Croydon; R (on the application of M)* v. *London Borough of Lambeth* [2009] UKSC 8 (House of Lords) at paragraph 27. For a review of how the law has been applied since this case, see the Children's Commissioner for England (July 2012) *The Fact of Age.* Available at www.childrenscommissioner.gov.uk/content/publications/content_590, accessed on 30 March 2014.

until her parents are traced. Depending on how Felicity became lost, she may go straight home or her case may turn into a child protection matter.

s20(1)(c) CA89 is wider than the other two subsections and is the most common ground for accommodation. The statutory draftsman did not even try to anticipate all the possible situations which might arise, instead expressing the subsection in broad terms to cover all eventualities. As Lord Hope said: 'the widest possible scope must be given to this provision.'[3]

Case Study: Circumstances prevent continued care

Seven children need the authority's help:
- Greg's mother has to go into hospital for an operation.
- Harry's mother cannot care for him until her mental health improves.
- Ian's father has been sent to prison.
- Jane's father is going into residential rehabilitation.
- Keith's parents are about to be evicted and will be homeless.
- Leon's disabilities mean his parents cannot meet his needs at home.
- Martin's parents cannot cope with his aggressive behaviour.

s20(1)(c) CA89 could apply to all seven.

The local authority must decide whether a child falling into any of the three categories appears to need accommodation as opposed to any other service. If so, there is a duty to accommodate. So it is for the authority to judge whether providing accommodation is the right way forward after an assessment carried out in accordance with the *Working Together* guidance. There is a specific statutory requirement to consult the child:

---

3   *R(G) v. Barnet LBC* [2003] UKHL 57 (House of Lords) at paragraph 100.

> s20(6) CA89 Before providing accommodation under this section, a local authority shall, so far as is reasonably practicable and consistent with the child's welfare –
>
> (a) ascertain the child's wishes and feelings regarding the provision of accommodation; and
>
> (b) give due consideration (having regard to his age and understanding) to such wishes and feelings of the child as they have been able to ascertain.

Exasperated parents of a rebellious teenager, for example, might want their offspring to be accommodated, but you might judge that it is better to try to work with the family with him staying at home. Provided assessments have been carried out correctly, that is an entirely legitimate response within the terms of s20 CA89.

16- and 17-year-olds

There is a specific duty[4] towards a 16- or 17-year-old in need where the local authority considers his welfare is 'likely to be seriously prejudiced' if he is not accommodated. This is a stronger test than for younger children, who must simply appear to require accommodation.

Young people needing accommodation may go to the housing department, not children's social care, so co-operation between departments is vital and each individual's case must be properly assessed.

Decisions can have far-reaching implications: if a young person is accommodated under s20CA89, she becomes 'looked after' and acquires rights to services continuing beyond the age of 18; if she is housed under housing legislation, she acquires no such rights. The authority cannot escape its obligations by labelling a placement as being a housing placement if in reality the young person should be accommodated under s20 CA89. If, however, contrary to the requirement for a joint protocol, the housing authority provides accommodation and children's social care are completely unaware of the case, they cannot later be deemed to have provided accommodation under s20.[5]

---

4   s20(3) CA89.
5   *R (M)* v. *Hammersmith and Fulham LBC* [2008] UKHL 14 (House of Lords).

The power to accommodate

There is a power to accommodate a child even if there is no duty to do so.[6] This power covers 'any child' within the area, in need or not, even where a person with PR is able to care for the child, if the local authority considers that accommodating the child would safeguard and promote his welfare. However, as a power, not a duty, it is entirely discretionary.

s20 CA89 and PR

The detailed provisions of s20 CA89 flow naturally from the local authority's role to support, not replace, the child's parents. Even if the child's usual carer requests accommodation, it makes sense that someone else with PR who is able and willing to look after the child should do so, instead of the authority stepping in. In this situation, the local authority is not allowed to accommodate the child[7]– a child's primary place is with a parent, not in substitute care. This does not apply, however, if there is an order for residence or special guardianship order in force[8] because the court's decision displaces the normal equality between those with PR in deciding where the child should live.

Once a child is accommodated, again it is logical that anyone with PR can remove him from accommodation at any time and without notice.[9] In practice you may ask a parent to give notice before discharging the child from accommodation to allow arrangements to be made, including preparing the child to move home, but such agreements, even if they are in writing and signed by the parent, have no legal force.

The child's views

As we have seen, it is not only good practice but a statutory duty to consider the child's views, but he does not have to consent to accommodation.

Once the child turns 16, he can be accommodated if he agrees, even if someone with PR wishes to take over his care. Likewise, he can refuse

---

6   s20(4) CA89.
7   s20(7) CA89.
8   s20(9) CA89.
9   s20(8) CA89.

to be discharged from accommodation by someone with PR against his will.[10]

The Act is, however, silent about what happens when a young person refuses to be accommodated or purports to discharge himself from accommodation. This Part of the Act gives no power to detain a young person against his will and, in reality, over-16-year-olds, who can leave school and support themselves, can vote with their feet. For under-16s, if persuasion is unsuccessful, the authority has to consider whether the grounds exist for care proceedings or, in an extreme case, a secure accommodation application under s25 CA89.

Case Study: Accommodation in action

Nigel, aged 12, lives with his mother, Olivia. His parents are separated and he is registered as a child in need. Olivia is going into a three-month residential drug rehabilitation programme and she asks the local authority to arrange foster care for Nigel while she undertakes her rehab.

Nigel tells his social worker, Peter, that he is 'OK' about going into foster care.

The local authority has a duty to accommodate Nigel under s20(1)(c) CA89 because:

- he is a child in need
- Olivia is temporarily prevented from looking after him
- he appears to need accommodation.

Peter draws up a placement agreement with Olivia including:

- Nigel is to be accommodated for at least the three months of Olivia's treatment.
- Olivia will give at least a week's notice before seeking to remove Nigel from the foster home.
- Olivia delegates to the local authority aspects of her PR, including giving day-to-day care, arranging routine and emergency medical treatment and agreeing to school trips.

---

10 s20(11) CA89.

Variation 1 – Nigel's father, Quentin, has PR. When Peter tells him of the accommodation plan, Quentin says he can care for Nigel and opposes foster care.

Peter may try to work with Quentin but he has no right to accommodate Nigel against Quentin's wishes – even if Quentin hardly knows his son and Nigel does not want to live with him. If Peter has evidence that Nigel is likely to suffer significant harm in Quentin's care, he must invoke child protection procedures but, if not, can only offer advice and support.

Variation 2 – Quentin has PR, but Olivia has an order for residence.

The order for residence changes the situation: Quentin cannot now veto Nigel's accommodation. He must go to court to discharge or vary the order for residence before he can oppose accommodation.

Variation 3 – Quentin has no PR. He is able and willing to care for Nigel, who wants to live with him, but Olivia objects.

Without PR, Quentin cannot veto accommodation. Only Olivia has PR so, even if Nigel would be better off with Quentin, he cannot be placed there against Olivia's wishes. Quentin must seek a PR order or an order for residence.

Variation 4 – Quentin has an order for contact.

Quentin's order for contact is unaffected by Nigel's accommodation and must be honoured.

Variation 5 – Olivia leaves rehab without completing her programme. She demands Nigel's immediate return.

Even though Olivia agreed to give notice before resuming Nigel's care, this has no legal force and she has the right to remove him at any time. Unless he can persuade Olivia to be reasonable, Peter can only block Nigel's return if circumstances justify emergency compulsory action.

Variation 6 – Olivia arrives at the foster home at 3 am in an unfit state to care for Nigel, demanding his instant return.

The foster father does not want to be pushed into an immediate decision and certainly does not want to hand Nigel back to Olivia in these circumstances. He can fall back on s3(5) CA89, as he is a person without PR but with the actual care of the child. He can 'do what is reasonable in all the circumstances of the case for the purpose of safeguarding or promoting the child's welfare'. This buys him enough time to try to persuade Olivia to wait until morning and talk to Peter, or to phone the out-of-hours service or police for them to decide whether to take emergency action to prevent Nigel's removal.

Variation 7 – Olivia's drug problem worsens and she is unable to care for Nigel in the foreseeable future.

Nigel can remain accommodated long-term, for the rest of his childhood if necessary. s20(1)(c) CA89 still applies as his mother is now permanently prevented from caring for him.

Variation 8 – Nigel is now 16 and settled in his foster home. Olivia is better and wants to have Nigel back home. He refuses to go.

As Nigel is 16, Olivia no longer has the right to discharge him from accommodation. He can refuse to leave, and the local authority can continue to look after him even against Olivia's wishes. Even a month before Nigel's sixteenth birthday, the provision would not apply and Olivia would have the right to discharge him against his wishes in the absence of a court order.

A looked after child

An accommodated child is a 'looked after' child, just as his counterpart who is in care. He therefore has to have a social worker, a care plan and regular reviews of his case. The local authority's duties to such children are spelled out in detail in CA89, regulations and accompanying guidance[11] and are summarised in Appendix 5.

Placement

Sections added[12] to CA89 make explicit the previous assumption that wherever possible and consistent with the child's welfare, a looked after child should be rehabilitated home, placed with a parent or other person with PR. If that is not possible, the most appropriate placement available should be chosen. The first choice is a relative, friend or other connected person, who must be assessed and registered as a local authority foster carer. Only if these options are not suitable should the child go to foster care, residential care or other provision (such as supported lodgings or living independently). As far as possible the placement should:

- be near the child's home

---

11   Such as the Care Planning Placement and Review (England) Regulations 2010 and Guidance.

12   s22A–G CA89 added by the Children and Young Persons Act 2008. The original s23 CA89 has been repealed.

- avoid disrupting his education or training
- be with a sibling
- be suitable to his particular needs if he is disabled.

Placing with family or friends

A particularly difficult legal situation arises when a child needs someone to care for her at short notice and the authority contacts a family member who takes the child on. Is the authority simply acting as a broker in a private family arrangement or is it placing a child in accommodation with a carer who happens to have a connection with the child? A string of cases[13] made it clear that where an authority takes an active role in arranging for a child who falls within s20 CA89 to live with a relative or friend, the chances are that it is accommodating and placing the child with all the consequential legal obligations, not to mention financial commitment, that entails. Authorities must take great care to be very clear of the legal basis of their actions.

It is clear that where a child is placed with family or friends, those carers must be assessed and registered as foster carers (albeit for the specific placement only). Temporary approval can be given for up to 16 weeks to allow assessments to proceed. They must be paid a fostering allowance which must not be less than that paid to other foster carers purely because it is a kinship placement[14] – to do otherwise is unlawful and several authorities have had their policies struck down by the court on judicial review.

Disagreements

The statutory scheme assumes that everyone will work in partnership and harmony. But what if there is a disagreement about what is best for the child? For a child in care, the answer is simple as the local authority has the final say. Not so where a child is accommodated: the parent(s)

---

13   Under the old s23 CA89, since repealed, including *R (SA)* v. *Kent County Council* [2011] EWCA Civ 1303 (Court of Appeal).

14   National Minimum Standards for fostering Standard 28.7; confirmed in *X (on the application of R)* v. *London Borough of Tower Hamlets* [2013] EWCA Civ 904 (Court of Appeal).

have PR but are not caring for the child while the local authority is caring for the child, but has no PR.

Just such a situation arose in the case[15] of a 12-year-old girl with multiple severe disabilities and other difficulties. She had been accommodated by the local authority for three years in a residential placement as her parents were unable to meet her needs. The local authority then proposed to move her to a foster home. Her parents opposed the move, but the local authority went ahead and commenced introductions.

The parents sought a judicial review of the local authority's actions. The High Court found that the authority had no right to move the child against the parents' wishes as it had no PR, but equally the parents had no right to dictate to the local authority how it used its resources or to demand a particular placement: there was a legal impasse. The local authority could not place the girl in the foster home and the parents could not insist that she stayed in the residential home.

Because this was judicial review, the court's job was done in simply declaring the authority's planned actions unlawful – it did not have jurisdiction to make an order resolving the problem. However, three options were suggested:

- the parties could negotiate a solution (a little optimistic when the dispute had already gone to court)

- the local authority should consider whether there were grounds to seek a care order, which would give it power to determine the child's placement (but this would require proof of significant harm)

- the authority could effectively say to the parents 'this is the service we are offering. If you are not happy, you can exercise your PR by taking on or arranging her care yourself.'

This case shows the potential practical difficulties arising from the legal characteristics of accommodation especially if the arrangement continues long-term. These challenges can be even more acute if accommodation is used where a child is in need because of a risk of harm and the relationship between the authority and parents is less than harmonious.

---

15   *R v. Tameside BC ex parte J* [2000] 1FLR 942 (High Court).

Ending accommodation

The CA89 says very little about how accommodation ends. The presumption is that the child simply returns to a parent's care, automatically ending the period of accommodation by the authority. The child may, however, remain 'in need' and a plan should be drawn up to identify the support and services required.

Accommodation and child protection

In the scheme of CA89, there is a clear distinction between support services, including accommodation, and child protection measures; they are in different Parts of the Act. In practice, boundaries are more blurred. Where a child needs to be accommodated because of serious inadequacies in parental care, a support service starts to blend into a protective measure.

Sometimes parents are asked to agree to have their child accommodated to avoid care proceedings. Reaching an agreement rather than resorting to compulsory measures is often said to be 'partnership with parents', consistent with the idea of minimum intervention and the 'no order' principle in s1(5) CA89. But is an agreement secured by an implicit (or even explicit) threat really an agreement at all? The idea of 'partnership' is stretched to breaking point when the balance of power is so unequal, as in a case[16] where the parents were visited by two social workers and four police officers (three in uniform) and the child was removed under what the judge described as an 'enforced s20 agreement' with the overt threat of police protection if they did not agree.

Accommodation, designed to be a truly voluntary measure, has none of the safeguards of care proceedings: parents have no automatic right to free legal advice, the child is not separately represented and there is no independent adjudication of the evidence by a court. All the cards are in the local authority's hand. Cynics might be tempted to believe that the accommodation route is chosen because it avoids court scrutiny and is quicker, easier and cheaper for the authority than going to court – not because it is the right thing to do.

---

16   *Re E (A Child)* [2013] EWHC 2400 (Fam) (High Court).

A striking illustration of the misuse of s20 CA89 occurred in the case[17] of the newborn baby of a mother with significant learning difficulties who had already had three children removed from her care. Pre-birth assessments were negative and the plan was made for permanent removal of the new baby. The mother knew of the plan. The very day that the baby was born, the mother was repeatedly asked to agree to her removal and accommodation under s20 CA89. The mother initially refused, then acquiesced at a time when she was medicated with morphine following a difficult birth.

Although ultimately the baby was made subject to care and placement orders, that did not justify the manner of her initial removal. Hedley J gave guidance:

- Every social worker has a personal duty[18] to be satisfied that the person concerned has the capacity to give consent; if in doubt, she should stop trying to obtain consent and take further advice.

- Even if the person has capacity, the worker must ensure that consent is informed. This includes the person knowing the choices available, the consequences of giving or refusing consent, and understands all the relevant issues.

- 'Willingness to consent cannot be inferred from silence, submission or even acquiescence. It is a positive stance.'[19]

- The authority should consider the parent's physical and psychological state, whether they have advice from a solicitor, family or friends, whether it would be fairer to go to court and whether it is necessary to remove the child.

- A baby should not be removed at birth using s20 CA89 when a court would not have ordered removal:

  > It can never be permissible to seek agreement to do that which would not be authorised by order solely because it is known, believed or even suspected that no such authorisation would be given and in order to circumvent that position.[20]

---

17   *Re CA (A Baby)* [2012] EWHC 2190 (Fam) (High Court).
18   Hedley J in *Re CA* at paragraph 46.
19   Hedley J in *Re CA* at paragraph 44.
20   Hedley J in *Re CA* at paragraph 35.

In this case, the risks to the baby were not such as to justify immediate removal at birth. The actions of the local authority were disproportionate and thus breached the Article 8 rights of both mother and baby. In something of an understatement, Hedley J said:

> local authorities may want to approach with great care the obtaining of Section 20 agreements from mothers in the aftermath of birth, especially where there is no immediate danger to the child and where probably no order would be made.[21]

Even if valid agreement is obtained, this is only the start. Thereafter, parental co-operation has to be secured at every stage as they retain exclusive PR – the local authority has no power to dictate to them or to make long-term plans, a particular problem if the parents are not always predictable or reasonable. The ultimate problem is that they have the power to remove the child at any time and without notice. The authority is then forced to fall back onto the compulsory measures it was trying to avoid, possibly in an emergency.

Child protection cases should be taken through the mechanisms designed specifically for them, not shoe-horned into a legal model which does not fit. Accommodation is there to help and support children and their families who are in need and should be kept for situations where agreement truly exists.

Points for practice

1. Always be clear whether a looked after child is accommodated or in care.

2. Make sure you know who has PR for an accommodated child.

3. Even if you are making arrangements at short notice, be clear with all concerned the exact legal basis on which they are made.

4. Record everything in writing, specifying the legal basis for your actions.

5. Use accommodation only for cases of true agreement, not for child protection cases.

---

21   *Re CA* at paragraph 46(x).

Part 4

Child Protection

Chapter 9

Child Protection Investigations

Child protection work goes on day in, day out, usually unnoticed by the general public and ignored by the media and politicians. It only hits the headlines when children are removed unnecessarily (as in Cleveland in the 1980s) or authorities fail a child in desperate need of rescue (such as Victoria Climbié or Peter Connelly). Then child protection suddenly becomes the centre of public and media attention. As Professor Eileen Munro wrote:

> ...the intensity of that reaction places enormous pressure on Government and professionals to act and act quickly in order to improve practice. This has meant that the majority of reform to the child protection system over the past forty years has taken place in the midst of a clamour for change.[1]

Indeed, the Cleveland report informed the Children Act 1989 (CA89) and the Climbié report influenced the Children Act 2004 (CA04). Professor Munro's own *Review of Child Protection* found that, while each reform, additional piece of guidance or extra procedure made sense in isolation, the cumulative effect created an over-bureaucratised system and 'a work environment full of obstacles to keeping a clear focus on meeting the needs of children.'[2]

---

1   Department for Education (2011) *The Munro Review of Child Protection: Final Report – A child-centred system*, paragraph 1.10. Available at www.gov.uk/government/publications/munro-review-of-child-protection-final-report-a-child-centred-system, accessed on 30 March 2014.
2   Munro Final Report, paragraph 1.16.

The Munro Review has led to a completely revised and substantially slimmer version of the key guidance on child protection, *Working Together*, initiatives to improve social work expertise and raise the status of the social work profession, amendments to the inspection system, changes to Serious Case Reviews, and an increased emphasis on early help.

However, no system is infallible. As Munro wrote:

> Determining how to improve the child protection system is a difficult task as the system is inherently complex. The problems faced by children are complicated and the cost of failure high. Abuse and neglect can present in ambiguous ways and concerns about a child's safety or development can arise from myriad signs and symptoms. Future predictions about abusive behaviours are necessarily fallible. The number of professions and agencies who have some role in identifying and responding to abuse and neglect means the co-ordination and communication between them is crucial to success.[3]

Ensuring that your cases fall in the category of unnoticed success rather than notorious disaster requires clear thinking, good judgment and a sound knowledge of the relevant law.

Strategic responsibilities

CA04 created the post of Director of Children's Services and the requirement to nominate a Lead Member for Children's Services. The Munro report urged that the importance of these senior roles with specific responsibilities for children's services should not be undermined[4] for example by combining these posts with other responsibilities, as appears to be happening in some areas.

Local Safeguarding Children Boards (LSCBs)

These were also established by CA04. The LSCB is a multi-agency body with a strategic role to co-ordinate and ensure the effectiveness of the represented bodies' actions to safeguard and promote children's welfare in their area. It is independent of its constituent agencies and all other local structures. It does not deliver or commission frontline

---

3   Munro Final Report paragraph 1.1.
4   Final report recommendation 7.

services and has no power to direct actions of agencies which remain autonomous. Rather, its function is co-ordination and scrutiny.

It must devise policies and procedures[5] covering:

- action to be taken in case of concerns about a child's safety or welfare
- thresholds for intervention (for support services and child protection)
- inter-agency procedures for enquiries (such as joint police and social work investigations)
- recruiting, training and supervising people working with children
- investigation of allegations against people working with children
- safety and welfare of privately fostered children
- co-operation with neighbouring authorities.

Other tasks include:

- communication and raising awareness about child protection
- monitoring and evaluating actions of the local authority and partner agencies and advising on improvement
- participating in planning children's services
- reviewing child deaths
- conducting Serious Case Reviews and advising the authority and Board partners on lessons to be learned
- developing a culture of information sharing between agencies.

The LSCB must have an independent Chair who can hold all agencies to account. The Chair produces an annual report on the performance and effectiveness of child safeguarding and welfare services in the area. Board members must be people senior enough to speak authoritatively for their agencies, commit them to policy and practice and hold them to account.

---

5   Local Safeguarding Children Boards Regulations 2006 SI 2006/90 regulation 5.

There should be close links between the Director of Children's Services and the LSCB Chair and the Lead Member should attend LSCB meetings and receive all its reports.

Significant harm

The key term in all CA89 child protection provisions from initial investigation through to care orders is 'significant harm'. Understanding this term is fundamental.

What is 'harm'?

s31(9) CA89 defines 'harm'. It tells us that 'harm' includes 'ill-treatment' which itself includes 'sexual abuse and forms of ill-treatment which are not physical', such as emotional abuse. Physical abuse itself is not explicitly included, but this is taken as read. This part of the definition therefore covers all forms of abuse.

'Harm' also includes 'the impairment of health or development'. Just as in s17 CA89, 'health' includes both physical and mental health, and 'development' includes physical, intellectual, emotional, social and behavioural development, so this part of the definition covers neglect cases.

A later amendment to CA89 added a separate reference to harm caused by seeing or hearing someone else being ill-treated (such as a sibling who is being abused or a parent subjected to domestic violence). This addition was perhaps unnecessary as such cases were arguably already covered by the broader definition but it serves to clarify matters.

What does 'significantly impaired' mean?

To assess whether health or development are being impaired, s31(10) CA89 tells us to compare the health or development of the child in question 'with that which could reasonably be expected of a similar child'.

What is a 'similar child'? Perhaps this was thought to be obvious – there are standard expectations for certain age groups and a developmental assessment will show whether a child is within the 'normal' range. Lord Wilson commented:

> whereas the concept of 'ill-treatment' is absolute, the concept of 'impairment of health or development' is relative to the health or

development which could reasonably be expected of a similar child. This is helpful but little more than common sense.[6]

But is it really so simple? The Act does not tell us which similarities to import from our actual child into our hypothetical 'similar' child – clearly there is no point comparing him with a child who is similar in all respects, including his neglectful or abusive upbringing. Lady Hale[7] commented that, unlike the standard of reasonable parenting which is objective, 'the level of development expected of the child is the subjective level to be expected of a child like him'. She quoted with approval Munby J who said: 'the court must always be sensitive to the cultural, social and religious circumstances of the particular child and family.'[8]

In a case from the very early days of CA89[9] which concerned significant harm caused by lack of education, the judge said: 'in this context a "similar child" means a child of equivalent intellectual and social development, who has gone to school.'

It seems, therefore, that we have to consider a hypothetical 'average' child of the same age, social and cultural background and potential, but factor out elements of abuse or neglect.

What does 'significant' mean?

The word 'significant' is not defined in the Act, nor do case law authorities provide much help. Indeed, in the Supreme Court, Lord Wilson said:

> In my view this court should avoid attempting to explain the word 'significant'. It would be a gloss; attention might then turn to the meaning of the gloss and, albeit with the best of intentions, the courts might find in due course that they had travelled far from the word itself.[10]

We must therefore look to the ordinary and natural meaning of the word. Lady Hale commended the dictionary definition: 'considerable, noteworthy or important'.

---

6   *In the Matter of B (A Child)* [2013] UKSC 33 (Supreme Court) at paragraph 25.

7   *In the Matter of B (A Child)* [2013] UKSC 33 (Supreme Court) at paragraph 178.

8   *In re K, A Local Authority* v. *N and Others* [2005] EWHC 2956 (High Court) at paragraph 26.

9   *Re O (A Minor) (Care Order: Education: Procedure)* [1992] 2FLR 7 (High Court).

10   *In the Matter of B (A Child)* [2013] UKSC 33 (Supreme Court) at paragraph 26.

It is clear that to be significant, harm must be, in the words of Hedley J, 'something unusual; at least something more than the common-place human failure or inadequacy'.[11] In that case, he found that the children had suffered 'harm' but it had not reached the level of 'significant harm'.

Is 'significant' the same as 'serious'?

Case Study: Not serious but significant?

Four-month-old Robert has bruises to his face. His father cannot see what all the fuss is about. Bruises are not serious – no medical treatment is needed, they heal quickly and they leave no scars. It is true that Robert's injuries are not medically serious, but that does not stop them being significant because of what they tell us.

In this context, the other dictionary definition of 'significant' – signifying or being indicative of something or having a particular meaning – may be particularly helpful.

How certain must we be?

At the outset of a child protection investigation, by definition only limited information is available, but by the final hearing of care proceedings the matter will have been investigated and assessed in minute detail. Not surprisingly, therefore, the law requires the existence of significant harm to be demonstrated with an increasing degree of certainty at each stage. We move from suspicion to belief and on to being 'satisfied'.

SUSPECT

The section dealing with child protection enquiries, s47 CA89, says that there must be a child protection investigation where there is 'reasonable cause to suspect' actual or likely significant harm. The need for 'reasonable cause' makes it clear that the authority cannot descend on a family at random to see if there is a problem – but the information

---

11   *Re L (Care: Threshold Criteria)* [2007] 1FLR 2050 (High Court) at paragraph 51.

only has to be enough to warrant suspicion. This is a much lower test than that required for a court order.

What if a court has already dismissed allegations against a person? Can the local authority still have reasonable cause to 'suspect' harm under s47? This question came to court in two cases. In the first[12] a man had been acquitted of sexual abuse charges in a criminal trial (where the standard of proof is the very high 'beyond reasonable doubt'). In the other,[13] the authority had unsuccessfully applied for a care order, failing to prove abuse to the requisite standard ('on the balance of probabilities').

In both cases, despite the evidence not being sufficient to satisfy the courts on higher tests, there were reasonable grounds 'to suspect' and the authorities were justified in continuing child protection enquiries. As Wall LJ said:

> Section 47 is about child protection, and the threshold which triggers the duties of a local authority to investigate are, for obvious reasons, lower than those which entitle a court to place a child in care. The Local Authority accordingly is entitled on the facts of this case to have 'reasonable cause to suspect' that the child is likely to suffer significant harm and to take appropriate steps both to investigate further into her circumstances and to monitor her well-being. This, in my view, includes her name remaining on the Child Protection Register.[14]

BELIEVE

By the time it comes to a court application, a higher level of certainty is expected. To obtain an emergency protection order (EPO),[15] the applicant must establish that 'there is reasonable cause to believe' that significant harm is likely. 'Believe' is a stronger word than 'suspect', so a greater level of evidence is needed.

For the next stage, an interim care order,[16] the court must be satisfied that 'there are reasonable grounds for believing' not only that significant harm exists, but also that it is attributable to inadequate care or the child being beyond control.

---

12   *R (ota S)* v. *Swindon Borough Council* [2001] 2FLR 776 (High Court).
13   *North Yorkshire CC* v. *S* [2005] EWCA Civ 316 (Court of Appeal).
14   *North Yorkshire CC* v. *S* at paragraph 30.
15   s44 CA89 – see Chapter 10 for more details.
16   s38 CA89 – see Chapter 11 for more details.

SATISFIED

To make a final care or supervision order, the court must be 'satisfied' on the balance of probabilities that the grounds for a care order (commonly known as the 'threshold criteria') exist. The House of Lords[17] explicitly said that suspicion is not enough to cross the threshold. Lord Nicholls said: 'The threshold is there to protect both the children and their parents from unjustified intervention in their lives. It would provide no protection at all if it could be established on the basis of unsubstantiated suspicions.'[18]

Section 47 – the duty to investigate

> s47(1) Where a local authority –
>
> (a)   are informed that a child who lives, or is found, in their area –
>
>   (i)   is the subject of an emergency protection order; or
>
>   (ii) is in police protection; or
>
> (b)   have reasonable cause to suspect that a child who lives, or is found, in their area is suffering, or is likely to suffer, significant harm,
>
> the authority shall make, or cause to be made, such enquiries as they consider necessary to enable them to decide whether they should take any action to safeguard or promote the child's welfare.

Most cases arise from subsection (b) which includes referrals from other professionals and members of the public.

The purpose of the enquiries is to decide whether 'any action' is needed to safeguard or promote the child's welfare, and in particular to consider whether court proceedings should be taken,[19] but court is not the only option. 'Any action' could include:

• calling a Child Protection Case Conference

---

17   *Re H & R (Child Sexual Abuse: Standard of Proof)* [1996] 1FLR 80 House of Lords. Affirmed by the House of Lords in *Re B (Children)* [2008] UKHL 35.

18   *Re H & R* at paragraph 54.

19   s47(3) CA89.

- taking emergency protection or care proceedings
- providing s17 services to the child and family or referring to other agencies for help
- helping the family resolve problems themselves
- taking no action at all.

If the authority decides that some action should be taken, then it must take it 'so far as it is both within their power and reasonably practicable to do so'.[20] If the authority decides not to make any court applications, it must consider whether to review the case at a later date.[21]

Seeing the child

> s47(4) CA89 Where enquiries are being made under subsection (1) with respect to a child, the local authority shall (with a view to enabling them to determine what action, if any, to take with respect to him) take such steps as are reasonably practicable –
>
> (a) to obtain access to him; or
>
> (b) to ensure that access to him is obtained, on their behalf, by a person authorised by them for the purpose, unless they are satisfied that they already have sufficient information with respect to him.

This section is backed up by the duty to apply for an EPO[22] if access to the child is refused or information as to his whereabouts is denied.

The importance of someone actually seeing the child cannot be overstated. One of the many haunting aspects of the Victoria Climbié tragedy is that, in Lord Laming's words:

> …in the last few weeks before she died, a social worker called at her home several times. She got no reply when she knocked at the door and assumed that Victoria and Kouao had moved away. It is possible that at the time, Victoria was in fact lying just a few yards away, in the

---

20   s47(8) CA89.
21   s47(7) CA89.
22   For more information on EPOs see Chapter 10.

prison of the bath, desperately hoping that someone might find her and come to her rescue before her life ebbed away.[23]

The child's wishes

Before deciding what action to take, the authority must:

so far as is reasonably practicable and consistent with the child's welfare –

a. ascertain the child's wishes and feelings regarding the action to be taken with respect to him; and

b. give due consideration (having regard to his age and understanding) to such wishes and feelings of the child as they have been able to ascertain.[24]

Other agencies

Other local authorities and education, housing and health authorities have a statutory duty to provide relevant information and advice to assist with s47 CA89 enquiries.[25] The concept of inter-agency working in child protection should be so deeply ingrained that a formal request for help should not be necessary – but it is useful to know the statutory basis for doing so if required.

Partner agencies can also be reminded that they also have their own statutory duty to have regard to the need to safeguard and promote children's welfare in discharging their functions.[26]

Time and again, enquiry reports and Serious Case Reviews highlight failures in inter-agency working and stress the need for close co-operation and information sharing. Individual agencies as well as the LSCB must put procedures in place and foster links at ground level so the theory of co-operation becomes second nature in practice.

---

23 Lord Laming (2003) *The Victoria Climbié Inquiry. Report of an Inquiry by Lord Laming*, paragraph 1.11. Available at www.official-documents.gov.uk/document/cm57/5730/5730.pdf, accessed on 30 March 2014.
24 s47(5A) CA89, added by CA04.
25 s47(9) CA89.
26 s11(2) CA04.

Working Together

Apart from the duties to see and to consult the child, s47 does not specify the nature or extent of enquiries. That is left to the authority's judgment, informed by the guidance contained in *Working Together*. As this was issued under s7 Local Authority Social Services Act 1970, it must be followed unless there are very good reasons to do otherwise.

The 2013 version replaces not only the old version of *Working Together* but also the *Framework for Assessment of Children in Need and their Families*. *Working Together* (2013) is a substantially slimmer volume than its predecessor, in line with the Munro Review's observation that the previous edition was 'too long to be practically useful' and the observation that 'thick manuals of procedures can be paralysing because they are hard to use and can prevent workers from moving quickly enough to seize opportunities'.[27] Munro also expressed the view that the proliferation of guidance 'has actually contributed to the de-professionalisation of child protection, as those working in the field feel increasingly obliged to do things "by the book" rather than use their professional judgment about children's needs'.[28]

Although *Working Together* is now less prescriptive and leaves more room for judgment, it remains statutory guidance and must be followed – it is easy to imagine the consequences if a case where it is not followed goes badly wrong.

Following Munro there is less emphasis on process, form completion and ticked boxes, but record-keeping remains crucially important, especially from a legal point of view. Information must be noted accurately to avoid imperfect recollection, miscommunication and misunderstandings. All decisions (including decisions not to take a particular course of action) and the reasons for them must be recorded. The best advice is always to imagine that every case you work will end up in court so you can be sure to explain, evidence and justify every step. Legal challenges (such as compensation claims) can arise years later, long after everyone involved has left the department or forgotten the case. You only have the records left to explain what happened and why. It is very important that Munro's justified comments about putting paperwork into perspective are not used to excuse poor record-keeping.

---

27   Munro Final Report at paragraph 3.13.
28   Munro Final Report at paragraph 3.14.

Enquiries and assessments

Working Together says:

High quality assessments:

- are child centred. Where there is a conflict of interest, decisions should be made in the child's best interests;

- are rooted in child development and informed by evidence;

- are focused on action and outcomes for children;

- are holistic in approach, addressing the child's needs within their family and wider community;

- ensure equality of opportunity;

- involve children and families;

- build on strengths as well as identifying difficulties;

- are integrated in approach;

- are a continuing process not an event;

- lead to action, including the provision and review of services; and

- are transparent and open to challenge.[29]

The document emphasises the need to remain child-centred, not being distracted by adult agendas, to reflect on latest research and to revise assessments as matters progress. Supervision plays an important role, the social work manager being prepared to challenge workers' assumptions.

Timescale for assessments

Timeliness is critical. The speed for any particular assessment depends on the individual case and is a matter for judgment, but *Working Together* prescribes that within one working day of receiving a referral, it should be acknowledged and a decision made by a social worker about the type of response required. If immediate action is needed, it should be taken. Alternatively, the case could require a s17 (child in need) or s47 (child protection) assessment. As information comes to hand, the nature of the case may change and it may move from one statutory category to

---

29 *Working Together* (2013) at paragraph 32.

another. Enquiries may also lead to concerns being discounted, leading to no further action.

The family should be informed (unless this would jeopardise the child's safety) and the child seen as soon as possible.

Action should be taken or services provided at any stage during the assessment if it becomes apparent that they are required; the child should not have to wait until the assessment is finished.

The timescale for completing assessments is set at a maximum of 45 days (unless an extension is required for good reasons which are discussed and recorded). The previous distinction between initial and core assessments has been removed.

Rather than detailed national prescription, the assessment process is to be the subject of a local protocol discussed between partner agencies and agreed by the LSCB.

Strategy discussion

In a s47 situation, there should be a strategy discussion between the local authority, police, health and other relevant bodies such as the referring agency. It does not have to be a meeting; discussions can, for example, be by phone. It is unfortunate that *Working Together* makes no reference to legal advice, although this may be covered in local protocols. Timely legal advice and effective team working with lawyers can prevent problems occurring later.

Case Conference

Case Conferences are not statutory, they only appear in the *Working Together* guidance.

WHEN?

The timing of a Case Conference depends on the urgency of the case and the child's needs but should not be more than 15 days after the strategy discussion. Conferences may be held pre-birth.

WHAT FOR?

Conferences are to bring together and analyse in a multi-agency meeting all relevant information and to plan how best to safeguard and promote the child's welfare. Crucially, the purpose is to plan for the future not simply to analyse past events.

WHO CHAIRS?

A person independent of operational or line-management responsibilities for the case, accountable to the Director of Children's Services, should chair the meeting. The same person should chair review conferences for the child.

WHO ATTENDS?

The parents/family and their supporters or advocates, the child, social worker and those professionals most involved with the child and family should attend. If necessary, parents can be excluded from part of the conference to allow information to be given which needs to be kept confidential (for example, to avoid jeopardising a criminal investigation). A full minute must still be taken of the confidential part of the meeting, but this is kept separate from the main minutes which themselves record the fact that confidential information was heard. The Chair must keep the need for continued confidentiality under review.[30]

WHO PROVIDES INFORMATION?

All professionals involved with the family should prepare a written report which, unless there is a good reason otherwise, is normally shared with the family in advance. The social work report should include analysis and recommendations.

WHAT DOES THE CONFERENCE DECIDE?

The Conference must assess whether the child is at ongoing risk of significant harm. If so it:

- appoints a lead social worker
- identifies professional and family members of the core group and the timetable for its meetings (the first being within ten days of the Conference)

---

30 *Re X (Emergency Protection Orders)* [2006] EWHC 510 (Fam) (High Court).

- agrees an outline protection plan specifying clear actions and timescales, expected improvements and timescales for change (the core group devises the detailed plan)
- fixes a review Conference, the first of which must be within three months.

WHAT IS A CHILD PROTECTION PLAN FOR?

The purpose of the plan is to ensure the child is and remains safe from harm, to promote her health and development and, where appropriate, to support parents and wider family to look after her.

CHALLENGING CONFERENCE DECISIONS

The LSCB must devise a procedure for complaints about Case Conferences and disagreements should be resolved by internal procedures. The courts are rarely involved although, as a last resort, judicial review is potentially available. In one case,[31] the court found that a Conference was wrong to enter the child's name on the Child Protection Register because it had heard no evidence about that individual child (information had centred on siblings). It is an important reminder that children within the same family do not come as a 'job lot' – each child must be considered individually.

The process must be fair and the courts can intervene if it is not. The Article 6 right to a fair trial applies to Conferences. Parents, children and relevant others should be appropriately informed, involved and enabled to participate in the process.

Legal action

Where a child is suffering or is likely to suffer significant harm, the local authority must consider the evidence and decide whether to take legal action. Whatever the recommendation of the Conference, the responsibility to take legal proceedings rests squarely and solely on the shoulders of the local authority. Unfortunately, *Working Together* makes no specific reference to the imperative need to seek specialist legal advice.

---

31   *R v. Hampshire County Council ex parte H* [1999] 2FLR 359 (High Court).

Child assessment orders

Imagine the situation: you suspect that a child might be suffering or likely to suffer significant harm but cannot be sure without a particular assessment. The parents refuse and the child is not old enough to consent to the assessment for herself. What can you do? You cannot go ahead with the assessment without parental consent and you cannot apply for an EPO or care order because, without the assessment, you have insufficient evidence.

This is precisely the situation for which Child Assessment Orders were designed.[32] On the local authority's application, the court can authorise a specific assessment to be carried out and require the child to be produced for that purpose, although the child can refuse to co-operate if she is of sufficient age and understanding.

These orders are rarely sought. Usually in practice either parental co-operation is secured, making an order unnecessary, or the case proceeds rapidly to the stage where, even without the assessment, evidence exists for an EPO or care proceedings.

Furthermore, there are limitations to the timescale for assessment (maximum seven days) and the type and scope of assessment – a single medical examination or initial psychiatric assessment could be covered but a full social work assessment is out of the question. An investigative interview with the child could be ordered, but applications can only be made on notice to the child's parents, allowing the opportunity for the child to be coached on what to say during the interview.

However, in spite of their shortcomings, it is important to remember that these orders exist and in an appropriate case can be a useful weapon in your armoury.

Particular situations
Joint police and social work investigations

An allegation of physical or sexual abuse or domestic violence involving a child triggers a local authority investigation under s47 CA89, which may lead to proceedings in the family court, but it is also a report of a crime leading to a police investigation which may lead to a criminal prosecution. It is often the case that the same set of facts gives rise

---

32   s43 CA89.

to two different investigations with very different approaches. Joint training can be very important to help police officers and social workers understand each other's procedural and evidential requirements as well as the different cultures of family and criminal justice.

Police and local authorities must co-ordinate their responses and share information from the moment a referral comes in. A comprehensive Protocol[33] provides detailed guidance on information sharing, procedures for the disclosure of evidence from one jurisdiction to another and arrangements for linked directions hearings in care and criminal cases. It is required reading whenever you have a case which involves police as well as social work investigation.

Once proceedings start, the Court of Appeal has emphasised the need for close liaison between police and local authority children's services.[34] Wherever possible, criminal and care proceedings should be co-ordinated with linked directions hearings.[35]

Criminal and care cases may arise from the same facts but the standards of proof, evidential rules, objectives and outcomes are quite different. Acquittal in a criminal court does not preclude findings of fact in the family court, as in a case[36] where the family court found that a man had raped his stepdaughter despite his previous acquittal in the criminal court. The reverse is also true, although far less common. One father was convicted of manslaughter even though the care proceedings judge had been unable to decide who was responsible for his baby's death. The Court of Appeal[37] rejected his appeal: care proceedings do not determine criminal cases or vice versa.

---

33   2013 Protocol and Good Practice Model: Disclosure of information in cases of alleged child abuse and linked criminal and care directions hearings. Issued in October 2013 by Association of Chief Police Officers, Association of Directors of Children Services, Association of Independent Local Safeguarding Children Board Chairs, Crown Prosecution Service, Department for Education, HM Courts & Tribunals Service, Local Government Association, President of the Family Division, Senior Presiding Judge for England and Wales, Welsh Government.
      In force from 1 January 2014. Available at www.cps.gov.uk/publications/docs/third_party_protocol_2013.pdf, accessed on 30 March 2014.

34   *R* v. *Levey* [2006] EWCA Crim 1902.

35   For more information see Hall, A. (ed.) (2007) *Related Family and Criminal Proceedings: A Good Practice Guide*. Available at www.judiciary.gov.uk/JCO%2FDocuments%2FFJC%2FPublications%2FRelatedFamCrimPro.pdf, accessed on 30 March 2014.

36   *W (Children)* [2009] EWCA Civ 644 (Court of Appeal).

37   *R* v. *Levey* [2006] EWCA Crim 1902 (Court of Appeal).

Conducting interviews

Interviewing alleged victims, perpetrators and potential witnesses is a key issue. Mistakes made even at the earliest stage of enquiries could taint evidence and jeopardise the prospects of successful action. For example, if an interview with an alleged perpetrator is not conducted under caution, any confession will be inadmissible in a criminal trial.

Is parental consent needed to interview a child? Usually parents decide who can speak to their child, but in child protection cases it may be essential to proceed without seeking prior parental consent, for example, where:

- the child may be threatened or otherwise coerced into silence
- important evidence will be destroyed
- a competent child does not wish the parent to be involved.

The decision and the reasons for it should be clearly recorded on the file.

Any discussions with the child from the very first contact must be handled professionally and with an eye to later court proceedings. It is vital to keep a careful and accurate record of every contact with the child, recording not just the child's answers but also the questions asked.

Case Study: Recording questions

Sally said 'Daddy punched me', but what was the question? It could have been:

- 'What happened?' – a non-leading question enabling Sally freely to recall events, giving her answer considerable evidential value
- 'Did Mummy or Daddy hit you?' – a 'forced choice' closed question, giving Sally two options, both presuming that a parent has hit her, greatly reducing the value of her answer
- 'Tell me how Daddy hurt you' – a wholly leading question just asking Sally to confirm the questioner's version of events, making her answer evidentially worthless.

If there is no record of the question asked or the context in which the statement was made, the court will treat the answer with caution and Sally's clear disclosure will be undermined.

Conducting a formal interview with a child is a particularly sensitive task. Detailed guidance on interviewing children (as well as other vulnerable witnesses such as people with a learning disability) is contained in the authoritative guidance *Achieving Best Evidence in Criminal Proceedings: Guidance on interviewing victims and witnesses, and guidance on using special measures.*[38] This is usually abbreviated to *Achieving Best Evidence* and the guidelines are known as the *ABE Guidelines*.

Key points to remember include the following:

- only people with specialist training and experience should conduct interviews
- interviewers should be appropriate to the case, including consideration of their gender
- the child should be able to communicate in his first language (spoken or signed) wherever possible
- any special needs must be taken into account, seeking specialist help or advice where necessary
- interviewers should have an understanding of relevant cultural or religious considerations
- no-one but the interviewer(s) should be present with the child
- leading questions should be avoided
- children should not be coached or offered incentives
- technical equipment must work efficiently, the room must be adequately lit and the video recording must show the child and the room clearly
- the purpose of the interview must be clear with no confusion between forensic and therapeutic interviews (therapeutic interviews usually have little evidential value).

If the guidelines are not followed, any video recorded interview with a child is likely to be ruled inadmissible in a criminal trial, so the child will have to attend court to give all his evidence in person or the evidence itself could be tainted. The rules of evidence in care proceedings may

38   Jointly issued by the Crown Prosecution Service, Department for Education, Department of Health and Welsh Assembly Government, March 2011. Available at www.justice.gov.uk/downloads/victims-and-witnesses/vulnerable-witnesses/achieving-best-evidence-criminal-proceedings.pdf, accessed on 30 March 2014.

be more flexible but a flawed interview can still undermine a case. This happened in a case[39] where the Court of Appeal found:

> the inadequacies of the ABE interview are manifest. Even allowing for a broad margin of latitude to anyone conducting such an interview, the departures from the Guidance are self-evident and glaring. There is, on the face of the interview (1) an inadequate establishment of rapport; (2) absolutely no free narrative recall by the child; (3) an abundance of leading questions; and (4) no closure. Everything is led by the officer, and nothing is introduced into the interview by the child.[40]

> … We regret to say that we were left with the clear impression from the interview that the officer was using it purely for what she perceived to be an evidence-gathering exercise and, in particular, to make LR repeat on camera what she had said to her mother. That, emphatically, is not what ABE interviews are about and we have come to the view that we can place no evidential weight on it.[41]

So an incompetent interview can mean that an offender goes free and attempts to protect the child and other children at risk are undermined. This is a great pity as children's evidence can be very powerful. In 2010, the Court of Appeal upheld the conviction of a man for anal rape of a child. The conviction rested solely on the evidence of the victim who was not yet three at the time of the offence and only four and a half at trial. The Lord Chief Justice on appeal said: '…the ABE interview shows an utterly guileless child, too naive and innocent for any deficiencies in her evidence to remain undiscovered, speaking in matter of fact terms. She was indeed a compelling as well as a competent witness.'[42]

Protecting children with disabilities

Clearly, in principle, a child with disabilities should receive the same protection from abuse and neglect as any other child. In practice, government guidance *Safeguarding Disabled Children*[43] tells us:

---

39   *TW* v. *A City Council* [2011] EWCA Civ 17 (Court of Appeal).
40   Wall P, *TW* v. *A City Council* at paragraph 50.
41   Paragraph 52.
42   *R* v. *B* [2010] EWCA Crim 4 (Court of Appeal) at paragraph 52.
43   DCSF (July 2009). Available at www.gov.uk/government/uploads/system/uploads/attachment_data/file/190544/00374-2009DOM-EN.pdf, accessed on 30 March 2014.

disabled children face an increased risk of abuse or neglect yet they are under-represented in safeguarding systems. Disabled children can be abused and neglected in ways that other children cannot and the early indicators suggestive of abuse or neglect can be more complicated than with non-disabled children.

Regrettably, unlike the former version, *Working Together* (2013) does not contain a specific section concerning children with disabilities. It is to be hoped that this will not lead to reduced awareness of the particular issues involved in protecting disabled children.

Investigation of alleged abuse or neglect of a disabled child demands strong inter-agency co-operation, often requiring specialist help, such as assistance with communication and advocacy services. Interviews with disabled children require particularly careful planning following the ABE guidelines. If a disabled child has to give evidence in the criminal court, special measures, including using intermediaries and communication aids, are available thanks to the Youth Justice and Criminal Evidence Act 1999.

Where in care proceedings concern turns on impairment of health or development, the definition of significant harm poses a particular challenge in the context of disability. Who is a 'similar child'? Clearly the hypothetical similar child must have the same disability as the actual child, but the effect of the same diagnosed disability can vary widely from one child to another. Precisely where on the spectrum does a 'similar child' lie? How can we establish whether our child's health or development is impaired by his innate difficulties or by inadequate, neglectful or abusive parenting? In cases of suspected abuse, how can we determine whether a child's challenging behaviour is part of her disability or an expression of the abuse she is suffering? These questions can be very challenging in practice and depend on close observation, detailed evidence-gathering and careful inter-agency co-operation, including seeking specialist advice.

How does the local authority's duty to support the child and family fit in with the duty to protect the child? Hedley J tackled this issue in a case involving a child with a major and life-long disability.[44] He expressed the view that the local authority cannot set up the family to

---

44   *LBH (A Local Authority v. KJ and Others)* [2007] EWHC 2798 (Fam) (High Court).

fail by not putting in support and then use that failure as grounds for compulsory intervention in the child's life. He said: 'a parent cannot be said to be responsible for falling below the standard of "reasonable care" if the public authorities cannot or do not provide what would be reasonably necessary to support that parent'.[45] Co-operating with that advice and support is part of responsible parenting, and failure to do so can be taken into account in assessing whether to move to child protection measures.

Disability in itself, and the very idea of the abuse of disabled children, can raise extra levels of sensitivity and emotional response amongst those involved, particularly amongst professionals inexperienced in disability issues (possibly including lawyers and judges). Those working with the family may have difficulty changing from a mindset of support and empathy to one of investigation and moving their focus from the carers to the child. These factors need to be acknowledged in the process.

Emotional abuse and neglect

All types of ill-treatment include an emotional element, but emotional ill-treatment can also cause significant harm on its own and can be grounds for a care order under s31 CA89. Emotional ill-treatment can cause profound and lasting damage and should not be under-estimated or given less priority than other more visible or acute forms of abuse. Emotional ill-treatment falls within Article 3 of the European Convention on Human Rights as 'inhuman' or 'degrading' treatment, so authorities are under a positive duty to protect against it.

Emotional ill-treatment can too easily be overlooked, simply because it usually takes place behind closed doors, is chronic, invisible and there is no straightforward tangible evidence – it does not show up on an X-ray. Emotional neglect can be particularly difficult to evidence as you are trying to prove an absence of an intangible form of care. However, with careful observation and close inter-agency working, it is possible to find evidence. Observations of interactions between parents and child, direct work with the child, school reports of a child's academic performance, behaviour and self-esteem and psychological assessments

---

45   LBH at paragraph 22.

can all build up an evidential picture which is not apparent to any single agency. Inter-agency co-operation is crucial.

Unborn babies

Sometimes concerns arise for a child even before birth because of the histories of older children in the family or because the parents' lifestyle or behaviour is likely to harm the baby. Court proceedings cannot be taken in respect of a child before birth, but child protection procedures can and should. This can include holding a Case Conference and making an unborn child subject to a child protection plan. In extreme cases, a plan may be needed to take emergency action as soon as the baby is born.[46] All relevant agencies and professionals (obviously including midwives) must be fully briefed. As even contemplating removal of a newborn baby is a drastic measure with clear human rights implications, careful reasoning and planning is required to ensure that any action is properly taken. Legal advice is indispensable.

Fabricated or induced illness

In these cases, parents may report non-existent illness, medical history or symptoms (the illness is fabricated) or the symptoms may be real but caused or exacerbated by the actions of parents or carers (the illness is induced). This relatively rare but potentially very serious form of child abuse is a highly sensitive issue to be approached with care, open-mindedness and clarity of analysis. If you come across such a case, it is essential to refer to the comprehensive government guidance *Safeguarding Children in whom illness is fabricated or induced* [47] and ensure that medical experts are aware of the current guidance from the Royal College of Paediatricians. In a case[48] where FII allegations were made then withdrawn, failure to refer to this authoritative guidance led a judge to criticise social workers, medical experts and lawyers involved and to order the authority to pay £100,000 costs.

---

46   See Chapter 10 for more information on emergency procedures.
47   DCSF (2008). Available at www.gov.uk/government/uploads/system/uploads/attachment_data/file/190235/DCSF-00277-2008.pdf, accessed on 30 March 2014. This guidance is issued under s7 Local Authority Social Services Act 1970 so must be followed unless there is good reason to do otherwise.
48   *Re X, Y and Z (Children)* [2010] EWHC B10 (High Court).

Particular questions for judgment include whether and when to involve parents in discussions, how to involve the child in the investigation and whether to use exceptional techniques such as covert video surveillance.[49]

Co-operation is vital and there should be a formal inter-disciplinary meeting to co-ordinate and assess available information. Accurate and detailed records are essential. Although medical and scientific evidence is often crucial, the wider context of social and emotional factors is also relevant.

Any decision to start care proceedings is the responsibility of the local authority alone and it must satisfy itself that the grounds exist, being prepared to test and challenge information provided by medical colleagues.[50] However, this does not mean that social workers can substitute their own judgment for medical advice; diagnosing fabricated or induced illness does not fall within social work expertise. Obvious as this may seem, it was not apparent to the social workers in one case[51] who obtained an EPO on the basis of their concerns of factitious or fabricated illness, formed without taking medical advice or raising the issue at Case Conference.

Cases where one parent has murdered the other

In one such case,[52] Hogg J took the opportunity to give general guidance for these rare but difficult situations:

- The threshold criteria are always met.

- The local authority should immediately consider issuing proceedings and should always allocate a social worker to offer immediate practical help and keep the decision as to proceedings under review.

- As the surviving parent is likely to be in custody and there will be strong emotions on all sides, it is critical for the local authority to be able to exercise PR.

---

49 Covert video surveillance is governed by the Regulation of Investigatory Powers Act 2000 and should only be undertaken by the police.
50 Emphasised by Theis J in *Re E (A Child)* [2013] EWHC 2400 (Fam) (High Court).
51 *Re X (Emergency Protection Orders)* [2006] EWHC 510 (Fam) (High Court), described in detail in Chapter 11.
52 *In the Matter of A and B* [2010] EWHC 3824 (High Court).

- The family should not be left to take private law proceedings themselves.

- A Children's Guardian should be appointed as soon as proceedings are issued.

- The case should be transferred to the High Court.

- Urgent consideration should be given to interim placement and contact issues – emergency arrangements made in the immediate aftermath of the event should not drift into becoming permanent.

- Consideration must be given to the effect of any media coverage on the children.

- Liaison is needed between concurrent criminal and care proceedings.

- Specialist psychiatric or psychological advice and appropriate therapy should be sought.

- Carers will need support, including immediate financial and practical support.

- Schools should be kept informed.

- If the home is a crime scene, liaison with the police will be needed to recover the children's possessions, toys, etc.

- Seek expert advice on contact.

- Consider a Family Group Conference to help family members communicate.

- There is no presumption against placement in the perpetrator's family. Another case[53] also confirmed that there is no presumption against contact between the children and the perpetrator – each case must be considered individually.

Dealing with parents

Child abuse and neglect is not limited to any social class, professional or educational background or level of ability. In practice many families involved in child protection investigations are already known to agencies and often come from a particular social sector. Articulate, affluent and able parents may be encountered less often, and can pose a particular

---

53   *Re T (A Child – murdered parent)* [2011] EWHC (High Court).

challenge in a child protection investigation. It should not be so, but Case Conferences can feel very different when the parents are able and assertive. Such parents often instruct lawyers at an early stage and challenge the legitimacy of every action, making some professionals feel intimidated and uncertain of their ground. Consciously or not, some people, even professionals, feel that such people could not have harmed their children and bring an inherent scepticism to the investigation. These cases demand a scrupulous regard to procedures, sound legal knowledge, a rigorous approach to investigation and a determination not to be deflected from protecting the child.

At the other end of the spectrum, socially or educationally disadvantaged parents and those with disabilities, learning difficulties, substance abuse or mental health problems or those from different cultures or who have limited English can all be vulnerable to the process exploiting their lack of knowledge, understanding, assertiveness or ability to cope.

Steps must be taken to ensure that the process is fair and parents' full participation is not impeded,[54] including where appropriate helping them understand information, using interpreters or advocates and taking specialist advice, while never compromising the child's best interests. The record must show how any special needs have been taken into account, otherwise the authority is left open to criticisms that the process is unfair, as in a case[55] where social workers failed to appreciate a mother's learning disability and seemed unaware of the existence of government guidance *Good Practice Guidance on Working with Parents with a Learning Disability*,[56] usefully explored by Baker J in his judgment.[57] In that case, the vulnerable mother was persuaded to agree to her children being accommodated with no indication that she was given proper assistance.

Not surprisingly, families caught up in child protection procedures can be unco-operative. The High Court has stressed 'lack of co-operation by parents is never a reason to close a file or remove a child

---

54 *Re G (Care: Challenge to Local Authority's Decision)* [2003] 2FLR 42 (High Court).
55 *Kent CC* v. *A Mother* [2011] EWHC 402 (High Court).
56 DoH/DES (2007) Available at http://webarchive.nationalarchives.gov. uk/20080814090248/dh.gov.uk/en/Publicationsandstatistics/Publications/ PublicationsPolicyAndGuidance/DH_075119, accessed on 30 March 2014.
57 *Kent CC* v. *A Mother* at paragraphs 132–135.

from the Child Protection Register. On the contrary it is a reason to investigate in greater depth.'[58]

One of the key features in the case of Peter Connelly was the manipulative, dominating and intimidating personality of his mother who, in the words of the second Serious Case Review 'constantly tested the safeguarding and child protection systems and they were always found wanting'.[59]

As the SCR said:

> The uncooperative, anti-social and even dangerous parent/carer is the most difficult challenge for safeguarding and child protection services. The parents/carers may not immediately present as such, and may be superficially compliant, evasive, deceitful, manipulative and untruthful. Practitioners have the difficult job of identifying them among the majority of parents who they encounter, who are merely dysfunctional, anxious and ambivalent. However, in this case the interventions were not sufficiently authoritative by any agency. The authoritative intervention is urgent, thorough, challenging, with a low threshold of concern, keeping the focus on the child, and with high expectations of parents and of what services should expect of themselves.[60]

In a significant Supreme Court case,[61] the parents were found to be 'fundamentally dishonest, manipulative and antagonistic towards professionals'.[62] Lord Wilson said:

> the characters of the parents disabled them from offering the elementary cooperation with professionals which Amelia's safety in their home would require. Family courts regularly make allowance for the negative attitude of parents towards the social workers who personify their employers' applications for care orders. But the level of the dishonest, manipulative, antagonistic obstructionism of the parents in this case was of a different order. Such attributes of course betokened a lack of insight into the needs of Amelia which raised wider concerns;

---

58   *Re E (Care Proceedings: Social Work Practice)* [2000] 2FLR 254 (High Court) paragraphs 257–258.
59   LSCB Haringey (February 2009) *Serious Case Review: Baby Peter.* Executive Summary at paragraph 4.8.5. Available at www.haringeylscb.org/executive_summary_peter_final.pdf, accessed on 30 March 2014.
60   Paragraph 5.8.3.
61   *In the Matter of B (A Child)* [2013] UKSC 33 (Supreme Court). For more analysis of this case, see Chapter 11.
62   *Re B* at paragraph 19.

but more immediately, they precluded the success of any rehabilitative programme, whatever its precise composition.

Although the parents evidently loved their child, their sheer inability to co-operate made rehabilitation impossible and the Supreme Court endorsed a care order with a plan for adoption.

Young people themselves may sometimes be less than co-operative with children's social care. Munby J commented about a young man who failed to co-operate in devising a pathway plan:

> The fact that a child is unco-operative and unwilling to engage, or even refuses to engage, is no reason for the local authority not to carry out its obligations under the Act and the Regulations. After all, a disturbed child's unwillingness to engage with those who are trying to help is often merely a part of the overall problems which justified the local authority's statutory intervention in the first place. The local authority must do its best.[63]

Complex investigations

Sometimes a case which starts with a single allegation grows beyond all expectations. Often, such cases turn on allegations of sexual abuse, with ever more potential victims and perpetrators coming to light, often linked to a particular institution, family or social group. Allegations may relate to current or historical abuse, and are unlikely to respect local authority boundaries, so issues of efficient sharing of information and resources arise.

Further complications arise if the media show interest in the case; careful handling of the media can be crucial to a successful outcome.

Such investigations demand careful co-ordination, strategic organisation and a rigorous attention to detail. High-level officers should be involved. Information needs to be shared, while scrupulously maintaining confidentiality to avoid jeopardising further investigations or, even more importantly, children's safety.

While co-ordinating the multiple angles of the case, it is important to remember that each child is an individual and, for a Case Conference or court proceedings, evidence must be gathered relating to the particular child. Each child's needs must be individually assessed.

---

63   *R (J) v. Caerphilly CBC* [2005] EWHC 586 (Admin) (High Court) at paragraph 56.

Back in 2002, the government issued guidance on handling such cases, *Complex Child Abuse Investigations: Inter-agency Issues.*[64] Although some of its references are in need of updating, it nevertheless contains useful strategic advice if one of your cases is in danger of expanding exponentially.

Points for practice

1. Child protection is built upon a detailed framework of statute, regulation and guidance. A sound knowledge of this framework is essential.

2. In difficult cases, go back to basics – remind yourself of the law and analyse the case applying those key principles.

3. Always assume every case will end up in court. Record everything promptly. Note every decision and reasons for it and always keep paperwork up to date.

4. Processes must be demonstrably fair to all involved.

5. Never allow emotions to cloud your judgment. Seek supervision and advice to remain objective. Keep your focus on the child; do not be distracted by adult agendas.

6. Foster inter-agency relationships. Real inter-agency co-operation depends on individual workers building links. Knowing who to call and being able to trust their response is worth a multitude of written policies.

---

64 Home Office (2002). Available at www.workingtogetheronline.co.uk/documents/ Complex_abu.pdf, accessed on 30 March 2014.

Chapter 10

Emergency Action

Child protection is an unpredictable business. Emergencies arise out of the blue. The stakes are high; failing to act swiftly and decisively could expose a child to serious harm, even death, but equally we must not forget that, as Munby J said: 'summarily removing a child from his parents is a terrible and drastic remedy'.[1] Such situations demand robust knowledge of legal provisions and procedure and sound professional practice.

Police protection and emergency protection orders

The two key provisions for the immediate protection of children are found in Part V of the Children Act 1989 (CA89): police protection,[2] an administrative power exercised by the police, and emergency protection orders (EPOs)[3] made by a court.

Under both provisions, we look ahead to see whether significant harm is likely if action is not taken to remove a child from an unsafe situation or to prevent him from being removed from a safe place (such as hospital). The fact that these sections should be invoked only in a situation of true urgency is implied rather than explicitly stated in the Act.

Given the similarities between the two provisions, how do you decide which to use? The clear presumption is that an EPO should be sought wherever possible so that the decision to remove a child is sanctioned by a court, not by an administrative procedure. *Working Together* says: 'Police powers to remove a child in an emergency should

---

1   *X Council v. B* [2004] EWHC 2015 (Fam).
2   s46 CA89.
3   s44 CA89.

be used only in exceptional circumstances where there is insufficient time to seek an EPO or for reasons relating to the immediate safety of the child.[4]

Police protection

> s46(1) CA89 Where a constable has reasonable cause to believe that a child would otherwise be likely to suffer significant harm, he may –
>
> (a) remove the child to suitable accommodation and keep him there; or
>
> (b) take such steps as are reasonable to ensure that the child's removal from any hospital, or other place, in which he is then being accommodated is prevented.

A Home Office Circular[5] gives detailed guidance to the police on how to exercise their powers. Proper procedures are particularly important given that police protection is a purely administrative matter; it is not an order and no court is involved. There is no independent scrutiny of the action taken or the grounds for it and no mechanism for parents or child to challenge or appeal against the decision. Human rights issues (Article 6, the right to a fair trial, and Article 8, the right to respect for private and family life) immediately spring to mind.

Police protection is purely a means of providing immediate safety for the child so the police do not obtain parental responsibility (PR). It is a short-term measure, lasting a maximum of 72 hours (in practice usually much less), and must be terminated earlier than that if the danger has passed.

The police must take reasonable steps to inform:

- the child
- his parents
- anyone else with PR
- the person the child was living with

---

4   *Working Together* (2013) at page 28.
5   Home Office Circular 017/2008.

of the action taken, reasons for it and what might happen next. The officer should also try to ascertain the child's wishes and feelings. In theory, he should grant such contact as is both reasonable and in the child's best interests to people including the child's parents, but in reality the case usually passes to the local authority before there is any realistic question of contact.

The police officer's first duties include informing the local authorities of the areas where the child was found and where the child normally lives (if different) and ensuring that the child is moved to local authority accommodation. In practice the local authority usually takes over responsibility for the child and the future conduct of his case very quickly. Police protection immediately triggers the duty to carry out a s47 CA89 investigation, so the local authority must urgently consider whether steps need to be taken to continue the child's protection. If not, the authority may decide to return the child home immediately.

It is always worth remembering that the police have other powers which may be of considerable assistance in an emergency. If it appears that a criminal offence has been or is being committed, or if there is a breach of the peace, the police may have power to arrest and remove from the scene the person who poses the immediate threat to the child. This may be preferable to removing the child and may make it possible to consider child protection measures in a more planned way.

Emergency protection orders
Grounds

One of the grounds for EPOs ties in with s47 CA89 and is available only to local authorities. If you are conducting a s47 CA89 investigation and you believe that you need urgent access to the child but the parent unreasonably refuses to allow you to see him, you can apply for an EPO.[6]

The more commonly used ground[7] for an EPO is available to anyone at all, although it is extremely rare for anyone other than the local authority to apply.

---

6   s44(1)(b) CA89.
7   s44(1)(a) CA89.

s44(1) CA89 ...the court may make the order if, but only if, it is satisfied that –

(a) there is reasonable cause to believe that the child is likely to suffer significant harm if:

(i) he is not removed to accommodation provided by or on behalf of the applicant; or

(ii) he does not remain in the place in which he is then being accommodated...

Just as for police protection, therefore, the focus for an EPO is on what is likely to happen if action is not taken, rather than what has already happened. The objective can be to remove the child from an unsafe place or to keep him in a safe one.

Court application

An EPO can only be made by a court. Unlike police officers, social workers have no power to remove a child by administrative decision. Failure to appreciate this led Nottingham City Council into serious and much publicised difficulties when a baby was removed at birth without either police protection or a court order. As Munby J said:

> The law is perfectly clear but perhaps requires re-emphasis. Whatever the impression a casual reader might gain from reading some newspaper reports, no local authority and no social worker has any power to remove a child from its parent or, without the agreement of the parent, to take a child into care, unless they have first obtained an order from a family court authorising that step.[8]

During the hearing, Munby J had put it bluntly: 'The professionals involved in this case should have known better.' The authority was ordered to return the baby to the mother's care (although she was removed again – lawfully – soon after and ultimately permanently removed), it was held to have acted unlawfully and to have breached the human rights of both mother and child, with damages to follow.

---

8   *G (R on the application of)* v. *Nottingham City Council* [2008] EWHC 152 (Admin) (High Court) Munby J at paragraph 15.

NOTICE

How much advance warning – if any – should the parents be given of an EPO application? The court rules provide for parents with PR and the child to have a minimum of one day's notice. If you are wondering how it is possible to give a day's notice in a true emergency, you are not alone. Arguably if parents can be given one day's notice, then it is not really an emergency and they could be given three days (the notice period for an interim care order), or the court could be asked to abridge that period. Whether the situation truly is urgent should be carefully considered in an immediate strategy discussion and legal advice should be sought.

It is, however, possible to proceed without any notice at all, at the discretion of the court. Whether notice should be given is a separate question from whether an order should be made – the court could agree to proceed without notice, but then, on hearing the application, decide not to make an order.

Proceeding without notice should be the exception, not the rule. As Munby J said: 'save in wholly exceptional cases, parents must be given adequate prior notice of…any application by a local authority for an EPO. They must also be given proper notice of the evidence the local authority is relying upon.'[9]

If a case does proceed without notice, the court only hears one side of the story and the parents know nothing of the application until the authorities arrive to remove the child. Can this be a fair trial? Is it a breach of human rights? The European Court of Human Rights has said:

> the court accepts that when action has to be taken to protect a child in an emergency, it may not always be possible, because of the urgency of the situation, to associate in the decision-making process those having custody of the child. Nor…may it even be desirable, even if possible, to do so if those having custody of the child are seen as the source of an immediate threat to the child, since giving them prior warning would be liable to deprive the measure of its effectiveness.[10]

So proceeding without notice can be justified provided the authorities can:

> …establish that a careful assessment of the impact of the proposed care measure on the parents and the child, as well as of the possible

---

9   *X Council* v. *B* at paragraph 57 (vii).
10   *Venema* v. *The Netherlands* [2003] 1 FLR 552 ECtHR at paragraph 93.

alternatives to the removal of the child from its family, was carried out prior to the implementation of a care measure.

Sometimes there is simply no alternative. In one such situation, Bury MBC[11] planned to remove at birth the baby of a highly disturbed woman who posed a real risk to her baby – she was, as the judge put it, 'capable of causing catastrophic injury to the child within a matter of moments.' The plan was for the police to take police protection as soon as the baby was born, swiftly followed by an EPO. Normally the authority would be required to discuss plans in advance with the mother, but this would 'expose the child to an utterly unacceptable degree of risk of potentially really serious physical harm.' The judge had no hesitation in agreeing that in this particular case, the 'draconian' and 'highly exceptional step' of proceeding without notification was 'entirely justified and indeed imperatively required'. The court found that this was an acceptable exception under Article 8 and therefore not a breach of human rights. The authority was commended for approaching the court (in the exercise of its inherent jurisdiction) to sanction the exceptional step in advance.

WHAT IS – AND WHAT IS NOT – AN EMERGENCY?

Working Together[12] suggests that immediate protection is required where there is a risk to life or the likelihood of serious immediate harm. The European Court of Human Rights[13] said that a child's immediate removal is justified in a case of 'imminent danger' which must be 'actually established'. It is a draconian measure requiring 'exceptional justification' and reasons which are 'extraordinarily compelling'. The strength of the language used is striking so it is clear that emergency action is to be reserved for cases of real urgency, where there is an immediate threat or imminent danger which cannot be managed in any other way. As Munby J said: 'However compelling the case may be, both the local authority which seeks an EPO and the justices in the FPC who grant such an order assume a heavy burden of responsibility.'[14]

---

11   *Bury MBC* v. *D* [2009] EWHC 446 (Fam) (High Court).
12   *Working Together* (2013) at page 28.
13   *P, C and S* v. *UK* [2002] 35 EHRR 31 (European Court of Human Rights) at paragraphs 116, 131, 133.
14   *X Council* v. *B* at paragraph 35.

Emergency action is most likely to be warranted in cases of physical harm, where there is real risk to life and limb. Neglect can justify emergency action at the stage of imminent risk – for example, a child neglected literally to the point of starvation. Bearing in mind that the notice period for care proceedings is just three days, unless there is specific information of immediate risk, many sexual abuse allegations are more suited to care proceedings than emergency action. Cases of fabricated or induced illness often involve a long course of action and do not warrant instant removal unless the allegation is that the parent provokes a medical emergency (such as asphyxiation or poisoning). In contrast, it is difficult to imagine a case of emotional abuse or neglect which justifies emergency action.

A chronic situation, however serious, does not become an emergency simply because professionals have just found out about it – it is the imminence of the danger which must be judged. Nor can simple lack of information or the need for assessment establish a genuine emergency unless there is other information to show imminent risk of serious harm.

EVIDENCE

An EPO application may be an unusual one, but it is still a court application and evidence must be produced and given on oath. If written evidence is available, it should be presented to the court, so if an emergency arises in a family where an assessment has already been carried out or a Case Conference held, the court should receive copies of reports and minutes.

Local authorities always have a duty to give full, frank and balanced information to the court, to present the case fairly and ensure that the court is objectively informed about both the facts and the relevant law. The responsibility to do this is even heavier when the local authority is the only party present in court. The need to act quickly does not absolve the authority from the duty to act properly.

Munby J said:

> The evidence in support of the application for an EPO must be full, detailed, precise and compelling. Unparticularised generalities will not suffice. The sources of hearsay evidence must be identified.

Expressions of opinion must be supported by detailed evidence and properly articulated reasoning.[15]

Even if parents are not present during the application, they should be given a full account of the evidence presented to the court as soon as possible thereafter. Inevitably in truly urgent cases most evidence is presented orally rather than in writing, so the Clerk's note of the evidence is particularly important.

WHO GOES TO COURT?

Judicial guidance is clear: the importance of a local authority lawyer on an EPO application should not be underestimated, even more so on an application without notice. Social workers should not be expected to apply for EPOs on their own. It is the lawyer's responsibility to advise before any application is made, to ensure that the case is presented properly and fairly to the court and to ensure that the parents are served with any order made and full information about the evidence presented to court.

REASONS

The court rules require the court to record not only its order but also the reasons for its decisions both on the question of notice and on the substantive application. In an urgent case, the decision can be announced and the reasons put in writing later.

LENGTH OF ORDER

An EPO can be made for a maximum of eight days, with the possibility of one extension on further application to court for up to seven days.[16] These are maximum times and the order ought to be made for the shortest period appropriate to the case – the doctrines of proportionality and minimum intervention require nothing less.

---

15   *X Council* v. *B* at paragraph 57 (vi).
16   s45(4) CA89.

Experience and research[17] show us that, in most cases, EPOs lead on to care proceedings, which take months. We are not, therefore, simply concerned with a week or two in a family's life: an EPO sets a case off on a particular track from which it can be difficult later to deviate. This very earliest step on the path therefore takes on even greater significance and requires even greater care and justification.

EFFECT OF EPOS

An EPO directs anyone who is in a position to do so to produce the child to the local authority which holds the order.[18] The authority has the immediate power to remove the child, or, if he is in a safe place, prevent his removal. But should it exercise this power? This must not be done unthinkingly or as a matter of course. According to Munby J, even after obtaining the order, the local authority must actively consider whether it still needs to act on it, or whether any less intrusive measure will suffice;[19] effectively there must be reflection and justification at every stage. If this is not done, even with an EPO in its pocket, the local authority could conceivably be acting unlawfully in removing the child.

As Munby J said: 'the [court] decides whether to make an EPO. But the local authority decides whether to remove.' He advised: 'Though no procedure is specified, it will obviously be prudent for local authorities to have in place procedures to ensure both that the required decision making actually takes place and that it is appropriately documented.'

The EPO gives PR to the local authority, shared with the parent(s). However, as it is only a short-term order, clearly this PR can only be exercised in such a way as is reasonably required to safeguard or promote the child's welfare for the duration of the order.[20]

A child should not necessarily be kept away from home for the entire duration of the EPO; on the contrary, there is a specific statutory duty to

17 Masson, J.M., Oakley, M. Winn, and Pick, K. (2004) *Emergency Protection Orders: Court Orders for Child Protection Crises.* Warwick: School of Law, Warwick University (funded by the NSPCC and Nuffield Foundation). Summary available at www.essauk.com/ pdf/epo-summary_wdf48088.pdf, accessed on 30 March 2014.

18 s44(4) CA89.

19 *X Council* v. *B* at paragraph 57 (xii).

20 s44(5) CA89.

return him home as soon as it is safe to do so.[21] The position should be subject to daily review, which should of course be duly recorded.

EXAMINATIONS AND ASSESSMENTS

The court can include in an EPO a direction for the child to be medically examined or psychiatrically assessed, subject to the child's right to refuse if he is of sufficient age and understanding.[22] The court can also forbid any such examination or assessment, for example in a case of suspected sexual abuse where the child has already had repeated intimate medical examinations.

CONTACT

During an EPO the child should have 'reasonable contact' with:

- his parents (with or without PR)
- anyone else with PR
- the person he was living with immediately before the order
- anyone with a contact order.[23]

Instead of leaving contact to the local authority's judgment as to what is 'reasonable', the court has power to direct what contact should or should not occur.[24] In an extreme case, it has the power to authorise the local authority to refuse contact.

EXCLUSION REQUIREMENTS

Where only one person poses a risk to the child, it might be better to remove that person from the scene rather than removing the child. The court has a power to do just that by attaching an exclusion requirement to an EPO.[25] The court must have reasonable cause to believe that excluding a named person from the child's home will remove the problem which gave rise to the EPO in the first place; that is to say that the child will no longer be likely to suffer significant harm, or the authority's s47 enquiries will no longer be frustrated. The court must

---

21   s44(10) CA89.
22   s44(6), (7) and (8) CA89.
23   s44(13) CA89.
24   s44(6)(a) CA89.
25   s44A CA89.

also be sure that there is someone else in the home who is able and willing to care for the child and that carer consents to the order.

The exclusion requirement requires the relevant person to leave and stay away from the home, and a power of arrest can be attached to the order. Alternatively, the court can accept a formal undertaking from the person concerned, but no power of arrest can be attached. A similar exclusion order or undertaking can later be attached to an interim care order[26] (but not a full care order). The local authority has a discretionary power to help the excluded person to find alternative accommodation.[27]

The idea is better in theory than in practice. You have to show that the risk to the child comes from only one identified person but that there is another competent carer in the home; situations are rarely so simple in real life. Even if this is so, you are effectively entirely dependent on the other person not only to care for the child but also to co-operate fully in keeping the other person out. Can you completely rely on the other carer? How can you police the arrangement?

Furthermore, the exclusion requirement can only ever be a short-term solution: it expires along with the EPO after a maximum of 15 days. Even if the case continues into care proceedings, a similar order can be attached to an interim care order, but not a full care order, so ultimately another solution must be found.[28]

As a result, exclusion requirements are used less often in practice than was originally hoped, but it is still important to remember that they exist as an option in an appropriate case.

WARRANTS

Not surprisingly, people whose children are being removed are not always fully co-operative. As a social worker, you do not have automatic powers to compel co-operation. It is always wise, therefore, to consider in advance whether you need to ask the court to add further provisions to the EPO, for example:

---

26 s38A CA89.
27 s17 and Schedule 2 paragraph 5 CA89.
28 Such as an injunction under the Family Law Act 1996.

- You do not know where the child is, but someone else does: the court can direct that person to give you information about the child's whereabouts.[29]

- You need to enter and search premises to find the child: the court can authorise you to do so,[30] although this does not give you power to force entry.

- You are refused or are likely to be refused entry to the premises or access to the child when you try to execute the EPO: the court can issue a warrant[31] authorising the police to help you, using reasonable force if necessary.

- You can show reasonable cause to believe that there is another child or children on the same premises who should also be subject to an EPO (for example, you obtain an EPO on a child trafficked for use in child prostitution and other children in the same situation are also likely to be on the premises): the court can authorise you to search the premises for the other child or children too, and, when you find them, if you are satisfied the grounds for an EPO exist for them, the court's order has the effect as if it were an EPO on them.[32] You can therefore remove all the children on the premises at the same time without having to go back to court.

Application to discharge EPOs

An application to apply to discharge the EPO can be made by:

- the child

- his parents

- anyone else with PR

- anyone he was living with at the time of the EPO

but this right does not arise until 72 hours after the order was made.[33] So, a child can be summarily removed from home and the parents can

---

29   s48(1) CA89.
30   s48(3) CA89.
31   s48(9) CA89.
32   s48(4) and (5) CA89.
33   s45(8) and (9) CA89.

do nothing about it for three days. Even that limited right is removed if the parents were given notice and were present at the hearing, even if they had no time to find a lawyer or to mount an effective opposition to the application. In practice, the timescales involved in EPOs mean that this provision is little used.

Appeals

In emergency action, where the stakes are high and the procedures swift, you might imagine that there would be a lot of appeals by parents angry at EPOs being granted or local authorities worried by EPOs being refused.

In fact the position is quite simple, if surprising: there is no appeal against either the granting or the refusal of an EPO.[34]

A CAUTIONARY TALE – LESSONS FROM RE X

If you wanted to invent a case study illustrating all the errors it is possible to make in an EPO application, you would struggle to improve on the true case of Re X.[35]

X was a nine-year-old girl, who had been the subject of two Child Protection Case Conferences, and whose name was on the Child Protection Register under the category emotional harm. The child protection plan involved a relatively low level of intervention. A legal planning meeting concluded that there were no grounds for care proceedings.

A further Case Conference took place at which no reference was made to any suggestion of factitious or induced illness. The Conference decided to continue the previous plan, and recommended a further legal planning meeting. Later that same afternoon, a hospital nurse contacted the social worker with an update, not a child protection referral. She reported that the mother had taken X to hospital with a stomach pain and was asking for X to be seen by a doctor, although a nurse had seen X and found no problem. The doctor was seeing X at the time and would telephone the social worker with the result later.

---

34 s45(10) CA89.
35 Re X (Emergency Protection Orders) [2006] EWHC 510 (Fam) (High Court).

Within two hours of the end of the Case Conference, and without waiting to hear from the doctor, the social worker and her manager had obtained an EPO. Why? Clearly uppermost in the social workers' minds was their suspicion of fabricated or induced illness, a suspicion never raised by any doctor, on which the social workers had never taken any medical advice and which had never been raised at Case Conference. McFarlane J must have felt he was stating the obvious when he said that this 'is not a diagnosis that can be made by social workers acting alone, it is matter that requires skilled medical appraisal.'[36]

The social worker took legal advice. The lawyer was 'not sure' that the grounds existed for an EPO, but the application went ahead regardless. McFarlane J deprecated the practice that allowed the social worker to override legal advice – any such decision should be made by someone above team manager level.

The team manager totally misunderstood the legal grounds for an EPO. Her evidence was: 'I could not say that X was 100% safe in that household.' As McFarlane J said, 'that assertion is nothing like the test needed to justify an EPO application.'[37] When, months later in the final care hearing, witnesses were asked to identify the imminent danger to X that afternoon, 'none of them could give a satisfactory reply'.[38] The judge concluded:

> The reality is that X was not in imminent danger of harm that in any way justified her removal from parental care that afternoon. There was, even on the evidence available to the social workers and the justices, no grounds for applying for, let alone making, an EPO… This was a long way from being an emergency protection order case.[39]

The lawyer attended court with the social work manager, but merely presented the social work evidence without doing anything to ensure that it was accurate or balanced or that the court was properly informed of the relevant law. This was a breach of the lawyer's duty to the court.

The court heard the application without any notice to the parents. It gave no reasons for this decision; indeed it did not seem to give the question of notice any separate consideration at all. The court was keen

---

36   *Re X* at paragraph 67.
37   *Re X* at paragraph 77.
38   *Re X* at paragraph 72.
39   *Re X* at paragraph 79.

to proceed quickly, conscious of a busy list of cases to follow. Instead of waiting for the social worker to arrive with the files, it proceeded without any written information on the oral evidence of the team manager, who had only a broad knowledge of the case. McFarlane J listed 13 assertions made by the manager in evidence[40] and described 'every single one' of them as 'misleading or incomplete or wrong'. 'The picture given to the magistrates by the team manager was, in my view, so seriously distorted that it is likely to have led the bench to have a totally erroneous view of the issues of the case.'[41] The magistrates were not even told that there had been a Case Conference that very day.

The magistrates' reasons for their decision were 'that the child would suffer imminent harm unless an EPO is made.' The judge described this as 'wholly inadequate and...in effect no more than a statement that the bench found the case proved.'[42] 'The emergency nature of the application, whilst requiring prompt determination, does not absolve the court of its duty to give a reasoned explanation for its decision.'

The parents and their representatives did not receive the details of the evidence presented at the EPO until the final hearing of the care proceedings 14 months later – 14 months in which the child had been placed away from home. The final painful twist in the case was that, at the end of the care proceedings, the judge found that there were insufficient grounds for a care order. There had never been a good reason to separate parents and child.

The judge did not doubt that the social workers acted in good faith for the best of motives, but their actions fell 'disastrously short of what was required'.[43] The local authority was ordered to pay £200,000 towards the parents' legal costs, but the real cost was the damage to the child and her family, which was incalculable.

Points for practice

1.   In a true emergency, there is no time to research the law and procedures. You need to know them – or where to find them.

---

40   *Re X* at paragraphs 47–48.
41   *Re X* at paragraph 50.
42   *Re X* at paragraph 54.
43   *Re X* at paragraph 60.

2. Keep in mind the key considerations at all times (see the aide-memoire in Appendix 6).

3. Keep a cool head – clear thinking is vital in an emergency.

4. Only take emergency action if it is truly justified. Carefully record everything including reasons. Keep all decisions under constant review.

5. Always take legal advice and insist on legal representation if you go to court.

6. Keep all parties' human rights in the forefront of your considerations, especially the child's rights to life (Article 2) and protection from ill-treatment (Article 3), the parents' right to a fair trial (Article 6) and everyone's right to respect for their family life (Article 8).

Part 5
Care Proceedings

Chapter 11

The Threshold Criteria

The philosophy underlying the Children Act 1989 (CA89) and underpinned by the Human Rights Act 1998 (HRA) was explained by Hedley J in a passage which has been approved by the Supreme Court:

> ...it is the tradition of the UK, recognised in law, that children are best brought up within natural families... It follows inexorably that society must be willing to tolerate very diverse standards of parenting, including the eccentric, the barely adequate and the inconsistent. It follows too that children will inevitably have both very different experiences of parenting and very unequal consequences flowing from it. It means that some children will experience disadvantage and harm, while others flourish in atmospheres of loving security and emotional stability. These are the consequences of our fallible humanity and it is not the provenance of the state to spare children all the consequences of defective parenting. In any event, it simply could not be done... Only exceptionally should the State intervene with compulsive powers and then only when a court is satisfied that the significant harm criteria in s31(2) is made out.[1]

The concept of the threshold

Unlike s8 orders, care and supervision orders can only be considered if the court has an application before it and if the specific grounds, commonly known as the 'threshold criteria', are made out. These orders

---

1   *Re L (Care: Threshold Criteria)* [2007] 1FLR 2050 (High Court) at paragraphs 50–51. This passage has subsequently been cited with approval by other courts including the Supreme Court in the seminal case of *Re B (A Child)* [2013] UKSC 33 where Lord Neuberger called these 'very wise remarks'.

cannot be made by the court of its own motion, even if it thinks it would be in the child's best interests to do so.

As Lady Hale explained, the idea is to strike a balance to enable the State to protect children from harm while protecting families from unwarranted intrusion: 'The threshold is designed to restrict compulsory intervention to cases which genuinely warrant it, while enabling the court to make the order which will best promote the child's welfare once the threshold has been crossed.'[2]

Two-stage process

In a final care hearing, the court has to answer two separate questions:

1. Are the threshold criteria met? If the answer is 'no', the matter ends there.

2. If 'yes', which order (if any) is in the child's best interests?

Even if the threshold is crossed, care or supervision orders are not inevitable: they are choices among a range of options to meet the child's needs. The court applies the s1 CA89 principles,[3] the child's welfare being paramount, and uses the welfare checklist to analyse his best interests. The court might make:

- a care order
- a supervision order
- a package of private law orders (such as an order for residence or special guardianship to grandmother, an order for contact to mother, no contact to father and prohibited steps preventing contact), possibly coupled with a supervision order
- no order at all.

The first step, therefore, is to look carefully at the wording of the threshold criteria.

---

2   *In the Matter of J (Children)* [2013] UKSC 9 (Supreme Court) at paragraph 2.
3   See Chapter 2 for more details.

Threshold criteria – definition

> s31(2) CA89 A court may only make a care order or a supervision order if it is satisfied –
>
> (a) that the child is suffering, or is likely to suffer, significant harm; and
>
> (b) that the harm, or likelihood of harm, is attributable to –
>
> (i) the care given to the child, or likely to be given to him if the order were not made, not being what it would be reasonable to expect a parent to give to him; or
>
> (ii) the child's being beyond parental control.

There are several elements in this wording to be considered, including: 'satisfied', 'is suffering', 'significant', 'harm', 'likely' and 'attributable'. At first glance, none of these words appears particularly complicated; however, the courts have had to work very hard to understand them.

Harm

As we saw in Chapter 9, 'harm' includes physical, emotional and sexual abuse as well as neglect causing impairment to health or development. It is deliberately wide. Hedley J said:

> ... it would be unwise to attempt an all embracing definition of significant harm. One never ceases to be surprised at the extent of complication and difficulty that human beings manage to introduce into family life. Significant harm is fact specific and must retain the breadth of meaning that human fallibility may require of it.[4]

Significant

State intervention in family life is only justified when harm reaches a level which is 'significant' or, as Hedley J put it, 'the exceptional rather than the commonplace'. The case which Hedley J was considering when he gave his helpful analysis of 'significant harm' concerned the children of parents with learning disabilities. He found that the children were

---

4   In *Re L* at paragraph 51.

suffering harm and would continue to do so. They were children in need. They were clearly disadvantaged and not doing as well as many of their peers. But the harm did not reach the level of 'significant harm', the threshold was not met and care orders were not an option.

In care proceedings, the local authority must file a 'threshold statement' which sets out clearly and concisely the essential nature of the case, specifying the significant harm it alleges. This requires clear thinking and careful analysis, often of an abundance of factual material.

Is suffering

Imagine a child is suffering significant harm. The local authority take care proceedings and he goes into foster care on an interim care order. At the time of the final hearing months later he is receiving excellent care in the foster home. Can the court say he 'is suffering' significant harm?

In normal English, the use of the present continuous refers to events in progress: 'is suffering' normally refers to what is happening now. But in the context of care proceedings, that would mean that as soon as the authority acted successfully to protect the child, the 'is suffering' element of the criteria could no longer be established. That cannot be right.

This very issue came to the House of Lords in the case of *Re M*.[5] Their Lordships decided that, when considering whether the threshold criteria are satisfied, the court must cast its mind back to the situation in existence at the 'relevant date' when protective measures started. So a child who was suffering significant harm at the start of the case, even though he is safe by the time of the final hearing, can still fall within the words 'is suffering significant harm'. For the sake of common sense, their Lordships had to change the rules of English grammar so that 'is' can mean 'was'.

The same problem and the same solution apply to the second alternative 'is likely to suffer'[6] – in such cases the court looks at what was likely at the relevant date.

---

5   *Re M (A Minor) (Care Order: Threshold Criteria)* [1994] 2FLR 557 (House of Lords).
6   *Southwark LBC v. B* [1998] 2FLR 1095 (High Court).

WHEN IS THE RELEVANT DATE?

Case Study: The relevant date

Bella's care proceedings start on 27 December. The final hearing is held the following June. Which is the relevant date for deciding if the threshold criteria are met? The key question is: when did protective measures start? Often, as here, this is the start of the care proceedings. So, in Bella's case the court looks not at the situation in June, but at what was happening the previous December.

Variation 1
Bella's care proceedings started on 27 December, following police protection taken on Christmas Day. Here we can see that protective measures started on Christmas Day; she was already safe by the time care proceedings started. So the court looks at her situation at Christmas.

Variation 2
Bella was taken into police protection on Christmas Day because her parents turned up, drunk and abusive, seeking to remove her from the foster home where she had been voluntarily accommodated since November while her parents sought treatment for their addiction problems. Here, although the arrangements were initially voluntary, Bella has been protected since her placement in the foster home, so in this case the court looks back to her situation in November. Measures do not have to be compulsory to be protective.

Does this mean that the court can only take into account information which was actually known at the relevant date? In practice, despite assiduous advance case preparation you rarely have all of the evidence the court will need to decide on threshold when you launch proceedings; information often comes to light during the course of proceedings. Can you use this information even though it was unknown at the relevant date? The Court of Appeal[7] confirmed that you can – it does not matter when the information becomes available provided it relates to the situation in existence at the relevant date.

---

7   *Re G (Care Proceedings: Threshold Conditions)* [2001] EWCA Civ 968 (Court of Appeal).

Case Studies: Information obtained
during proceedings

Carl has been sexually abused. During care proceedings, he discloses the abuser's name. Although this was not known at the start of the case, it clearly relates to the situation at the relevant date when protective measures began, so it can form part of the evidence to cross the threshold.

David's case is based on physical and emotional abuse. During the proceedings, his mother is diagnosed with a bipolar affective disorder. Again, the diagnosis might be new, but the condition is unlikely to be so. It relates to the situation at the relevant date so can be used.

Ellie's case starts as one of physical abuse. After she is taken into care, it transpires that she has also been sexually abused. This is a different type of harm of which we previously knew nothing. As long as the evidence shows the sexual abuse happened when she lived at home and not since she has been in care, it is material relevant to the threshold and must be placed before the court – the local authority has a duty to do so even though it was not the original basis for proceedings.[8]

Fiona is in foster care. On contact visits, the superviser observes little attachment between Fiona and her parents. These observations are primarily evidence of Fiona's relationship with her parents now. They may give some indication of the relationship before but we must be careful not to draw too many conclusions – supervised contact is artificial and the situation is very different from that at the relevant date. Its value in terms of establishing the threshold is limited.

George was failing to thrive at home, but blossoms in foster care. This implies that there is nothing organically wrong with him and his previous failure to thrive was due to the care he was receiving. We must be careful, though – as Hedley J said, if children are removed from low-functioning parents and placed with competent foster carers 'it would be really very surprising indeed if some changes, particularly on the educational front, were not to be apparent.'[9] The fact that children do better with excellent foster carers does not of itself prove that their parents' care was not good enough – the level of George's failure to thrive at home must in itself constitute significant harm.

8   *Re A (Children: Split Hearing)* [2006] EWCA Civ 714 (Court of Appeal).
9   *Re L* at paragraph 19.

What if something completely new happens during the proceedings? Can new events be taken into account in assessing the threshold? Unless they relate to the situation at the 'relevant date', the answer is 'no'.

Case Study: New events

Baby Harry suffers fractures diagnosed as non-accidental, so care proceedings are started. There are no other concerns for him. The strain of the proceedings causes Harry's mother to suffer a breakdown and the parents' marriage to break up.

These matters did not exist at the relevant time; indeed, they have been caused by the proceedings themselves so they cannot count towards establishing the threshold. They may be relevant in the court's decision as to what order, if any, to make if – and only if – the threshold criteria are made out. If the parents' medical experts show that Harry's fractures were due to a rare medical condition, not ill-treatment, the case falls apart and the threshold criteria are not met – regardless of the fact that Harry now has a mentally unstable mother and separated parents.

Satisfied

How 'satisfied' does the court have to be? As we saw in Chapter 9, 'suspicion' is enough for a s47 CA89 enquiry and 'belief' justifies an EPO, but neither is enough for a care or supervision order. The court must be 'satisfied' on the evidence that the threshold criteria are proven.

Care cases are civil proceedings so the case must be proven 'on the balance of probabilities'. This is a lower level than criminal trials, where the case must be proven 'beyond reasonable doubt'. In *Re B* Lord Hoffman explained that the standard of proof is 'the degree of persuasion which the tribunal must feel before it decides that the fact in issue did happen' and in care proceedings, the court 'must be satisfied that the occurrence of the fact in question was more likely than not.'[10]

Before *Re B* was decided, there was a series of cases which suggested that the more serious the allegation, the higher the standard of proof. In *Re B* their Lordships were emphatic. Baroness Hale was determined to:

---

10   *Re B (Children)* [2008] UKHL 35 (House of Lords) at paragraph 4.

...announce loud and clear that the standard of proof in finding
the facts necessary to establish the threshold under s31(2) or the
welfare considerations in s1 of the 1989 Act is the simple balance of
probabilities, neither more nor less. Neither the seriousness of the
allegations nor the seriousness of the consequences should make any
difference to the standard of proof to be applied in determining the
facts.[11]

So we are clear: the facts which establish the threshold criteria must be
shown to be more likely than not to be true. This can only be established
on evidence, so it is the local authority's job to produce the evidence to
satisfy the court of the statutory criteria, building up the whole picture.
An apparently minor piece of information might be the piece of the
puzzle which makes everything else fall into place. Lord Nicholls said:

the range of facts which may be taken into account is infinite. The facts
include the history of members of the family; the state of relationships
within a family; proposed changes within the membership of a family;
parental attitudes and omissions which might not reasonably have
been expected, just as much as actual physical assaults. They include
threats and abnormal behaviour by a child and unsatisfactory parental
responses to complaints or allegations and facts which are minor or
even trivial if considered in isolation, when taken together may suffice
to satisfy the court of the likelihood of future harm...[12]

Often, to decide what is true the court must assess contradictory
evidence and different versions of events. As Baroness Hale said: 'I do
not underestimate the difficulty of deciding where the truth lies but that
is what the courts are for.'[13]

How likely is likely?
We do not have to wait until a child has actually suffered significant
harm before we can protect her. The threshold criteria also cover the
situation where she is 'likely to suffer significant harm'. What does
'likely' mean? The House of Lords[14] decided that 'likely' means ' a real

---

11   *Re B* at paragraph 70.
12   *Re B* at paragraph 59.
13   *Re H & R (Child Sexual Abuse: Standard of Proof)* [1996] AC 563 (House of Lords) at
     page 101B–C.
14   *Re H & R*, Lord Nicholls at p585F.

possibility, a possibility that cannot sensibly be ignored having regard to the nature and gravity of the feared harm in the particular case.' The harm does not have to be 'more likely than not' to happen; that phrase refers to a different concept, the level of evidential proof required to establish the case.

So, to be 'likely' there must be a real possibility of that harm happening. How do you prove it? The difficulty with the 'likelihood' part of the threshold criteria is that you are trying to establish something which, by definition, has not happened yet and which you hope never will. But this is not an exercise in speculation; the court must have evidence on which it can act. As Lady Hale put it, judging likelihood is:

> a prediction from existing facts, often from a multitude of such facts, about what has happened in the past, about the characters and personalities of the people involved, about the things which they have said and done, and so on.[15]

The evidence must be robust enough to 'satisfy' the court 'on the balance of probabilities'. In other words, the facts on which the case is based must be 'more likely than not' to be true; only then can the court go on to judge the degree of likelihood of future harm. Suspicions, beliefs or fears:

> …can no more form the basis of a conclusion that the second [likelihood of harm] threshold condition in section 31 (2)(a) has been established than they can form the basis of a conclusion that the first [present harm] has been established.[16]

Lady Hale was at pains to make this point very clear in Re J:

> Care courts are often told that the best predictor of the future is the past. But prediction is only possible where the past facts are proved. A real possibility that something has happened in the past is not enough to predict that it will happen in the future. It may be the fact that a judge has found that there is a real possibility that something has happened. But that is not sufficient for this purpose. A finding of a real possibility that a child has suffered harm does not establish that he has. A finding of a real possibility that the harm which a child has suffered is 'non-accidental' does not establish that it was. A finding of a real

---

15   *Re B (Children)* [2008] UKHL 35 (House of Lords) at paragraph 22.
16   Lord Nicholls, *Re H & R* at page 589E.

possibility that this parent harmed a child does not establish that she did. Only a finding that he has, it was, or she did, as the case may be, can be sufficient to found a prediction that because it has happened in the past the same is likely to happen in the future. Care courts need to hear this message loud and clear.[17]

Case Study: Likely harm

Kate is 16. She alleges sexual abuse by her stepfather. It is her word against his; there is no other evidence. Her mother and stepfather have a younger daughter, Linda. Is she likely to suffer significant harm?

Linda's case depends entirely on Kate – Linda is only likely to suffer significant harm if the evidence shows that it is more likely than not that Kate has been abused, not just that it is possible that she has been.

If there is insufficient evidence to prove Kate's allegations on the balance of probabilities there is also insufficient evidence to show that Linda is 'likely' to be abused, however many suspicions there may be and however uncomfortable people feel.[18] The threshold cannot be crossed for either girl.

Attributable

Significant harm on its own does not satisfy the threshold criteria. A child with the best parents in the world might suffer significant harm – he could have a serious accident – but it does not justify care proceedings. The State only needs to step in if there is a link between the harm and parental failure. The threshold criteria are therefore only met if the significant harm is attributable either to inadequate parental care or lack of control.

AN OBJECTIVE STANDARD

When cases concern allegations of inadequate care, CA89 sets an objective standard, comparing the care the child is actually receiving (or is likely to receive) to what 'it would be reasonable to expect a parent to give'. The wording refers to 'a parent', that is, a hypothetical reasonable parent, not 'this' parent or a 'similar' parent.

---

17   *In the Matter of J (Children)* [2013] UKSC 9 (Supreme Court) at paragraph 49.
18   This scenario closely follows the situation in *Re H & R*.

It is important to realise that the 'attributability' element is about establishing a causal link; it is not about blame, still less about punishing parents. Although some cases involve deliberate harm, more often parents are doing their incompetent best, their parenting ability impaired by mental ill-health, drug use, learning disability or their own abusive childhoods. Their inadequate care may not be morally blameworthy – indeed, it may arouse considerable sympathy – but it can still satisfy the statutory criteria.

Wilson LJ said:

> one of the most difficult categories is that in which the case against the parents is not that they have actively mistreated their child but simply that, by reason of their learning difficulties or other such deficits, they lack the mental and other resources with which to provide him with adequate emotional or physical care.[19]

WHOSE STANDARDS?

The care it would be 'reasonable to expect a parent to give' sounds at first blush like a clear, objective standard; but it is value-laden and, at least to a degree, culturally determined. Courts increasingly find themselves having to apply the standard to families from very different backgrounds with varying cultural norms. How do they impose an objective standard in a diverse society?

One case involved ritual harm to a child associated with a traditional Congolese belief in witchcraft, although the court heard that physically harming a child is not part of the traditional belief. Ryder J said: 'this court has no hesitation in condemning ritual practices that cause physical or emotional harm to children.'[20] Thus, there is a bottom line below which the court will not go whatever the claimed cultural justification.

However, that is not to say that no variation can be allowed. Munby J had to deal with a case of an alleged forced marriage. He said:

> the task of the court considering threshold for the purposes of s31 of the 1989 Act may be to evaluate parental performance by reference to the objective standard of the hypothetical 'reasonable' parent, but this does not mean that the court can simply ignore the underlying

---

19 *Re L (Children) (Care Proceedings: Significant Harm)* [2006] EWCA Civ 1282 (Court of Appeal) at paragraph 2(a).
20 *Haringey LBC v. S* [2006] EWHC 2001 (High Court) at paragraph 3.

cultural, social or religious realities. On the contrary, the court must always be sensitive to the cultural, social and religious circumstances of the particular child and family. And the court should, I think, be slow to find that parents only recently or comparatively recently arrived from a foreign country – particularly a country where standards and expectations may be more or less different, sometimes very different indeed, from those with which we are familiar – have fallen short of an acceptable standard of parenting if in truth they have done nothing wrong by the standards of their own community.[21]

He was nevertheless quite clear that in any cultural setting forced (as opposed to arranged) marriage is a gross abuse of human rights and a form of domestic violence: 'no social or cultural imperative can extenuate and no pretended recourse to religious beliefs can possibly justify a forced marriage.'[22]

A delicate but clear balance needs to be struck. Cultural, social and religious considerations must be taken into account but ultimately child abuse is child abuse and we must not shy away from protecting children whatever the family context.

Who must the harm be attributable to?

Sometimes, it is clear who abused a child. In other cases, there may initially be several candidates but investigations clarify matters – medical evidence reveals the timing of injuries, a confession is made or further evidence comes to light. The standard of proof to determine who is responsible for non-accidental injuries is the simple balance of probabilities, no more, and the court should make a finding wherever it is possible to do so.[23]

But what if a baby is injured, all the potential perpetrators deny abuse and even when all the investigations are complete, it is still impossible for the court to determine who did it?

A criminal prosecution is probably ruled out – the CPS cannot prosecute several defendants on an either/or basis. The only exception to this covers cases at the most serious end of the spectrum where

---

21   *Re K (A Local Authority* v. *N and Others)* [2005] EWHC 2956 (Fam) (High Court) at paragraph 26.
22   *Re K* at paragraph 85.
23   *In re S-B* [2010] 1 AC 678 (Supreme Court), a case unusually decided by no less than seven Justices.

prosecution is possible for 'causing or allowing' death or serious physical injury to a child.[24] This was the offence for which Peter Connelly's mother, her boyfriend and his brother were all convicted; it was not possible to establish which one(s) of them actually killed Peter so nobody could be charged with murder.

But care proceedings are different. As a matter of policy, we cannot deny a child protection because we cannot identify the perpetrator of abuse – but how does this fit with the 'attributability' wording of the Act?

Imagine two couples, A and B, who both have babies of about the same age. Mrs B is a childminder who looks after baby A. So baby A spends time in both households; baby B does not. Baby A suffers serious shaking injuries. The evidence cannot establish whether the injuries occurred when baby A was at home with the As or being looked after by Mrs B. So there are three possible perpetrators in two different households and two different babies to worry about.

If you were the social worker, would you take care proceedings on baby A, baby B or both? When a similar situation arose in Lancashire, care proceedings were commenced on both children – baby A for actual harm and baby B for likely harm.[25] The judge who first heard the case expressed his dilemma like this:

> If the criteria are met and orders are made, I am exposing one child to the possibility of removal from parents who are no risk and have done no wrong... If the applications are dismissed then I will undoubtedly be causing one child to be returned to a parent, or parents, one or both of whom are an obvious and serious unassessed risk.

The case went to the Court of Appeal. Baby B's case ended there. On analysis, it was a 'likelihood' case, so B's case depended on A's case: baby B was only at risk if it was Mrs B who injured baby A. That was a matter of suspicion but, as we have seen, suspicion is not enough; there was no proof on the balance of probabilities that Mrs B posed a danger. So the threshold was not crossed for baby B.

What about baby A? That question went all the way to the House of Lords. It was clear beyond doubt that baby A had suffered actual significant harm. But the parents argued that there was no proof that the

---

24   s5 of the Domestic Violence, Crime and Victims Act 2004 (as amended by the Domestic Violence, Crime and Victims (Amendment) Act 2012, s1).
25   *Lancashire County Council* v. *B* [2001] 1FLR 583 (House of Lords).

harm was 'attributable' to their care so the threshold was not crossed. If this was right, it would mean that a baby who had been seriously injured by one of his carers could not be protected unless the perpetrator could be identified. Lord Nicholls described such a conclusion as 'dangerously irresponsible'.

Their Lordships looked at the precise words of CA89. It says that the care 'given to the child' must be not what it was reasonable to expect a parent to give – it does not say by whom that care must be given. Lord Nicholls said it primarily refers to parental care but, where there is shared care, it can include the care given by any of the carers if the court cannot determine which part of the care network has failed. So the threshold was crossed for baby A.

Of course crossing the threshold does not necessarily lead to a care order and removal; that is only one option depending on the outcome of assessments and the application of the welfare principle.

This ruling allows us to protect children where the perpetrator is uncertain. The downside is that, as the threshold can be crossed where the parents are only 'possible' perpetrators, wholly innocent parents may face losing their children – and children may be permanently separated from parents who have done nothing.

SUBSEQUENT CHILDREN

If Mr and Mrs A went on to have another baby together, the findings for the first baby would be enough to establish likelihood of harm for the new baby, regardless of the inability clearly to identify the perpetrator.

But what happens if, in the future Mr and Mrs A separate and Mrs A has a new baby with a different partner? Is that baby likely to suffer significant harm on the basis of what happened to baby A?

It is important to note that cases which turn only on the history of an injury to another child are 'very rare';[26] usually there are many other elements to take into account. However, this very question came to the Supreme Court in Re J.[27] Here, a previous child had died from non-accidental injuries and the mother was found to be one of the possible perpetrators. She separated from her partner and formed a new relationship. The local authority took care proceedings on the

---

26   Lady Hale, In the Matter of J (Children) [2013] UKSC 9 (Supreme Court) at paragraph 5.
27   In the Matter of J (Children) [2013] UKSC 9 (Supreme Court).

three children of the reconstituted family, basing the case solely on the possibility that the mother had injured the previous child, not on failure to protect or any other risk factors; the case was therefore presented in an artificially narrow way, allowing the Supreme Court to make a clear declaration of the law.

The case turned on the question of likelihood. As we know, likelihood can only be established on the basis of findings of fact made on the standard of the 'balance of probabilities'.

So what were the findings of fact? There was no doubt that another child had been seriously abused; that was a proven fact. The mother had been found to be a 'possible' perpetrator, but no more than that. The finding that she may have caused injuries in the past could not somehow mutate into a finding that she did so. So her role in the abuse was a matter of suspicion, a real possibility, no more. And as we know, suspicion is not enough.

Effectively the J case was the same as the case of the childminder's baby: another child had suffered abuse but there was no more than a possibility that the mother was responsible. The threshold could not be crossed. The Supreme Court has now twice confirmed 'a real possibility that this parent has harmed a child in the past is not, by itself, sufficient to establish the likelihood that she will cause harm to another child in the future.'[28]

The words 'by itself' are very important. Lady Hale was at pains to stress the importance of considering the 'innumerable other facts' which may be relevant to a consideration of likelihood: 'There may, or may not, be a multitude of established facts from which such a likelihood can be established. There is no substitute for a careful, individualised assessment of where those facts take one.'[29]

In another Supreme Court case,[30] Lord Wilson pointed out that the parents' character in so far as it affects their parenting is relevant to every stage of the enquiry including threshold.

Lord Hope[31] was also very clear that the court does not discount the fact that the carer was a possible perpetrator; it remains part of

---

28   Lady Hale in *Re J* at paragraph 54, citing with approval the Supreme Court decision in *Re S-B* [2010] 1 AC 678.

29   *Re J* at paragraph 54.

30   *In the Matter of B (A Child)* [2013] UKSC 33 (Supreme Court) at paragraph 31.

31   *Re J* at paragraph 87.

the evidence, perhaps prompting further enquiry or, in combination with other facts about her behaviour or attitudes, providing evidence to cross the threshold, looking at the evidence as a whole. Do not think, therefore, that the Supreme Court was saying for one moment that the fact that a parent was a 'possible' perpetrator of past abuse is irrelevant; simply that on its own it is not enough to cross the threshold.

Their Lordships recognised that these decisions caused 'consternation' among child protection professionals. Lord Reed considered this an over-reaction, pointing out the rarity of cases which truly turn on one fact; indeed, the *Re J* case only did so because the local authority chose to restrict its case to the single legal issue.

Wilson LJ acknowledged: 'No doubt there are hard and worrying cases. But the requirement of proven factual foundation is a bulwark against the State's removal of a child from his family, which I consider very precious.'[32]

Points for practice

1. Never lose sight of the threshold criteria amidst all the issues, agendas and distractions raised in care proceedings.

2. Be clear and precise about exactly how you allege the threshold is crossed. Close liaison with your legal team is crucial.

3. Evidence every point of your case carefully. Remember the courts can only proceed on evidence.

4. You can take care proceedings even if you cannot prove who the abuser was. However, the court should be urged to make a finding wherever possible.

---

32   *In re F (Interim Care Order)* [2011] EWCA Civ 258 (Court of Appeal).

Chapter 12

Care Proceedings
Interim Stages

Care proceedings application

The decision whether or not to take care proceedings lies with the local authority.[1] However strident partner agencies or a Case Conference may be in their opinions, they cannot make the local authority take a case to court. The local authority must exercise its own judgment and apply objective analysis to the information and views of partner agencies; Theis J[2] was critical of an authority which submitted that it had 'little option' but to take proceedings on the basis of information provided by health professionals without challenging or testing it, putting it into context or balancing it against other factors.

Even the court '...cannot require the local authority to take proceedings. The limit of [the court's power] is to direct the authority to undertake an investigation of the children's circumstances.'[3] This direction under s37 Children Act 1989 (CA89)[4] can be coupled with an interim (not a full) care order, but if the local authority then decides not to apply for a care order, the court can do nothing. The boundary between the roles of courts and local authorities is clear, but can cause tension, as in a case[5] of an intractable contact dispute which everyone

---

1   CA89 also empowers the NSPCC to take proceedings; in practice the role falls to local authorities.
2   *Re E (A Child)* [2013] EWHC 2400 (Fam) (High Court).
3   Wall J in *Re M (Intractable Contact Dispute: Interim Care Order)* [2003] EWHC 1024 (Fam) (High Court).
4   See Chapter 4 for more details on s37 reports.
5   *CP v. AR* [2009] EWCA Civ 358 (Court of Appeal).

agreed had caused emotional harm to the eight-year-old child who had been subject to proceedings for six years. Even though the local authority agreed that the threshold had been crossed, it refused to take proceedings. The judge could not force it to do so even though he thought care proceedings and a foster placement would be in the child's best interests. Whether the child in future years might have a claim for the authority's refusal to act remains to be seen.

Which court?

From the start of the Act it was decided that cases should be heard at the appropriate level of court according to the gravity and complexity of the case. So a case which concerns poor hygiene and failure to feed or clothe a child properly can perfectly well be decided by magistrates, whereas a case which involves complex and contradictory expert evidence about factitious or induced illness needs the expertise of a High Court judge.

Previously there were distinct courts – the Family Proceedings Court (FPC) (part of the magistrates' court), the County Court and the High Court – and cases could be transferred from one to the other until they reached the correct level. With the advent of the Family Court,[6] we have a single family court with a unified administration and where possible a single location, comprising magistrates, County Court judges and High Court judges (all known as 'Judges of the Family Court'). The principle, however, remains the same: each case is to be decided at the appropriate level for its particular characteristics. It is to be hoped that streamlining administration will improve the practical experience of taking a case to court. The High Court also retains a separate identity for certain matters which are reserved to the High Court's jurisdiction.[7]

Who takes part?

Party status is important. Parties to proceedings have the right to:

- attend all hearings
- be represented by a lawyer (although not necessarily the right to Legal Aid)

---

6   Introduced by the Crime and Courts Act 2013, in force from 22 April 2014.
7   Such as wardship, some cases with an international element and judicial review.

- be served with copies of all applications, orders and evidence
- submit their own evidence in writing and, if necessary, give oral evidence at a contested hearing.

In care proceedings, the local authority is the applicant. The respondents are:

- everyone with parental responsibility (PR)
- the child.

Parents without PR and the people with whom the child was living when proceedings commenced are not automatic parties, but they must be formally notified of the proceedings so they can apply to become parties if they wish. The court will then decide if that is appropriate.

A married father has PR and is a party to care proceedings, and the mother's husband is presumed to be the child's father unless there is evidence to the contrary. In one case,[8] the mother did not want her husband to be involved in proceedings, saying he was unaware of the baby, who was the product of rape. The Court of Appeal referred to the strong presumption that a child born in a marriage is legitimate and found there was insufficient evidence that this husband was not the father so he was entitled to be party to the proceedings. Rules about service and party status should only be relaxed in exceptional circumstances.

If in doubt, ask the court. Do not make assumptions as in one case[9] where, although both mother and putative father confirmed paternity, the local authority and Guardian thought they knew better, and did not notify him or include him in assessments. This serious error and injustice led to the care order being set aside and the whole case being re-heard, causing delay, stress and expense to all concerned.

Other people can be added as parties in the court's discretion. So, for example, it may be appropriate for grandparents to become parties but this will only happen if they have a separate case to advance, for instance if they seek to care for the child. If they are just supporting

---

8   *Re AB (Care Proceedings: Service on Husband Ignorant of Child's Existence)* [2004] 1 FLR 527 (Court of Appeal).

9   *Re B (Care Proceedings: Notification of Father without Parental Responsibility)* [1999] 2 FLR 409 (High Court).

their daughter they can participate as witnesses, they do not need party status.

Curiously, there is nothing in CA89 or court rules directing how the court is to exercise its power to confer party status. The child's welfare is not paramount as it is not a decision determining the child's upbringing. The Court of Appeal[10] said the factors vary from case to case, but the provisions of s10(9) CA89[11] (the criteria for giving leave to make a private law application) highlight some matters of particular relevance – the nature of the proposed application, the applicant's connection with the child, any risk of disruption to the child, the local authority's and parents' positions, as well as the motivation for the application and the prospects of success.

Intervenor

What if allegations are made against someone who is not a party? Clearly, as a matter of justice, that person must have the right to answer the allegations, but equally clearly he should not have access to all the highly sensitive information in the case. The solution is to make him an intervenor – he has the right to see the parts of the evidence which relate to him and to challenge that information in court, but not to participate in the rest of the case.

The child as party

The child is automatically a party to care proceedings and is represented by both a Children's Guardian (provided by CAFCASS) and a solicitor. The Guardian gives instructions to the solicitor and they work as a team unless the child is competent to instruct the solicitor himself. If so, and if his wishes are different from the Guardian's view of his best interests, the solicitor represents the child and the Guardian puts her own case.

The participation of older children in the proceedings has been the subject of much anxious consideration and is still evolving. In the past it was simple – children did not attend court in care proceedings. In contrast, child witnesses in criminal proceedings have always had to

---

10   *B (A Child)* [2012] EWCA Civ 737 (Court of Appeal).
11   See Chapter 4 for more information.

attend court for cross-examination in person. Increasingly, child care professionals, judges and children themselves have been asking why children should not have the opportunity actively to participate in cases which determine their future, or indeed why adult parties should not have the chance to test evidence children give against them.

Although the primary responsibility for representing the interests of children involved in proceedings lies with CAFCASS and children's lawyers, as a social worker you may have important information to contribute to discussions about a child's wishes and feelings, his capacity to give evidence and whether attending court is in his best interests.

Can a child give evidence in care proceedings?

It is clear that a competent child can give evidence. Even if the child does not understand the oath, s96(2) CA89 says that the court can hear his unsworn evidence provided that he understands that he must tell the truth and has sufficient understanding to justify the court hearing his evidence.

Should a child give evidence in care proceedings?

There used to be a presumption against children giving evidence. That was overturned by the Supreme Court case of Re W,[12] a case of care proceedings in respect of five children which turned on the allegations of serious sexual abuse made by the eldest child, a 14-year-old girl. The court considered the requirements of the European Convention on Human Rights and found that there is a balance to be struck between the right to a fair trial (Article 6), which includes the right to challenge evidence, and everyone's right to respect for private and family life (Article 8). Neither right automatically outweighs the other; it is a question of balance in each case. Baroness Hale said:

> When the court is considering whether a particular child should be called as a witness, the court will have to weigh two considerations: the advantages that that will bring to the determination of the truth and the damage it may do to the welfare of this or any other child...[13]

---

12   W (Children) [2010] UKSC 12 (Supreme Court).
13   Re W, Baroness Hale at paragraph 24.

... The essential test is whether justice can be done to all the parties without further questioning of the child.[14]

To decide where the balance lies, the court must consider many factors including:

- the issues in the case
- the other evidence before the court
- the quality of any ABE interview
- the nature of the other party's challenge
- the age and maturity of the child
- the length of time since the relevant events
- the Guardian's views
- the risk of delay.

The child's own wishes and feelings are an important factor and the Supreme Court said: 'We endorse the view that an unwilling child should rarely, if ever, be obliged to give evidence.'[15] Although there is no longer a presumption against the child giving evidence, the Supreme Court anticipated that in most cases the result of the balancing exercise will be that the child should not be called to attend court.

If, however, a child does have to give evidence, every possible measure should be taken to improve the quality of that evidence and decrease the risk of harm to the child. In the family court, this includes but is not limited to the 'special measures' prescribed in criminal trials; Baroness Hale suggested possibilities including video recorded cross-examination, questions through an intermediary or questions asked by the judge herself, not necessarily by a respondent's lawyer. As a social worker who knows the child, you may have useful suggestions to make.

After the W case, the Family Justice Council issued guidelines[16] to be followed in care proceedings when children are to give evidence,

---

14 *Re W* at paragraph 30.
15 *Re W* at paragraph 26.
16 Working Party of the Family Justice Council (December 2011) *Guidelines in relation to children giving evidence in family proceedings.* Available at www.judiciary.gov.uk/ JCO%2FDocuments%2FFJC%2FFFJC_Guidelines_+in_relation_children_+giving_ evidence_+in_+family_+proceedings_Dec2011.pdf, accessed on 30 March 2014.

including practical considerations to prepare for the hearing, how the evidence should be given and how children should be questioned. Familiarise yourself with these guidelines if any child you work with has to go to court.

Judges should always be prepared to take an active role to control proceedings. As Lady Hale said in the case of a vulnerable witness:

> The Court's only concern in family proceedings is to get at the truth. The object of the procedure is to enable witnesses to give their evidence in the way which best enables the Court to assess its reliability. It is certainly not to compound any abuse which may have been suffered.[17]

Pauffley J promised robust case management in a case involving a 17-year-old girl with significant learning difficulties:

> I would not shrink from stopping cross examination altogether if it became too onerous for G or, indeed, if the process ceased to have value. I have done so in other cases because the needs of the young person plainly required swift, decisive and radical intervention. Limiting the subject areas for questioning likewise may become necessary according to G's responses; and I would react as the needs of the situation demanded.[18]

What if the child positively wants to give evidence? A 15-year-old subject to care proceedings[19] desperately wanted to return home and wanted to give evidence via video link to convey the strength of his feelings. However, his lawyer and his Guardian had already made his views very clear, and the judge was worried about a damaging emotional outburst from the mother if her son gave evidence. The Court of Appeal weighed up the potential benefits and risks, found that oral evidence would not add to the court's knowledge, and confirmed the decision not to allow the young man to give evidence.

Can a child meet the judge?

Some children want to meet the judge who will decide their case, even if there is no question of them giving evidence in court; equally some judges want to meet the children whose cases they are deciding. This is

---

17   *A (A Child)* [2012] UKSC 60 (Supreme Court).
18   *Re G and E (Children) (Vulnerable Witnesses)* [2011] EWHC 4063 (Fam) (High Court).
19   *P-S (Children)* [2013] EWCA Civ 223 (Court of Appeal).

becoming more common and there are guidelines[20] for such meetings. It must be absolutely clear that the purpose is not to gather evidence; it is to help the child to understand the proceedings better and to reassure her that the judge has understood her. The parties all have a right to express their views before the judge decides whether or not to meet the child. If a meeting goes ahead, considerations include:

- where and when it should happen
- who should prepare the child (usually the Guardian)
- who will bring the child to the meeting
- who will be present (obviously, the judge must never see the child alone)
- who is to keep a note of the meeting, which must be approved by the judge and communicated to the other parties.

At any such meeting the judge must make it quite clear to the child that:

- he cannot keep secrets and the other parties will know what she says
- making a decision is the judge's job, not the child's responsibility, and he has many factors to consider.

Procedure

After the introduction of CA89, there was a steady growth in the volume of paperwork. Documentation often filled several lever arch files, even in relatively routine care cases. Proceedings frequently took over a year to complete. Expense, complication and delay had grown out of proportion. Something had to be done. A series of regulations and initiatives in case management culminated in the imposition in the Children and Families Act 2014[21] of a statutory 26 week limit for the completion of care proceedings (with a provision for exceptions to be made where necessary for the child's welfare).

---

20 Family Justice Council (April 2010) *Guidelines for Judges Meeting Children who are subject to Family Proceedings*. Produced by the Family Justice Council and approved by the President of the Family Division. Available at www.fnf.org.uk/downloads/Guidelines_for_Judges_Meeting_Children.pdf, accessed on 30 March 2014.

21 Time limit imposed by s14 of the Children and Families Act 2014. Extensions require specific justification and may not be for more than eight weeks at a time.

This book is not the place for a detailed exposition of procedure in care proceedings, but it is important to be aware that every stage of the process, starting before proceedings are issued, is regulated with increasingly standardised procedure[22] and strict timescales. Judges are increasingly expected to be active case managers, making sure cases stay on track.

The tight timetable for proceedings means that more preparatory work needs to be done before the case starts (except in emergencies, of course). Clear, focused thinking and analysis before starting the court process help considerably thereafter. Teamwork with your lawyers is vital. The role of local authority lawyers is given little prominence – they barely receive a mention in enquiry reports or even *Working Together*. But they have a key role to play and cases proceed far more smoothly when the social work and legal teams co-operate in a spirit of mutual respect for and understanding of each other's roles and responsibilities. Child care lawyers need to have some knowledge of social work practice and procedures to understand your perspective of a case and to interpret your instructions; they need your help with that. Effective team working also includes being prepared to question and challenge each other where necessary; it is far better to receive probing enquiry and constructive criticism from someone on the same side than to see a case collapse in court.

Pre-proceedings letter and meeting
Wherever possible, the local authority must send the child's parents a letter explaining clearly that care proceedings are contemplated and the reasons for concern. The parents with their legal representatives then attend a meeting to discuss the matter. Research[23] has indicated that this process is surprisingly successful in diverting cases from court, whether thanks to improved care and co-operation or a kinship care placement being arranged. However, where cases did go to court

---

22 Practice Direction 36C and Public Law Outline 2014, implementation of final version 22 April 2014. Available at https://www.justice.gov.uk/downloads/protecting-the-vulnerable/care-proceeding-reform/pd12a.pdf, accessed on 17 April 2014.

23 Masson, J., and Dickens, J. (2013) *Partnership by Law? The pre-proceedings process for families on the edge of care proceedings.* Universities of Bristol and East Anglia. Available at www.bris.ac.uk/law/research/researchpublications/2013/partnershipbylaw.pdf, accessed on 30 March 2014.

after the pre-proceedings process, there was a delay in the application being made and there was no discernible effect on the proceedings, in particular no reduction in the length of proceedings.

Issuing proceedings

The application must be accompanied by a bundle of documents including a threshold statement which sets out concisely (no more than two pages) and precisely how the authority alleges that the s31 CA89 criteria are met. Although drafting this is a job for your lawyers, it is obviously vitally important that it accurately reflects social work concerns. Also required at the very start are:

- social work chronology
- social work statement (following a prescribed structure) and genogram
- current assessments of the child and family
- a care plan.

Evidence

All evidence in care proceedings is put in writing. It is 'filed' (sent to the court) and 'served' (sent to the other parties) following the timetable set by the court. Evidence must be submitted on time. All parties see all evidence in advance of any hearing and no-one can rely on evidence which has not been disclosed: there are no surprise witnesses or dramatic courtroom revelations in care proceedings.

The court can and frequently does accept evidence in written form without the witness coming to court to give oral evidence; indeed, oral evidence is usually only necessary where the evidence is disputed. Careful preparation of written evidence is therefore essential. The focus must be on quality, not quantity.

Stages in proceedings

The court gives standard directions (such as appointing a Guardian) without anyone going to court. The usual hearings are:

- a case management hearing (CMH) preceded by an advocates' meeting – to draw up a timetable through to final hearing within 26 weeks, identify key issues and the evidence required including considering whether expert evidence is needed

- a further case management hearing (FCMH), but only if necessary
- an issues resolution hearing (IRH), again preceded by an advocates' meeting – to resolve or narrow issues, identify the evidence necessary on the remaining issues in dispute and to give directions for the final hearing. If it is possible to do so, the IRH can be used as a final hearing
- final hearing.

Interim orders

Even the best managed care proceedings take months from beginning to end. What happens to the child in the meantime? The local authority has the option of seeking an interim care order (ICO) or interim supervision order (ISO) but this is by no means inevitable – it is quite possible for the child to remain at home with no order throughout the case until final hearing.

There must be a good reason to apply for an interim order so the local authority must consider as separate issues:

- whether care proceedings should be started at all; if so,
- whether an interim order should be sought; and if an ICO is made,
- whether the child should be removed from home.

None of these decisions should be made lightly. An interim order does not in any way pre-judge the final hearing but a child could be away from home for months under interim orders. The implications for the child, family and for the assessments to be undertaken are enormous. For this reason the Court of Appeal[24] stressed that the standard required to justify the interim removal of a child is 'very high' and cannot be founded on speculative evidence.

---

24   Re M (Interim Care Order: Removal) [2005] EWCA Civ 1594 (Court of Appeal).

Case Studies: Interim orders

In Ali's case, care proceedings are started on the grounds of neglect. In spite of months of work, the standard of basic care – feeding, clothing, hygiene, school attendance and so on – is not good enough. The long-term plan may be to remove Ali from home if nothing changes, but there is no need to remove him in the interim; indeed it will be beneficial for the Guardian to see him at home in his mother's care and there is always the possibility that the proceedings themselves will finally prompt Ali's mother to make the necessary changes.

Four-year-old Ben, on the other hand, has suffered significant injuries which medical evidence suggests are non-accidental. His parents deny all knowledge. The social worker cannot keep Ben safe at home pending the completion of proceedings so she seeks an ICO with view to moving Ben into foster care until matters are resolved.

The grounds for interim orders are set out in s38(2) CA89.

> s38(2) CA89 A court shall not make an interim care order or interim supervision order…unless it is satisfied that there are reasonable grounds for believing that the circumstances with respect to the child are as mentioned in s31(2).

The reference to the s31 threshold criteria means that the local authority must demonstrate to the court reasonable grounds to believe the case can be made out in respect of both significant harm and attributability. Even then, an ICO does not automatically follow – the court must exercise its discretion applying the welfare test. The Court of Appeal[25] has stressed that a child's removal from parents is not to be sanctioned unless the child's safety requires interim protection. 'Safety' is not limited to physical safety; the Court of Appeal[26] has made it clear that it can also include emotional safety or psychological welfare.

If an ICO application is opposed, a contested interim hearing must be arranged. Given the purpose of an ICO, such hearings must be limited

---

25 *Re K and H* [2006] EWCA Civ 1898 (Court of Appeal).
26 *Re B and KB* [2009] EWCA 1254 (Court of Appeal).

to the issues relevant to the interim stage which cannot wait for the final hearing. Interim hearings are not a dress rehearsal for a full trial.

Black LJ summarised the position:

> The interim care order regime is designed...to ensure that the child is kept safe in the period prior to the court's full consideration of the local authority's care application. The focus of an interim care hearing is upon what may happen to the child during the interim period if he or she continues to live with or returns to live with his or her parents. An interim care hearing is not designed for the purpose of evaluating the longer term future except in so far as that is necessary to give directions for the management of the case. And it should not lead to the making of an interim order that will, as a matter of fact, afford an advantage to the local authority...or prejudice a parent's ability to put forward proposals to care for their child.[27]

In that case, an ICO was refused, requiring the return of a four-month-old baby to a mother whose previous children had been permanently removed and who was in prison at the time. The prison mother and baby unit would secure the baby's safety pending a final hearing. The longer-term issues were matters for a final hearing, which should not be prejudged at the interim stage. Black LJ said:

> the relationship of A and M should have been preserved pending a final adjudication of the issues in the care proceedings. Concern as to delay should have been addressed by making arrangements for this final adjudication to take place promptly rather than by foreshadowing its determination by the making of an interim care order which kept M and A apart.[28]

When CA89 was introduced, interim orders were subject to a statutory time limit (eight weeks maximum for the first order, four weeks for subsequent orders). Those limits are removed by the Children and Families Act 2014,[29] leaving the judge to determine the length of orders and eliminating the administrative burden of the need for regular renewals.

---

27   L (A Child) [2013] EWCA Civ 489 (Court of Appeal) at paragraph 53.
28   L (A Child) [2013] EWCA Civ 489 (Court of Appeal) at paragraph 60.
29   s38 CA89 amended by s14(4) of the Children and Families Act 2014.

Effect of an ICO

An ICO gives the local authority PR which lasts as long as the order. PR is shared with the parent(s), but not equally as, just as under a full care order, the local authority can restrict the parents' exercise of their PR where necessary to safeguard and promote the child's welfare. So, the local authority decides on contact arrangements (subject to any interim contact order made by the court) and, most importantly, it decides where the child lives during the ICO. This could be in foster care, a children's home, in an extended family placement, or at home. The ICO gives the local authority, not the court, the power to decide on the child's placement and this placement can be changed during the ICO.

However, as any other local authority power, this power must be exercised properly, fairly and with due regard to the various parties' human rights. In one case,[30] the authority obtained an ICO with a plan to place the children with their grandparents pending an assessment of their ability to care for them longer term. When that assessment was negative, the authority decided to move the children to foster care during the course of an ICO. Crucially, the decision was made without consultation; the parents and grandparents were simply informed of a decision which had already been taken.

There was no remedy available in the family court. The family could not ask the court to decide on placement as that is beyond the court's powers and, given that an ICO was already in force, the family would have no opportunity to contest until the expiry of that order, which would be too late.

So an application was made for judicial review. It is wholly exceptional for the Administrative Court to intervene when there are ongoing family proceedings, but this was an exceptional case. The judge quoted Munby J from a previous case: '...the removal of a child from a parent (and I would add any other family member) should not be countenanced unless and until there has been due and proper consultation and an opportunity to challenge the proposal.'[31] Of course, an exception can be made for emergencies, and it must be remembered that the duty is to consult and take views expressed into account –

---

30   *R (on the application of H)* v. *Kingston upon Hull City Council* [2013] EWHC 388 (Admin) (High Court).

31   *Re G (Care: Challenge to Local Authority Decision)* [2003] EWHC 551 (Fam) (High Court).

not necessarily to follow them. The local authority's decision-making processes must always be rational and fair, whether or not a court order is in force.

Interim assessments

During the interim phase of proceedings, s38(6) CA89 gives the court control of assessments of the child, although it cannot force a competent child to co-operate against his will. Assessments of the adults involved do not come within s38(6) CA89 although they form an important part of the evidence in care proceedings. No-one can compel an adult to co-operate, but if they do not, it has obvious implications for their case. Directions under s38(6) can only be made if the assessment is necessary to help the court decide the case justly. Factors include the impact on the child's welfare, the issues to be considered in the assessment, whether other evidence is or could be available on these issues, the impact on the timetable and the cost involved.[32]

> s38(6) CA89 Where the court makes an interim care order, or an interim supervision order, it may give such directions (if any) as it considers appropriate with regard to the medical or psychiatric examination or other assessment of the child; but if the child is of sufficient understanding to make an informed decision he may refuse to submit to the examination or other assessment.
>
> (7) A direction under subsection (6) may be to the effect that there is to be –
>
> (a) no such examination or assessment; or
>
> (b) no such examination or assessment unless the court directs otherwise.

Residential assessments

One way to conduct an intensive assessment of a family's functioning is through a residential assessment. Can the court insist on such an assessment even if the local authority does not agree? The answer

---

32   s38(7)(A) CA89 added to CA89 by the Children and Families Act 2014.

depends on whether the assessment proposed falls within the wording of s38(6) CA89. If not, the court has no power to order it, even if it would be in the child's best interests: s1 CA89 does not apply to this subsection as it concerns an interim evidential issue, not the child's upbringing.

A series of cases[33] has decided that the court has power to order residential (or other) assessments which involve the child's participation and which are required so that the court can reach a proper decision at the final hearing. It must be an assessment, not treatment or therapy, and must always have the aim of providing necessary information to the court within a realistic timescale. It is important to note that the assessment must be 'required' and the evidence 'necessary', not just that it might be of assistance.

Some cases were thought to suggest that parents facing the loss of their child always had a right to an assessment by someone other than the local authority so that they had a chance to advance a positive case. This interpretation was roundly rejected by Black LJ who said:

> Such a principle is unworkable not least because, sadly, there are cases in which the parents are plainly not able to care for their children and in which no amount of assessment or evidence gathering will enable them to put forward a positive case.[34]

The increased emphasis on the speedy resolution of proceedings seems likely to favour time-limited, focused assessments over the lengthy and expensive residential assessments of the past in the majority of cases.

Experts

The involvement of expert witnesses in care proceedings is undergoing radical change. It had become almost the norm for outside experts to be consulted in care cases, leading to increased delay and ballooning costs[35] with little return in terms of the information before the court.

---

33 Most importantly *Re C (A Minor) (Interim Care Order: Residential Assessment)* [1997] AC 489 and *Re G (Interim Care Order: Residential Assessment)* [2005] UKHL 68, both decided by the House of Lords.
34 *Re S* [2011] EWCA Civ 812 (Court of Appeal) at paragraph 93.
35 £52 million in the year to October 2011 according to government figures.

The Family Justice Review[36] noted 'weaknesses' in the quality of evidence. This was highlighted by a study[37] of psychological reports for court which found reports to be of variable quality (two-thirds were rated 'poor' or even 'very poor'), compiled by experts who were sometimes inadequately qualified for the task and who were too often full-time experts with no clinical practice. It found that some psychological evidence was presented as fact when it was conjecture or speculation, based on untested theories, and experts strayed beyond the limits of their expertise. Many practitioners have in any event long argued that psychologists have been instructed to provide what is rightfully social work evidence. Not surprisingly, this has led to the introduction of National Standards for Expert Witnesses.[38]

In his 'View from the President's Chambers' in June 2013, Sir James Munby P wrote:

> What is required is a major change of culture. Three things are needed: first, a reduction in the use of experts; second, a more focussed approach in the cases where experts are still needed; and, third, a reduction in the length of expert reports.

REDUCTION IN USE OF EXPERTS

In the past, the test was whether an expert report was 'reasonably required'. Now, it must be 'necessary',[39] clearly a stiffer test. 'Necessary' was explained by the Court of Appeal as: 'something between "indispensable" on the one hand and "useful", "reasonable" or "desirable" on the other hand...', having '...the connotation of the imperative,

---

36   An independent review carried out by Sir David Norgrove.

37   Ireland, J. L. (February 2012) *Evaluating Expert Witness Psychological Reports: Exploring Quality*. February 2012. Research carried out by the University of Central Lancashire, part-funded by the Family Justice Council. Available at http://netk.net.au/ Psychology/ExpertReports.pdf, accessed on 30 March 2014.

38   Ministry of Justice and Family Justice Council Response to consultation published November 2013. Available at http://socialwelfare.bl.uk/subject-areas/services-activity/criminal-justice/ministryofjustice/158364experts-standards-consultation-response.pdf, accessed on 30 March 2014. Implementation April 2014.

39   Family Proceedings Rules from 2013 and placed on a statutory footing by s13 of the Children and Families Act 2014.

what is demanded rather than what is merely optional or reasonable or desirable.[40]

The Court of Appeal was considering the case of a child who had a rare genetic disorder affecting the development of the bones in the back and ribs. She also had bruising that was thought to be non-accidental. The question arose as to whether her condition made her particularly susceptible to bruising. The local expert who had filed a report in the case candidly said this question was beyond his expertise.

The mother applied for three expert reports – from a geneticist, a haematologist and a paediatrician – to give a general overview of the case. In the past she may well have been allowed to seek all three, but in the new climate only the geneticist was approved; the other two applications 'did not begin to get off the ground' as the issues were already covered in the evidence. However, the geneticist's evidence was necessary to enable the court to deal justly with a key question; without it the right to a fair trial could be breached. Importantly, the geneticist was able to provide a short report on a targeted paper exercise (without examining the child) within the timetable already fixed for the case.

Thus, whenever an expert report is requested, the court must be satisfied that the evidence is necessary, adding something important to the information already before the court which is not within the expertise of someone already in the case, including the social worker and the Guardian. It is now clear beyond argument that social workers are 'experts'. As Munby P wrote:

> One of the problems is that in recent years too many social workers have come to feel undervalued, disempowered and de-skilled. In part at least this is an unhappy consequence of the way in which care proceedings have come to be dealt with by the courts. If the revised PLO is properly implemented one of its outcomes will, I hope, be to re-position social workers as trusted professionals playing the central role in care proceedings which too often of late has been overshadowed by our unnecessary use of and reliance upon other experts.

---

40   *Re H-L (A Child)* [2013] EWCA Civ 655 (Court of Appeal) approving the definition of the same word in a different statutory context (adoption) in the case *Re P (Placement Orders: Parental Consent)* [2008] EWCA Civ 53 (Court of Appeal).

This chimes with the drive to enhance social work expertise endorsed in the Munro report. The time is right for a newly confident social work profession to re-claim its rightful place in the court process.

MORE FOCUS

The precise issues which the expert is asked to consider must be clearly identified. Questions must be kept to a manageable number, relate to the key issues in the case and of course must be within the ambit of the expert's specialist area. The timetable for the report must be fixed at the outset.

SHORTER REPORTS

Munby P urged experts to concentrate less in their reports on history and narrative and more on analysis and opinion. Reports should be succinct, focused, analytical and evidence-based. Pauffley J complained that it had become '...the norm for experts (particularly paediatricians and psychologists) to produce absurdly lengthy reports...'[41] She roundly criticised a long, repetitive paediatric report which in part duplicated questions already addressed by another expert:

> The modern way exemplified by Dr R's over-inclusive and doubtless expensive report is no longer acceptable. Experts must conform to the specifics of what is asked of them rather than, as here, provide something akin to a 'paediatric overview.' I struggle to recall a single instance when such expansive and all inclusive analysis has been of real utility in a case of this kind.[42]

Time will tell how matters change in practice. However, it would be no surprise to see parents' (and possibly children's) representatives challenging decisions. From the parents' perspective, the cumulative effect of the changes in the system is that they have less time to prepare their case, less Legal Aid funding to do so and a restricted opportunity to instruct an independent expert to challenge the local authority's evidence. It will feel unfair and, bearing in mind the life-changing issues involved, no doubt cases will be brought alleging a breach of the right to a fair trial.

---

41   *IA (A Child)* [2013] EWHC 2499 (Fam) (High Court).
42   *Re IA* at paragraph 115.

The role of expert evidence

There will, inevitably, be cases where there is a genuine necessity for expert opinions and parties including the local authority must be prepared to push for such evidence where it is needed to enable the court to do the right thing for the child. But even in these cases an expert's report, however authoritative, is only part of the evidence. The court, not the expert, decides the case on all of the material before it. As Ryder J said: 'a factual decision must be based on all available materials, i.e. be judged in context and not just upon medical or scientific materials, no matter how cogent they may in isolation seem to be.'[43]

Evolving knowledge

Scientific understanding progresses and expert evidence must keep pace. As Dame Elizabeth Butler Sloss P put it: 'The judge in care proceedings must never forget that today's medical certainty may be discarded by the next generation of experts or that scientific research may throw a light into corners that are at present dark.'[44]

This comment was made in a case following a series of criminal cases in which mothers were convicted of killing their babies on the basis of medical evidence which later proved unreliable. There have also been care cases, including the case of the Webster family,[45] where three children were removed and adopted on the basis of medical evidence given honestly, competently and in good faith at the time but which later transpired to have missed an alternative innocent possible explanation for the injuries.

Experts instructed in care proceedings must be up-to-date with latest developments in their field, and we must all guard against jumping to conclusions based on our experience in previous cases; thinking may have moved on. For example, it seems that subdural haematomas are caused by less force than was previously thought, albeit still a level of

---

43   *A County Council v. A Mother and others* [2005] EWHC Fam (High Court) at paragraph 31.
44   *Re U, Re B (Serious Injuries: Standard of Proof)* [2004] EWCA Civ 567 (Court of Appeal).
45   *W (Children)* [2009] EWCA Civ 59 (Court of Appeal).

force which is unacceptable.[46] Experts now acknowledge that there is still much to learn in this field.[47]

We must not assume that it is always possible to find an explanation and we must guard against the false logic that, because all known innocent explanations have been ruled out, the only conclusion left is a sinister one; sometimes we do not and cannot know. As Hedley J said:…it is dangerous and wrong to infer non-accidental injury merely from the absence of any other understood mechanism. Maybe it simply represents a general acknowledgement that we are fearfully and wonderfully made.[48] A case[49] in point involved a happy, smiling baby girl with 'spectacular' skull fractures but no brain injuries and no clinical symptoms, leaving an array of leading experts baffled.

At the end of the court's forensic examination it may be found that the cause of injuries cannot be proven to be non-accidental as initially thought or that there is another innocent explanation, or even that there is no explanation at all. This does not mean that the local authority was wrong to bring the case in the first place. It is the court's job to decide and the authority is acting properly to put the matter before the court.

Split hearings

As we have seen, there are two questions for the court in care proceedings: whether the threshold is crossed; then, if so, what order (if any) should be made. In most cases the two questions are considered together, all the evidence being heard in one final hearing and the judgment passing seamlessly from one question to the next. But sometimes the court splits the issues, holding a fact-finding hearing and making the welfare decision later. Ryder LJ[50] has made it clear that separate hearings should only be held where deciding a discrete, stark issue will expedite the case, for example where the threshold criteria would not exist if findings were not made, or in complex medical cases where an accurate diagnosis

---

46 *Re A & D (Non-accidental Injuries: Subdural Haematomas)* [2002] 1FLR 337 (High Court).
47 For a very clear and interesting summary on current thinking on subdural haematomas and retinal haemorrhages, see the judgment of Black J in *Re JS* [2012] EWHC 1370 (Fam) (High Court) at paragraphs 48–64.
48 *Re R (Care Proceedings: Causation)* [2011] EWHC 1715 (Fam) (High Court) at paragraph 19.
49 *Re M (Children)* [2012] EWCA Civ 1710 (Court of Appeal).
50 *Re S (A Child)* [2014] EWCA Civ 25 (Court of Appeal).

is key to the child's future. It is not appropriate to use a split hearing to assist in social care assessments. Where a welfare recommendation depends on a factual finding, social workers may have to provide alternative formulations.

Case Study: Split hearing

Baby Alexander, previously unknown to the authorities, has serious injuries but there are no other causes for concern. His parents say he was injured accidentally but the paediatrician suspects abuse. Was it an accident or not? If there was abuse or negligence, can the court determine who was responsible? If the injuries cannot be shown to meet the threshold criteria, the case ends there, so it could be a suitable case for a split hearing.

The two parts of the hearing should be heard by the same judge. What happens if new evidence comes to light or a party changes her story between one hearing and the next? The Court of Appeal confirmed that given that a split hearing is merely part of the whole process of trying a case and not a separate exercise, the court can revisit findings later in the case in the light of subsequent developments.[51]

Once the court has spoken, all parties must proceed on the basis of the facts found. Great Ormond Street Hospital was roundly criticised[52] when it continued to work with children on the basis they had been sexually abused when the judge had concluded that the allegations were untrue and originated by the mother. All professionals must respect the court's authority and responsibility for decision making.

Family courts and the media
There is a public interest in preserving the confidentiality of proceedings; we also need a system which is open to scrutiny and understood by the public. Article 8 rights to privacy conflict with Article 10 rights to freedom of expression. Practice is fast evolving. Whereas family courts were previously closed to the media, now the media can attend unless it

---

51   *A and L (Children)* [2011] EWCA Civ 1205 (Court of Appeal).
52   *Re N (Sexual Abuse Allegations: Professionals Not Abiding by Findings of Fact)* [2005] 2FLR 340 (High Court).

is necessary to exclude them. The court controls the right to report cases and s97 CA89 prohibits the publication of anything intended or likely to identify the child. Practice guidance now establishes a presumption in favour of publication of suitably anonymised judgments in family cases unless there is a compelling reason to withhold publication. While the identities of children and families are protected, local authorities and experts can expect to be named in reports.[53]

The High Court weighed up conflicting applications of the police and *The Times* in the case[54] of children whose parents and grandmother were murdered on a family holiday in France. Balancing the various rights, the judge decided that media presence at the hearings would not increase the risk to the girls, but an injunction was made to ensure that nothing would be published which might reveal their whereabouts.

The advent of the internet has added further complications. When aggrieved parents posted on the internet a film of social workers removing their baby, complete with offensive and threatening comments about the named workers, the local authority applied for an injunction. Weighing up all the competing rights, Munby P decided:

> ...the balance between the public interest in discussing the workings of the system and the personal privacy and welfare interests of the child is best and most proportionately struck by restraining the naming of the child while not restraining the publication of images of the child.[55]

This area of law will no doubt continue to evolve and the courts will need to be alert to the ever-changing world of social networking and new media.

Points for practice

1. Care proceedings increasingly require clear analysis, careful preparation and timely presentation. Work closely with your legal team.

---

53 Practice Guidance on Transparency in the Family Court, in force from 3 February 2014.
54 *Re Al-Hilli (Children)* [2013] EWHC 2190 (Fam) (High Court).
55 *Re J (A Child)* [2013] EWHC 2894 (Fam) (High Court).

2. Carefully consider any application for an interim order and be able to justify any plan to remove a child from home.

3. Be prepared to contribute to discussions about the child's role in proceedings.

4. Social workers are experts. Claim your expertise and resist applications to instruct experts to duplicate social work evidence.

5. Expert witnesses should only be used where absolutely essential.

Chapter 13

Care Proceedings
Care Orders, Care Plans and Contact

Which order?

Crossing the threshold is just the first step in care proceedings. The next question is which order, if any, should be made. In many cases, there is little or no dispute about the threshold – the key question is to decide where the child's future lies.

How does the court approach this task? The legal principles are clear:

- The child's welfare is paramount (s1 CA89).

- The welfare checklist applies (s1(3) CA89).

- The court must consider the full range of its powers, not just the orders sought by the parties (s1(3)(g) CA89).

- The court must not make any order unless it is better for the child than making no order at all (s1(5) CA89).

- The parties' human rights are engaged, especially Article 8 (respect for private and family life).

- Any interference with family life must be proportionate.

Proportionality is key; the court must go as far as necessary to protect the child, but no further. The stronger the order, the greater the justification required. This idea was succinctly put by Lady Hale: 'a court can only separate a child from her parents if satisfied that it is necessary to do so, that nothing else will do.'[1] This principle was endorsed by all

---

1   *Re B (A Child)* [2013] UKSC 33 (Supreme Court) at paragraph 145.

the Supreme Court Justices, although Lady Hale disagreed with her colleagues on its application to the facts of the case. Interestingly, the majority approved the highest level of interference with Article 8 rights (care order and placement order for adoption) on facts at the lower level of the child protection spectrum (the likelihood of future emotional and psychological harm).

Court orders
Understanding the options

The appropriate order flows from the assessment of the child's best interests and the plan devised following assessments before and during proceedings. You can only recommend an order to the court if you understand the nature and effect of all the legal options available, including private[2] as well as public law orders, while not overlooking the possibility of no order at all.

Care orders and supervision orders

Care (CO) and supervision orders (SO) can only be made if the threshold is crossed. The grounds, standard of proof and degree of evidence required are exactly the same for the two orders, but their characteristics could hardly be more different.[3] In practice, local authorities rarely apply for SOs; they are generally made in cases which started as applications for COs but which move on in the course of proceedings.

PR

A CO confers parental responsibility (PR) on the local authority. The parents do not lose their PR but the authority can overrule them where necessary to safeguard or promote the child's welfare,[4] so the local authority has a 'senior partner' role. Under a CO the local authority decides where the child lives and it can change the child's placement without returning to court, although of course proper administrative

---

2   s1(3)(g) CA89. For more information on private law orders, see Chapters 4–6.
3   See Appendix 7 for an 'at a glance' summary of similarities and differences between COs and SOs.
4   s33(3) and (4) CA89.

procedures must be followed. By making a CO, the court entrusts the child's future to the local authority.

A SO does not give the local authority PR; its role is to 'advise, assist and befriend' the child.[5] So the parents, not the authority, decide where the child lives and the authority has no power to remove him. If removal becomes necessary, it is back to square one with police protection, an EPO or fresh care proceedings. The court cannot simply 'scale up' a SO to a CO, although it can on application vary a CO down to a SO.[6]

DURATION

A CO lasts until the child turns 18 unless the court discharges it[7] or makes another order (such as an order for residence, special guardianship or adoption) which automatically ends it. Ending the CO early requires an application and a court decision.

In contrast, a SO lasts for up to one year, with a possibility of extension on application to the court for up to three years in total.[8] If there is no application to extend it, the SO simply fades away. In practice, SOs are rarely extended; either matters improve making a further order unnecessary, or the SO proves insufficient so a different response – perhaps a CO – is needed.

Thus, a CO continues unless the court ends it; a SO ends unless the court extends it.

The contrast between the two orders is thrown into sharp relief when the proposal is to place the child at home. This could be done under a CO or SO. Which should it be? Factors to consider include:

- Does the local authority need PR? If so, only a CO will suffice.

- Is it appropriate for the authority to have power to remove the child without returning to court? If so, only a CO will suffice, but this is a draconian power so would need clear justification.

- How long should the order last? If the maximum three years of a SO is inadequate, a CO is needed.

- Which order is proportionate?

---

5   s35(1)(a) CA89.
6   s39(4) CA89.
7   s39(1) CA89.
8   Schedule 3 paragraph 6 CA89.

Placement at home under a CO can seem anomalous: it seems contradictory to entrust the parents with the child's day-to-day care yet still retain the ultimate power to remove him by administrative action without returning to court. Furthermore, apart from social work visits, the practical care and control is left to the parents, yet the local authority is legally responsible. Ultimately, proportionality is the key – the court should make the least interventionist order consistent with the child's needs. In most cases this will be a SO unless there is a good reason to the contrary. If your plan is to leave or place the child at home, this should be your starting point.

Care plan

By making a CO, the court entrusts the child's future to the local authority. Not surprisingly, it needs to see a care plan first. The authority has a statutory obligation[9] to file a care plan; indeed, it is one of the documents be filed at court at the very outset of proceedings and must be updated throughout. The plan details key elements of the authority's proposals for the child's future including the crucial elements of placement and contact. Plans must be made for each child individually; siblings may have similar plans but they must not be unthinkingly duplicated.

The court must[10] consider the care plan and cannot make a CO until it has done so. The proposals for placement and contact form part of its assessment of the available options and its decision as to which order (if any) to make.

But the court cannot dictate the care plan. The division of roles is clear: the court decides whether or not to make a CO, the local authority decides how it will put a CO into effect. Once a CO is made, the court has no further role unless and until another application is made in respect of the child.

What if the court does not like the care plan proposed? In most cases, the matter is resolved by discussion. As Wall LJ said:

---

9   s31A CA89.
10   s31(3A) CA89. An amendment made by the Children and Families Act 2014 limits the court's obligation to the placement and contact elements of the plan.

Care proceedings are only quasi-adversarial. There is a powerful inquisitorial element. But above all, they are proceedings in which the court and the local authority should both be striving to achieve an order which is in the best interests of the child. There needs to be mutual respect and understanding for the different role and perspective which each has in the process. We repeat: the shared objective should be to achieve a result which is in the best interests of the child... In the overwhelming majority of cases in which there is a disagreement between the local authority and the court over a child's care plan, that disagreement is resolved by careful reconsideration on both sides. In our experience, as a consequence, such disagreements are extremely rare. That is as it should be. It is patently not in the interests of the already disadvantaged children involved in care proceedings for there to be a stand-off between the court and the local authority, the result of which, as here, is still further delay in resolving the children's future placements.[11]

But if judicial pressure does not persuade the authority to change its mind, the court has few options. In the past, courts could consider making interim care orders instead of a final order to wait for issues to become clearer; for example to adjourn to see whether parents stay free of drugs. That option is now likely to be severely limited by the imperative to complete cases swiftly other than in wholly exceptional circumstances. The court is therefore likely to be limited to granting or refusing orders within its repertoire.

Case Studies: Court's choice of orders

The local authority seeks a CO for Amir with a plan for long-term fostering. The judge agrees he cannot go home but takes the view that Amir should live with his grandmother. He can achieve this by making an order for residence or special guardianship order to the grandmother instead of a CO.

The local authority seeks a CO and plans to place Boris in foster care with contact to his mother twice a year. The court agrees that Boris needs to be in care, but considers that contact should be monthly. The court can achieve this by making a contact order alongside the CO.

---

11   *Re S & W* [2007] EWCA Civ 232 (Court of Appeal) at paragraphs 35–38.

Carla has remained at home during the proceedings, which are based on neglect, but the authority seeks a CO and plans a foster placement. The judge concludes that although the threshold is crossed, removing Carla would be disproportionate – the harm caused by removing her would outweigh the harm at home, which could be mitigated by the provision of services. He can achieve this by making a SO instead of a CO.

The local authority plan to rehabilitate Darius to his parents' care. The judge believes they pose too great a risk to Darius and he should remain in foster care. There are no suitable friend or family carers. The judge has a problem: there are no orders available to him to achieve his objective. Balcombe LJ discussed just this situation:

> the judge is therefore faced with the dilemma...that, if he makes a care order, the local authority may implement a care plan which he or she may take the view is not in the child or children's best interests. On the other hand, if he makes no order, he may be leaving the child in the care of a wholly irresponsible, and indeed wholly inappropriate parent. It seems to me that, regrettable though it may seem, the only course he may take is to choose what he considers to be the lesser of two evils...[12]

Care plan – placement options

Before a final hearing in care proceedings, the local authority must be ready with its proposals for the child having reasoned through the various options available. It can be a tall order to comply with tight court timetables, especially in a case which begins as an emergency involving a family previously unknown to the authorities. Sound, focused work is essential.

Assessments of several options must be undertaken at the same time; there is no time to work through the options one by one. This gave rise to the terms 'twin-track' or 'parallel' planning, a practice given judicial approval by Bracewell J.[13] It must be clearly explained to the family that considering several options does not pre-empt the final decision and the fact that the possibility of adoption is being explored does not mean that rehabilitation has already been ruled out. It can sometimes be

---

12   *Re S and D (Children: Powers of Court)* [1995] 2FLR 456 (Court of Appeal) pages 634D–635C.

13   *Re D & K (Care plan: twin track planning)* [1999] 2FLR 872 (High Court).

difficult for families to believe that the authority is doing anything other than going through the motions before reaching a foregone conclusion.

Parallel planning is not to be confused with 'concurrent planning', a term which refers to a specific scheme whereby the child is placed with carers who will adopt the child if rehabilitation or other options are ruled out. Similarly, fostering for adoption has had renewed government impetus and regulations have been changed to allow a person approved as an adopter to be temporarily approved as a foster carer for a named child without separate fostering assessment and approval.[14] The idea is that the child will have more stability by being placed at the interim stage in a placement which will become permanent if other options fail.

HIERARCHY OF PLACEMENT

The proportionality principle of the least interference in family life consistent with the child's welfare is reflected in a statutory presumption for placement.[15] Unless it is not consistent with his welfare, a looked after child (in care or accommodated) must be placed with a parent, other person with PR or a person who had a residence order before any CO was made. If this is not possible, the authority must make 'the most appropriate placement available',[16] but preference must be given to friends or family approved as foster carers before placing with unrelated foster carers or other options. Adoption is the last resort.

Although there is a clear hierarchy of placement, McFarlane LJ[17] has counselled against the courts using a linear approach to identifying the appropriate order. The tendency is to look at each option individually, starting with the least interventionist and progressing up the scale as each is eliminated because of some deficiency in that option. He argued that this creates a bias towards the most draconian option which is then chosen because it is the only one left, without looking at its own de-merits. Instead, he counselled a 'global, holistic evaluation of each of the options'. He explained:

> what is required is a balancing exercise in which each option is
> evaluated to the degree of detail necessary to analyse and weigh its

---

14   Regulation 25A Care Planning, Placement and Case Review (England) Regulations 2010, in force since July 2013.

15   s22C(2) CA89.

16   s22C(5)–(7) CA89.

17   *G (A Child)* [2013] EWCA Civ 965 (Court of Appeal) at paragraphs 49–51.

own internal positives and negatives and each option is then compared, side by side, against the competing option or options.[18]

It is also useful to remember Balcombe LJ's realistic assessment: 'There is very rarely a right answer in relation to children – it is usually a case of trying to decide which is the less wrong one.'[19]

The Court of Appeal has indicated[20] that it demands from local authorities a rigorous analysis of all available options and fully reasoned recommendations, with particular justification if adoption is recommended. You need to be ready for a probing examination by the court of your reasoning.

PARENTS FIRST

The presumption that a child should live with his parents, or one of them, can cause particular tensions in re-constituted families where there are half-siblings. There can be a conflict between the siblings' need to stay together and the presumption that, in general, children should be with their parents. It is a question of welfare, to be decided on the facts of each case. In one case[21] the grandmother wanted to care for all three half-siblings together, whereas the plan was to place the two eldest with her and the youngest with his father. The Court of Appeal considered whether there were any compelling factors to override the presumption of placement with a parent and found that this was not a case where the value of the sibling bond outweighed that presumption. The Supreme Court[22] has emphasised that the key question is one of welfare, not rights. However, sometimes the court has the dilemma of resolving cases where the welfare of each of the children is paramount but their needs conflict.

If a child is to be placed at home under a CO, detailed regulations[23] must be followed and the placement agreement must contain information

---

18 *Re G* at paragraph 54.
19 *Re S and D (Children: Powers of Court)* [1995] 2FLR 456 (Court of Appeal) page 635.
20 *Re B-S (Children)* [2013] EWCA 1146 (Court of Appeal); see Chapter 16 for more information on this case.
21 *Re D (Care: Natural Parent Presumption)* [1999] 1FLR 134 (Court of Appeal).
22 *B (A Child)* [2009] UKSC 5 (Supreme Court).
23 Care Planning, Placement and Case Review (England) Regulations 2010 SI 2010/959. Lengthy statutory guidance is also available in Volume 2 Children Act 1989 Guidance and Regulations, DCSF March 2010.

including details of the support and services to be provided, the parents' obligation to keep the authority informed of any changed circumstances, and the circumstances in which the placement will be terminated.

FAMILY PLACEMENTS

If parents cannot care for the child, the next option to consider is a placement with friends or family or other people connected with the child. This is often referred to as 'kinship care' but this term is not a legal one and does not connote any particular legal status.

Family Group Conferences have no statutory status but can be very helpful in identifying options for placement or support within the child's existing network.[24] No-one should be automatically ruled out. For example, in a case[25] where the children's father killed their mother, the judge confirmed that there is no presumption against a perpetrator's family and each case must be considered individually (in that case the paternal grandparents took on the children's care).

'Family' is not limited to blood relationships, confirmed by the Court of Appeal in a case[26] where the proposed 'family' member was the mother's foster sister – that was not a problem, but delay was, as the potential carer only came forward at the final care hearing. Wall LJ said the local authority 'plainly should have called a family group conference', adding 'it is equally plain that KB should have put herself forward at a much earlier stage'. As he put it:

> The moral of the case, yet again, is that the available options for a child should be teased out as early as possible, and if a family member wishes to be considered to care for a child, he or she should come forward at the earliest possible opportunity.[27]

In some families, there may be several potential carers and it can be impossible to carry out a full assessment on every one, so the practice has developed of undertaking a 'viability assessment' to see whether proceeding to a full assessment is justified. Such assessments must be

---

24   For an explanation of Family Group Conferences see Appendix C of the Statutory Guidance on Family and Friends Care. *R (on the application of X)* v. *London Borough of Tower Hamlets* [2013] EWHC 480 (Admin) (High Court).
25   *In the Matter of A and B* [2010] EWHC 3824 (High Court).
26   *G & B (Children)* [2007] EWCA Civ 358 (Court of Appeal).
27   *Re G & B* at paragraph 42.

carried out professionally and fairly, unlike one which the court[28] found to be flawed and inadequate to the extent that it ordered a thorough independent assessment in its place.

As always, procedures must be fair. In one case,[29] an authority assessed the aunt and uncle of a boy subject to care proceedings. The assessment was positive save for the need for them to move away to avoid the risk of bumping into the family. Unfortunately, a move was not possible. The couple were not given a copy of the report and no-one discussed with them the possibility of engaging with the court process until the day before the final hearing when they were told to come to court (which proved impossible due to work commitments). The Court of Appeal found the process was unfair. McFarlane LJ said his concern was:

> ...above all the need for A's welfare to be determined by a process which accorded to the requirements of a fair trial. This was a watershed decision in A's life; it would be hard to underestimate the importance of it or the impact of it upon his future. It was therefore necessary for a procedurally sound approach to be applied.[30]

The care and placement orders which had been made were overturned and the case went back for re-hearing, building in more delay, expense and stress for all concerned.

If a placement with family or friends is approved, the appropriate legal order must be identified, according to all the circumstances of the case. The options are:

- as foster carers under a CO
- an order for residence
- a special guardianship order
- adoption.

---

28   Re M-H (Assessment: Father of half brother) [2006] EWCA Civ 1864 (Court of Appeal).
29   P (Children) [2012] EWCA Civ 401.
30   At paragraph 18.

If the child is 'looked after', related or family carers must be assessed and approved as local authority foster carers,[31] albeit under a specific approval for a named child. Temporary approval for up to 16 weeks is possible while an assessment is undertaken. They are entitled to fostering allowances and several authorities have had their policy of paying related carers substantially less than other carers quashed as unlawful and discriminatory.[32]

The government has issued detailed authoritative guidance[33] on placement with friends and family. As it was issued under s7 LASSA 1970, it must be followed unless there is a good reason not to do so.

Contact

Contact is a key element in a care plan. It is of course a wide term covering the whole spectrum from staying contact at one end to letter box contact at the other. Contact in the context of COs is governed by s34 CA89, not s8. Before it can make a CO, the court must consider contact arrangements and invite the parties to comment on them.[34]

Contact should be an integral part of the plan, not an afterthought as it sometimes appears to be. The child's relationships and contact needs should form part of the holistic assessment of her best interests. The reasons for and purpose of contact should be analysed to inform recommendations as to the nature and level of contact between the child and each relevant person, remembering that the child may need contact with each parent, grandparents, siblings, extended family members, former foster carers or any number of other people. Each relationship needs to be considered separately but without forgetting the whole picture – it is hardly in the child's interests to be passed around like a parcel from one contact visit to the next.

---

31   Assessment and approval is governed by the Fostering Services (England) Regulations 2011. For more information on fostering services, including the assessment and approval process see also Statutory Guidance for Fostering Services 2011 and National Minimum Standards for Fostering Services.

32   See for example *R (on the application of X)* v. *London Borough of Tower Hamlets* [2013] EWHC 480 (Admin) (High Court).

33   Department for Education (2010) *Family and Friends Care: Statutory Guidance for Local Authorities.* Available at www.education.gov.uk/aboutdfe/statutory/g00200350/family-carers-2011, accessed on 30 March 2014.

34   s34(11) CA89.

Contact must also be seen in the context of the child's placement; indeed, the two factors are often intertwined. Sometimes contact needs have to be sacrificed to meet more important placement needs, although this should never be lightly done; restrictions on contact may constitute a breach of Article 8 rights, so must always be justifiable and proportionate.

Although the legal basis for contact with a child in care is different from private law contact, many of the considerations are the same and the aide-memoire in Appendix 3 applies equally to both.

The statutory presumption

The local authority has a statutory duty[35] to allow a child in care 'reasonable contact' with his parents, including a father without PR, guardians or special guardians, step-parents with PR and anyone who had an order for residence which was discharged by the CO.

What is 'reasonable'? This depends on all the circumstances of the case. The local authority must exercise its discretion properly and fairly, taking relevant considerations into account and ignoring irrelevant factors. As for any decision about a looked after child, there is a statutory obligation[36] to consult relevant people (including the parents and child) and to give their views due consideration. This is reinforced by the human rights requirements for fairness in all procedures.

The child's best interests are the key consideration – contact should not be dictated by the availability of premises, supervisors or other resource issues. Nor should a formulaic response be adopted – a particular level of contact should not be suggested simply because that is the authority's usual practice for children of that age. The rationale for and reasonableness of the decision should be clearly demonstrable and documented on the file. If not, the authority risks challenges to increase contact or proceedings for breaches of human rights.

'Reasonable' is a flexible word, but it would be stretching it too far to argue that it includes no contact at all. If contact is to be severely restricted or denied, the local authority must seek an order under s34(4) CA89 giving it permission to refuse contact.

---

35   s34(1) CA89.
36   s22(4) CA89.

Contact with others

As a child in care is a 'looked after' child, the authority has a statutory duty[37] 'unless it is not practicable or consistent with his welfare' to 'endeavour to promote' contact between the child and his parents, anyone else with PR and, in a phrase striking for its breadth, 'any relative, friend or other person connected with him'. Contact with the child's parents is often such a difficult and pressing issue that it can be easy to overlook other relationships that may be just as important for the child, including contact with siblings.

Contact orders

Rather than leaving contact to the local authority's discretion, the court has power to make a defined contact order. This can be made at the same time as the CO or on a separate application later. The court can make a contact order[38] of its own motion, or application can be made by the local authority or child, anyone with a statutory presumption of reasonable contact, or anyone else with the court's permission. The court can include such conditions[39] as it thinks appropriate in any contact order, if necessary prescribing the precise details of when, where and how contact should take place.

Contact proposals form an important part of the local authority's care plan, but it is for the court to decide. The court is not bound by the local authority's care plan and can make a contact order of its own motion, even one which is incompatible with the plan if it is in the child's best interests.[40] This will inevitably require the authority to adjust the care plan.

There must be no doubt that a contact order is binding and must be complied with, however much the local authority or its agents disagree with it. In a case where the local authority foster father was hostile to the children's father and sabotaged contact, it was made clear by the Court of Appeal[41] that the court has power to attach a penal notice to a contact order. If the order is not complied with, it is contempt of court.

---

37   Schedule 1 paragraph 15 CA89.
38   s34(2), (3) and (5) CA89.
39   s34(7) CA89.
40   *Berkshire CC* v. *B* [1997] 1FLR 171 (High Court).
41   *P-B (Children)* [2009] EWCA Civ 143 (Court of Appeal).

There could be committal proceedings whereby the officer responsible for the order – or conceivably the Director of Children's Services – could be sent to prison.

Refusing contact

The local authority can refuse contact to anyone who has neither a statutory presumption nor a court order in his favour, provided that it is a reasonable exercise of its discretion and the decision is taken properly.

However, the local authority cannot simply refuse contact to someone who has a statutory right to reasonable contact; it needs court permission to do so. The court can, on application by the local authority or the child or of its own motion, make an order under s34(4) CA89 authorising the authority to refuse contact between the child and a named person. If you are clear from the outset that an individual should not have contact, seek a s34(4) CA89 order at the same time as the CO to avoid having to make a separate application to court later.

A s34(4) order is not an order forbidding contact (which is possible, albeit highly exceptional). Instead, as Munby J explained:

> an order under section 34(4) only 'authorises' the local authority to refuse to allow contact. It does not forbid such contact and a local authority, even if clothed with authority under section 34(4), is, of course, under a continuing duty to keep matters under review and to allow contact to resume as soon as it is safe and appropriate to do so.[42]

So the power to refuse contact must be exercised properly, reasonably and fairly with an eye to human rights and it must be kept under review. As always, decisions and the reasons for them should be clearly recorded on the file.

Emergencies

In an emergency, the local authority can suspend contact which it is otherwise bound to grant (either under the statutory presumption or an order) for up to seven days where necessary to safeguard or promote

---

42   *Re K* [2008] EWHC 540 (Fam) at paragraph 29.

the child's welfare.[43] Regulations[44] detail procedural requirements which include serving written notice on:

- the child (unless inappropriate given his age and understanding)
- parents
- others with PR
- anyone whose order for residence was discharged by the CO
- the child's Independent Reviewing Officer (IRO)
- anyone else the authority considers relevant.

The notice must specify:

- the decision
- the reasons for the decision
- its duration
- the date it was taken
- remedies in case of dissatisfaction.

If the problem is not resolved within the seven-day maximum period of suspension, the authority must apply to court for an order authorising continued refusal of contact.

Interim refusal

In some cases, contact is not safe even during the interim phases of proceedings. Needless to say, refusing contact when by definition the threshold criteria are yet to be adjudicated is a major decision with significant implications for the rest of the case. If contact is refused at an interim stage, this inevitably affects the relationship between parent and child and impacts assessments; for example, the Guardian may have no opportunity to observe parents and child together. The human rights considerations are obvious. However, you should never shy away from seeking such an order where the child's safety demands it.

The Nottingham case, which started with the unlawful removal of a newborn baby,[45] continued into care proceedings where a residential

---

43   s34(6) CA89.
44   Care Planning, Placement and Case Review (England) Regulations 2010, reg 8.
45   See Chapter 10.

assessment broke down disastrously. The authority sought permission to refuse contact at an interim stage. Munby J said:

> It is a very drastic thing indeed to interfere with a young mother's contact with her newborn baby, and his contact with her, particularly at a time when 'threshold' (see section 31(2) of the Act) is yet to be established. It is an even more drastic thing to deny contact altogether, and something which lies at the very extremities of the court's powers. Extraordinarily compelling reasons must be shown to justify an order under section 34(4) at this early stage in the proceedings.[46]

In that case the circumstances were so extreme that the baby's safety imperatively demanded such an order, to last to the next hearing when it would be reviewed.

Contact where the plan is adoption

If the care plan is adoption, the local authority must seek a placement order under the Adoption and Children Act 2002, wherever possible at the same time as the CO. The court must consider contact within the placement order application.[47]

Points for practice

1. Carrying out all necessary steps in time requires strong organisation and clear thinking.

2. Proportionality is key.

3. Placement with unrelated carers is only appropriate if rehabilitation to parents or family placement are unsuitable.

4. Have a clear understanding of the nature and effect of the different orders available. Fit the order to the case; never try to make the case fit the order.

5. If a child is to remain at home, start with a presumption of a SO and only seek a CO if you have clear reasons to justify it.

---

46   *Re K* [2008] EWHC 540 (Fam) (High Court) at paragraph 25.
47   For more information about adoption and placement orders see Chapter 16.

6. If you ask the court to entrust a child to your authority's care, you owe it to the court and the child to present a carefully drawn up, realistic care plan.

7. Contact is an integral part of a care plan. Ensure your plans are carefully reasoned.

8. Contact should not be refused lightly but do not shy away from an application if it is necessary to protect the child.

Chapter 14

Care Plans

Obtaining a care order (CO) is the not the end of the story. Courts, Guardians and lawyers leave the stage unless another application is made. The local authority, parents and child then begin a new chapter in which legal obligations are every bit as important, albeit not under the spotlight of the court.

Looked after children

The local authority has duties[1] to all looked after children, whether they are in care or voluntarily accommodated, not just to place them but to take care of them and promote their welfare in all other respects. To achieve this, all looked after children must have a care plan which must be kept under regular review. Detailed government guidance and regulations apply.[2]

Care plans must include:

- the permanence plan (long-term planning including timescales)

- details of the placement and why it was chosen

- any court orders

- the name of the Independent Reviewing Officer (IRO)

- contact with parents and other relevant adults

- contact with siblings

- personal health plan

---

1   s22 A and B CA89.
2   Care Planning, Placement and Case Review (England) Regulations 2010.

- personal education plan
- contingency plan, a plan B in case plan A is not achievable.

Fostered children also have a placement plan to help the carer look after the child appropriately.

Placement plans include information about:

- the child's family
- race, religion and religious practice, cultural and linguistic heritage
- disabilities or other special needs
- circumstances leading to placement
- long-term plan and timescale
- anticipated duration and objectives of placement
- who has authority to take particular decisions for the child (most day-to-day decisions should be delegated to the carer).[3]

As looked after children approach adulthood, there must also be a pathway plan which, as the name suggests, is to prepare the way towards moving to independence. The authority's duty to looked after children does not end at 18; there are ongoing statutory duties to young people after they leave care or accommodation.

Consultation

Parents retain their PR even when a child is under a care order and have full PR if he is accommodated. They and the child have a right to be informed and consulted about all decisions, especially about significant developments or changes.

In *Re G*,[4] children were rehabilitated to their parents' care in accordance with the care plan. Two years later the social workers became concerned about the children's care. A meeting, which did not involve

---

3   The Care Planning, Placement and Case Review (England) Regulations 2010 as amended by the Care Planning, Placement and Case Review and Fostering Services (Miscellaneous Amendments) Regulations 2013.

4   *Re G (Care: Challenge to Local Authority's Decision)* [2003] EWHC 551 (High Court).

the parents, decided to remove the children from home. Unsurprisingly, the parents took the matter to court. Munby J held:

> The fact that a local authority has parental responsibility for children pursuant to s33(3)(a) of the Children Act 1989 does not entitle it to take decisions about children without reference to, or over the heads of the children's parents. A local authority, even if clothed with the authority of a care order, is not entitled to make significant changes in the care plan, or to change the arrangements under which the children are living, let alone to remove the children from home if they are living with their parents, without properly involving the parents in the decision-making process and without giving the parents a proper opportunity to make their case before a decision is made. After all, the fact that the local authority also has parental responsibility does not deprive the parents of their parental responsibility.

The authority had forgotten the fundamental principles of CA89 and it had breached the family's Article 8 rights. The duty to act fairly applies to all dealings with children and their families from the very first contact to the very last.

Does this mean that even the most abusive and undeserving parents must always be fully informed and involved? The presumption is that they must, although for example there is a provision[5] allowing the authority to withhold the placement address of a child in care (but not an accommodated child).

In an extreme case, the court can absolve the local authority from the responsibilities it would otherwise have. In one case,[6] a 13-year-old girl was desperate that her father (who was serving a long sentence for raping her) should not be informed or consulted about her future. She had already successfully applied to have his PR discharged. The High Court made a declaration absolving the local authority from any obligation to consult him: her rights prevailed over those of her father. The local authority was directed to provide him with limited annual information on her general well-being and progress and to inform him only of very significant events such as life-threatening illness or proposed adoption.

---

5   Schedule 2 paragraph 15(4) CA89.
6   *Re C (Care: Consultation with Parents Not in Child's Best Interests)* [2005] EWHC 3390 (High Court).

It is worth bearing this possibility in mind. If you have a case extreme enough to justify such an order, raise the matter with your lawyers. It may be best to deal with the issue during the care proceedings, rather than having to return to court later.

The child's role

The voice of the child must be heard in care planning. Her views must be sought and taken into account. But this does not mean that her wishes must be followed; the duty is to serve her best interests.

In one case[7] a troubled teenager from London was placed under an ICO in a children's home in Devon, where she was doing well. A psychiatrist recommended she should remain there until she was 16. The local authority's placement panel decided instead to return her to London. This decision was reached without reading reports or consulting the girl's mother, Children's Guardian or the children's home. The court found the process was fundamentally defective; such a significant decision should not be taken without reading the papers and consulting relevant people. The mother's human rights had been breached, and the care plan would expose the child to further harm. Munby J observed that the authority had placed too much weight on the wishes of an out-of-control and wayward teenager set on self-destruction and had too much regard for 'government inspired targets and expressions of ministerial view'. The authority maintained it was in the right, but wisely decided to back down graciously to move things forward – if it had not done so, judicial review was likely.

Reviews

Reviews are to oversee the implementation of the care plan, monitor progress and to take decisions to make any necessary changes. Review meetings must be held within prescribed maximum intervals:

- first review within 20 days of the child first becoming looked after
- second review within three months of the first

---

7   *Re X, London Borough of Barnet v. Y and X* [2006] 2FLR 998 (High Court).

- third and subsequent reviews within six months of the previous review.

These are maximum timescales and meetings should be held as often as necessary. In fact each child's case should be under constant review; it is a process, not an event. Furthermore, simply holding meetings in accordance with the regulatory timetable does not of itself fulfil the authority's duty or protect it from liability. It is not a question of ticking boxes; meetings must be effective. A child's human rights can still be breached regardless of an immaculate list of review meetings.

The court's role

Accommodated children have no court involvement in their lives, but the court's role in care planning is limited even for a child in care. The court must consider the proposed care plan before making the CO but once the order is made, its role ends. Unless and until another application is made (perhaps for contact or discharge of the CO) the court has no way of knowing whether the beautifully constructed care plan presented to it is actually put into effect.

Not surprisingly, judges have often been frustrated that they cannot ensure that the orders they make are properly implemented. At one stage, the Court of Appeal invented a concept of 'starred milestones', which were elements in the care plan so key that if they were not implemented then the case had to be brought back to court. But the House of Lords[8] 'respectfully but emphatically' found that the Court of Appeal had taken judicial creativity too far. Going back to first principles, Lord Nicholls reminded us: 'Interpretation of statute is a matter for the courts; the enactment of statutes and amendment of statutes are matters for Parliament.'

---

8   *Re S (Minors) (Care Order: Implementation of Care Plan); Re W (Minors) (Care Order: Adequacy of Care Plan)* [2002] 1FLR 815 (House of Lords).

So the matter fell to Parliament. The response[9] was the creation of the role of IRO by amending s26 CA89, fleshed out by detailed statutory guidance in the form of the *IRO Handbook*.[10]

Every looked after child must have an IRO, a qualified and experienced social worker whose role is to monitor how well the local authority does its job as a corporate parent, to ensure plans meet the child's needs and are implemented and that the child's voice is heard. IROs have a key role in the review process including chairing reviews. The local authority must inform the IRO of any changes, or any failure to implement review decisions.

IROs also have a strategic role within the authority. The IRO service manager should deliver an annual report to the lead member for Children's Services identifying good practice and areas for improvement, highlighting any matters needing urgent attention.

IROs are independent of line management or budgetary responsibility for children's cases but they remain within the local authority. This may seem an unhappy compromise; they are neither truly within nor outside the local authority. They cannot actually make any decisions or implement any action for the child, nor are they truly independent inspectors.

What can IROs do?

If there is a problem in a child's care plan the IRO must take the matter up within the local authority – all the way to chief executive level if necessary. If that does not work and the IRO considers that the child's human rights may be being breached he should:

- help a competent child who wants to take a case to court herself to get appropriate legal advice; or

- see if a suitable adult (possibly, but not necessarily, a parent or carer) is willing to pursue a case on the child's behalf; or

---

9   Introduced by the Adoption and Children Act 2002, further amended by Children and Young Persons Act 2008.

10   DCSF (2010) IRO *Handbook: Statutory guidance for independent reviewing officers and local authorities on their functions in relation to case management and review for looked after children.* Available at https://www.gov.uk/government/publications/independent-reviewing-officers-handbook, accessed on 2 April 2014.

- if no-one else is available, refer the matter to CAFCASS which decides whether to take a case to court. An application could be under CA89 (for instance for contact or discharge of a CO), a free-standing application for breach of human rights or for judicial review.

Is the system working?

Ofsted reviewed the effectiveness of IROs. The report[11] was not encouraging. One key finding stated: 'In nearly all authorities, review recommendations and the subsequent monitoring of progress by IROs were not consistently rigorous, leading to poor planning for children's futures and unnecessary delay in some children's cases.' Many IROs had excessive workloads; not surprisingly this compromised their effectiveness.

The sanction of legal action by CAFCASS is used remarkably rarely: between 2007 and 2011 there were only eight cases referred by IROs nationally. It is difficult to believe that only eight cases warranted referral.

Over the years, the law reports have recounted many cases of children drifting in care and being failed by the system. In one case, the IRO was described by the High Court[12] as 'supine and ineffective'.

Nor did an IRO help two boys looked after in Lancashire.[13] They were removed from home in 1999 when they were aged only two years and six months respectively. It was the start of an appalling catalogue of failure. In 2001 they were freed for adoption,[14] but they were never adopted. Instead, one boy moved 77 times including 12 main placements, the other 96 times with 16 main placements. They were physically and sexually abused in two foster homes. They had no contact with their

11 Ofsted (7 June 2013) *Independent Reviewing Officers: Taking up the Challenge?* Available at www.ofsted.gov.uk/resources/independent-reviewing-officers-taking-challenge, accessed on 30 March 2014.
12 *S (A Child Acting by the Official Solicitor)* v. *Rochdale Metropolitan Borough Council and the Independent Reviewing Officer* [2008] EWHC 3283 (Fam) (High Court).
13 *A and S* v. *Lancashire County Council* [2012] EWHC 1689 (Fam) (High Court).
14 When a child was freed for adoption under the Adoption Act 1976 (no longer in force), all legal relationships with the birth family were extinguished. Children freed for adoption but never adopted are often described as 'legal orphans'. There remains a small number of children under this unenviable legal status. Their cases should be urgently reviewed.

family despite their requests. From 1999 to 2011 there were 35 reviews, 16 of which were chaired by the IRO, none of which managed to move their cases on.

Not only were the children failed by the local authority, the IRO himself acknowledged that, although he was the only independent person in a position to protect the boys' rights, he had not done so and had not addressed or monitored the social workers' repeated failures (including assurances that proceedings to revoke the freeing order had been commenced when they had not). The case report contains long extracts of the IRO's honest and heartfelt account of his own failings and the difficulties of his role, including an excessive case load, inadequate supervision and lack of training and legal advice.

The court found that the boys' human rights had been breached. The local authority was liable under Article 3 (protection from torture or inhuman or degrading treatment) in respect of the abuse in the foster homes. There were also breaches of Article 6 (right to a fair trial) for the inadequate monitoring processes and failure to take the case back to court as well as a breach of Article 8 (respect for family life) in failing to provide a stable home or to re-establish contact with the birth family. But those breaches were not just the responsibility of the local authority – the IRO himself was also found responsible. A claim for substantial damages will follow but nothing can repair the harm done to two boys who were supposed to have been 'looked after'.

The judge took the opportunity to offer a lengthy analysis of the genesis and details of the IRO role and the difficulties in its implementation. He sent a copy of his judgment to the Children's Commissioner and the President of the Family Division. He reminded us:

> ... s11 of the 2008 Act includes a power to confer the delivery of IRO services on a national body, outside the control of local authorities, if the measures to strengthen the IRO function do not now contribute to a significant improvement in outcomes for looked after children.[15]

Time will tell if further amendments will be introduced, taking the IRO role out of local authorities and into a truly independent body.

---

15   *Re A and S* at paragraph 196.

Legal options

There are various legal options if a care plan is not implemented or parents or child are unhappy, for example:

- an application for a contact order to increase contact, or change its nature. This is not limited to contact between parents and children but could involve others such as siblings or grandparents

- an application for judicial review if decisions are not taken properly, following the correct law and procedures, are unlawful or unreasonable

- a free-standing human rights application for a declaration, injunction or damages

- an application to discharge the CO or for another order which has the same effect (order for residence or special guardianship order).

Case Studies: Challenges to care plans

Jackie is in care. The care plan was for services to be provided to rehabilitate her to her mother's care. This has not happened and Jackie wants to go home. Jackie, or someone on her behalf, could apply under s39 CA89 for the care order to be discharged. (Jackie's mother could also apply; indeed, she might be the more appropriate applicant.)

Keith is in care, placed separately from his sister Lily. He wants to see her more often. The local authority fails to increase contact. Keith, or someone on his behalf, could apply for a contact order. In such an application, Lily's welfare is the court's paramount concern – if there is a conflict, her interests supersede Keith's.

Michael is a teenager in care. He can be threatening, rude and unco-operative. He is not invited to reviews because of his disruptive behaviour. A review decides to change his placement and reduce contact to his parents. Michael could argue that his human rights were breached by failing to involve and consult him about plans and seek an injunction to stop the changes and/or damages.

Nicola has multiple disabilities and challenging behaviour. An expert devises a care plan for her, including a specialist residential placement requiring joint health, social and educational funding. The funding cannot be agreed, so instead the authority proposes to place her in a less specialist unit, with piecemeal health and education services. Nicola's representative might seek a judicial review of the decision, arguing it is unreasonable, and asking the court to quash the decision and order a rethink.

Discharge of COs

The court can discharge a CO on an application made under s39 CA89 by the local authority, parent or child. The decision is made on the child's welfare which is paramount.

In *Re O*[16] the children were at home under a CO. The care plan included therapy and shared care with a foster family, neither of which were arranged. The social worker failed to visit for five months. Then, on the advice of a psychiatrist who had seriously inaccurate information, the authority decided to place the children in residential care with limited contact to mother. Unsurprisingly, the CO was discharged and replaced by a residence order and SO.

Penal notice

It must be remembered that obligations to looked after children are mandatory, not optional. The Court of Appeal[17] was furious when a seriously disabled child's case was brought to the court for a discharge of the CO. The application was surprising as she was nearly 18 at the time, but it soon became apparent that the main objective was just to bring the case before the court to force the authority to fulfil its statutory duty to draw up a pathway plan. The judge ordered such a plan and, trusting the authority to comply, dismissed the application for discharge. Once again, nothing was done.

The case went to the Court of Appeal to try to reinstate the application. Ward LJ said the case was 'lamentable, totally lamentable… the local authority have utterly neglected their duty in a way which is worthy of the highest condemnation and that is what I give it.'

Wall LJ's fury leaps off the page of the court report. The authority's failure was compounded by the fact that senior managers responsible for the decision were not in court to answer to it; instead the case was

16   *Re O (Care: Discharge of Care Order)* [1999] 2FLR 119 (High Court).
17   *S (A Child)* [2008] EWCA Civ 1140 (Court of Appeal).

handed to, as Wall LJ put it, 'some wretched social worker … put forward as a sacrificial lamb, as a victim to this court's anger and legitimate wrath.'

An order was made for a pathway plan to be filed and a penal notice was attached to the order. This meant that if the order was not obeyed, it was contempt of court and committal to prison could and, the court warned, probably would follow. And the person to be sent to prison would not be the social worker – it would be the Director of Children's Services. It is safe to assume that the order was rapidly complied with.

Cases should never, ever, be allowed to deteriorate to this level. Statutory duties are mandatory, not optional. Court orders must be obeyed and ultimately no-one, not even a Director, is above the law.

It is worth remembering Munby J's words:

> The State assumes a heavy burden when it takes a child into care… If the State is to justify removing children from their parents, it can only be on the basis that the State is going to provide a better quality of care than that from which the child has been rescued.[18]

Points for practice

1. Care plans must be properly and realistically drawn up.

2. Care planning is a duty, not an optional extra. The authority is liable if care plans are not properly implemented.

3. Processes must be fair. Parents and children must be consulted, informed and involved.

4. Holding review meetings and writing plans is not enough on its own. Cases must be actively monitored and action taken to ensure the child's needs are met.

---

18   *Re F; F v. Lambeth LB* [2001] 1FLR 217 (High Court) at paragraph 43.

Chapter 15

Adoption Fundamentals and Adoption by Consent

What is adoption?

Adoption is governed by the Adoption and Children Act 2002 (ACA).[1] It is the most far-reaching order a court can make in respect of a child as it represents the complete transfer of a child from one family to another. Its qualities of permanence and security make it the plan of choice, particularly for young children taken into care where rehabilitation and kinship care are ruled out, and for children relinquished by their parents. For that reason there has been a considerable government impetus to encourage and support[2] adoption and to reduce delays in the system.

Adoption is unique and quite unlike orders under CA89.[3] It:

- terminates birth parents' parental responsibility (PR)[4]

- transfers exclusive PR to the adopter(s) – the child is treated in law as if born to them[5]

- has life-long effect

- is irrevocable

---

1   Adoption and Children Act 2002. Stationery Office, London. Available at www. legislation.gov.uk/ukpga/2002/38/contents, accessed on 30 March 2014.
2   See, for example, the Adoption Support Fund to be rolled out by 2015.
3   For a summary of the contrast between adoption, special guardianship and residence orders, see Appendix 2.
4   s46(2)(a) ACA.
5   s67(1) ACA.

- ends the child's relationship with the entire birth family
- creates new relationships with the whole adoptive family.

Case Study: Effect of adoption

Chardonnay's mother is Debbie, who has an older son, Chandler. Chardonnay is made subject to a CO and placement order and is placed for adoption with Angela and Adam Smith, who already have an adopted son, Alexander. The moment the judge makes the adoption order:

- all court orders and rights under CA89 disappear
- Debbie loses her PR – she is no longer Chardonnay's mother
- Chandler is no longer her brother
- Angela and Adam become Chardonnay's parents with exclusive PR
- Alexander becomes Chardonnay's brother
- Angela and Adam can choose Chardonnay's name. She becomes Charlotte Smith
- Charlotte is now part of the Smith family for the rest of her life.

Debbie's and Adam's mothers both die. Each leaves all her money 'to my grandchildren'. Chardonnay/Charlotte inherits nothing from Debbie's mother, as she is no longer her granddaughter, but takes her share of Adam's mother's fortune.

Security

The unique characteristics of adoption make it secure. It lasts for life, not just to 18. The birth parents are no longer 'parents' and so cannot make applications to court to disrupt the placement. The adopters have exclusive PR so no-one, neither local authority nor birth parents, can interfere.

Irrevocability

Adoption is permanent and irrevocable, unlike orders under CA89. This has been emphasised, for example, in the case of the Webster[6] family who were not able to set aside adoption orders, even though later medical evidence raised doubts over the whole basis for the CO and adoption. Similarly a local authority[7] was unable to overturn an adoption order where the placement had irretrievably broken down and it seemed appropriate to be able to revive the child's previous identity. Courts preserve the principle that adoption is final.

Proportionality

The drastic effect of an adoption order means that a child and her adoptive family have permanence and security. But it is also clear that adoption orders are the most draconian in terms of human rights – there can be no greater interference with family life than terminating relationships forever. Clear justification is needed to show that adoption is proportionate, especially where it is opposed by the parents. As Lord Clarke said: 'Only in a case of necessity will an adoption order removing a child from his or her parents be proportionate.'[8] Make sure you address human rights issues whenever adoption is a possibility.

Contrast with other orders

A long-term placement could be achieved by way of adoption, long-term fostering, an order for residence or special guardianship. Black LJ[9] urged local authorities always to analyse and explain in written evidence or reports to court the reasoning behind the recommended legal option for a child. She summarised some differences between adoption and long-term fostering including:

- the adopters' permanent commitment giving adoption a different feel'

---

6   *Re W: Webster & Anor* v. *Norfolk County Council* [2009] EWCA Civ 59 (Court of Appeal).
7   *Re W* [2013] EWHC 1957 (Fam) (High Court).
8   *In the Matter of B (A Child)* [2013] UKSC 33 (Supreme Court) at paragraph 135.
9   *Re V (Children)* [2013] EWCA Civ 913 (Court of Appeal).

- permanence and security as the parents cannot apply for discharge
- different contact provisions
- routine life is different as an adopted child is not a 'looked after child'.

Adoption agencies

Adoption is of such significance that it can only be arranged by an adoption agency. It is illegal to make a private arrangement[10] or for money to change hands.[11] Non-agency adoptions are permitted only in limited cases such as step-parent adoptions and placements which start otherwise (e.g. private fostering or residence orders) and evolve into adoption.

Local authorities and registered adoption societies are 'adoption agencies', governed by detailed regulations[12] supplemented by statutory guidance.[13]

Basic principles

The fundamental principles set out in s1 ACA closely resemble those of CA89, which is helpful in practice as most children reach adoption via CA89. However, there are two key differences:

- s1 ACA principles apply to the adoption agency's decisions as well as the court's (s1 CA89 applies to the court alone).

- s1 ACA is adapted to reflect the specific characteristics of adoption, particularly its life-long nature and the termination of birth family relationships.

---

10   ss92 and 93 ACA.
11   s95 ACA.
12   Adoption Agencies Regulations 2005 (AAR05) as amended by the Adoption Agencies (Miscellaneous Amendments) Regulations 2013.
13   Department for Education (July 2013) *Statutory Guidance on Adoption.* Available at http://media.education.gov.uk/assets/files/pdf/s/adoption%20statutory%20guidance%202013%20final%20version.pdf, accessed on 30 March 2014.

> s1(2) ACA The paramount consideration of the court and of adoption agency must be the child's welfare throughout his life.

The last three words of s1(2) remind us that in adoption we must take a very long-term view when judging a child's best interests.

Delay

s1(3) ACA provides: 'in general, any delay in coming to the decision is likely to prejudice the child's welfare.' We know that in adoption the need to act swiftly (while still getting it right) is particularly acute: children over five wait more than a year longer than their younger counterparts to be adopted.[14] The chances of adoption being a viable care plan decline rapidly once a child passes school age.[15]

Welfare checklist

When determining the child's best interests, the court and agency must consider the matters set out in the checklist which mirrors the CA89 list, adapted to the context of adoption. Just as in CA89 the list is not exhaustive, so other relevant factors must also be considered. Nor does the list determine the priority to be given to each element – that depends on the circumstances of the particular case.

---

14   Department for Education (July 2013) *Quarterly Adoption Survey.* Available at www. gov.uk/government/uploads/system/uploads/attachment_data/file/212438/ Quarterly_adoption_survey_Q3_2012-13.pdf, accessed on 30 March 2014.

15   Ofsted figures indicate that only 6% of the children adopted in 2011–12 were more than five years old.

s1(4) ACA The court or adoption agency must have regard to the following matters (among others) –

(a) the child's ascertainable wishes and feelings regarding the decision (considered in the light of the child's age and understanding),

(b) the child's particular needs,

(c) the likely effect on the child (throughout his life) of having ceased to be a member of the original family and become an adopted person,

(d) the child's age, sex, background and any of the child's characteristics which the court or agency considers relevant,

(e) any harm (within the meaning of the Children Act 1989) which the child has suffered or is at risk of suffering,

(f) the relationship which the child has with relatives, and with any other person in relation to whom the court or agency considers the relationship to be relevant, including:

   (i) the likelihood of any such relationship continuing and the value to the child of its doing so,

   (ii) the ability and willingness of any of the child's relatives, or of any such person, to provide the child with a secure environment in which the child can develop, and otherwise to meet the child's needs,

   (iii) the wishes and feelings of any of the child's relatives, or of any such person, regarding the child.

(The word 'relative' includes parents, and 'relationships' are not restricted to legal relationships.)

Race, religion and culture

Matters such as racial origins, religion and culture are already covered by heading (d) of the checklist, but their significance in adoption was thought to warrant a separate subsection in the ACA. Following the implementation of the Children and Families Act 2014, this subsection now applies only in Wales.

> s1(5) ACA In placing the child for adoption, the adoption agency must give due consideration to the child's religious persuasion, racial origin and cultural and linguistic background.

When placing a child in a new family for life, the child's origins and identity are obviously important but they have never overridden other factors, and have only ever formed part of the child's welfare overall. s1(5) ACA never justified a child drifting in care waiting for a perfect match that never came, but was repealed in England[16] to remove any possible misunderstanding.

We know that black and minority ethnic children wait longer for adoption than others.[17] We also know that the majority of approved adopters are white.[18] Government guidance is emphatic: 'Any practice that has the effect of stopping a child from being adopted primarily because the child and prospective adopter do not share the same racial or cultural background is not child-centred and is unacceptable.'[19]

Range of powers and no order

The court and agency must consider the whole range of options available,[20] including orders under CA89, which the court can make of its own motion without application. Another option is no order at all.

Case Study: Range of orders

Linda is subject to care proceedings. Rehabilitation is ruled out but her aunt is a suitable carer and wants to adopt her. The agency and the court must weigh up all the options – long-term fostering, residence order, special guardianship or adoption. Adoption brings more security and permanence than the other options but at the price of the distortion of family relationships (aunt becomes mother; mother becomes aunt).

---

16 Repealed by s3 of the Children and Families Act 2014.
17 *Quarterly Adoption Survey* (see above).
18 Ofsted figures for all prospective adopters approved in 2011/12.
19 *Statutory Guidance on Adoption*, July 2013 (see above).
20 s1(6) ACA.

All the circumstances have to be considered to choose the right option for Linda.

Who can be adopted?

Any child can be adopted provided he is:

- under the age of 18 at the date of the application[21]
- under 19 at the date of the order[22]
- not married.[23]

Who can adopt?

A single person or a couple can adopt.[24] The usual minimum age is 21 but there is no statutory maximum. In practice adoption agencies operate policies as to adopters' ages but like all policies these must leave room for discretion in exceptional cases or they could be subject to judicial review.

A single person is usually neither married nor in a civil partnership. Someone who is in a subsisting marriage or civil partnership can only adopt alone if the couple is permanently separated, or the other half of the couple cannot be found or is incapable of applying through physical or mental ill-health.[25]

What is a couple?

Under ACA the word 'couple' includes couples (gay or straight) 'living as partners in an enduring family relationship.'[26] They do not have to be married or in a civil partnership. It is somewhat anomalous that informal couples are eligible to apply for the most drastic order, but not for less extreme options such as step-parent orders under CA89.

---

21   s49(4) ACA.
22   s47(9) ACA.
23   s47(8) ACA.
24   Ofsted figures reveal that for prospective adopters approved in 2011–12, 75% were married couples, 3% in a civil partnership, 8% unmarried opposite sex couples, 2% same sex couples, 10% single people.
25   s51(3) ACA.
26   s144(4) ACA.

Same sex couples are eligible to become adopters like any other couple and adoption agencies may not discriminate against potential adopters on the basis of their sexuality.[27]

Agency role

The agency has three main decisions:

- Is adoption in the child's best interests?
- Is a person/couple suitable to adopt?
- Is the proposed match of child/ren and adopter(s) the right one?

The Adoption Panel

Every agency must have an Adoption Panel (which can be shared with another agency). Panels do not make decisions; they make recommendations which must be taken into account by the agency's decision maker. The recommendations are:

- whether adoption is the right plan for the child in cases of parental consent (not where a placement order is required: these cases go straight to the decision maker[28] and then on to court)
- whether an applicant is a suitable person to be an adopter
- whether a proposed 'match' of child and prospective adopter(s) is the right one.

The Chair must be suitably qualified and experienced and independent of the agency.

The agency must maintain a list of people suitable to be on a Panel, including:

- one or more social workers with at least three years' experience including adoption experience
- the agency's medical adviser

---

27 Equality Act (Sexual Orientation) Regulations 2007 SI 2007/1263. Available at www.legislation.gov.uk/uksi/2007/1263/regulation/4/made, accessed on 30 March 2014. Ofsted figures reveal that 6% of adopters approved in 2011–12 were lesbian or gay (for a further 6% no information is available).
28 This means that cases in care proceedings where the care plan is for adoption do not go to Panel. The change was introduced on 1 September 2012 to eliminate duplication.

- others including people who are independent of the agency, those with relevant expertise (for example in education, mental health, race and cultural issues) and people with personal experience of adoption.

To be quorate, at least five members must be present including a suitably qualified social worker and the Chair or vice-chair. At least one person must be independent (this may be the Chair).

The Panel must take legal advice and may seek other specialist advice as necessary.

Careful minutes must be kept of all Panel meetings, their recommendations and reasons. Prospective adopters must be invited to a Panel meeting before a recommendation is reached on their case. Parents, children and prospective adopters should be notified immediately of relevant recommendations and reasons, with the clear caveat that these are recommendations, not decisions.

Agency adviser

The agency must appoint as agency adviser[29] a social worker of at least five years' standing including experience in management and adoption. The adviser is not a Panel member and does not make decisions. Instead, her role is to advise the decision maker where requested, to advise on policies and procedures and to monitor the quality of reports. She also keeps the Panel informed of the progress of cases they have considered.

Decision maker

The decision maker must be a senior person in the agency. Decisions must be much more than a rubber stamp of any social work plan or Panel recommendation. The High Court[30] has said that decision makers should consider:

- s1 ACA

- all the information in the case, including reports to Panel (first checking that these comply with regulations)

---

29 Adoption Agency Regulations 2005 reg 8.
30 *Hofstetter v. London Borough of Barnet and IRM* [2009] EWHC 3282 (Admin) (High Court).

- the stability and permanence of the relationship of any couple proposed as adopters
- the recommendation, reasons and minutes of any Panel meeting.

Then she should:

- list the material taken into account
- identify the key arguments
- consider whether the process has been fair and any Panel has addressed issues properly
- consider whether any new information impacts the decision
- state the reasons for the decision.

If the decision maker does not have sufficient information, she must ask the agency to rectify this. She should seek medical or legal advice wherever necessary.

Parents, the child and prospective adopters must be informed of relevant decisions, orally within two days and in writing within five days.

Approving a child for adoption

A permanence plan should be decided for a looked after child no later than the second statutory review (that is, after four months). The review must consider all available options to meet the child's needs. An agency can only place a child for adoption 'if it is satisfied that the child ought to be placed for adoption',[31] a conclusion which necessarily involves considering and rejecting other possibilities.

For siblings, the usual starting point is to place them together but in some cases this is not possible because of conflicting needs or simple practical reality. One mother appealed[32] against a plan that proposed adoption for the youngest two of seven siblings and foster care for the others. The Court of Appeal acknowledged that there was a fundamental difference in the plans for the siblings, but the court has to

---

31   s18(2) ACA.
32   *S-C (Children)* [2012] EWCA Civ 1800 (Court of Appeal).

do its best for each child and sometimes this requires different solutions for different children.

Where a child may be difficult to place, the agency can widen the pool of potential carers for the child by considering long-term foster carers as well as adopters.[33]

If the review decides on adoption, an adoption case record must be set up for the child. Information and counselling must be provided to the child, parents and other family members (such as siblings or grandparents) and their wishes and feelings must be sought. The agency must obtain detailed information about all aspects of the child's history, characteristics, background and personality, the report of a medical examination and full information about the birth parents including details of their health history, background, religion and culture. A detailed report known as the 'child's permanence report' (CPR) must be prepared. This report forms the basis of decisions about adoption and matching, it informs the adopters and it can be seen by the adopted person when adult. It is a vital document.

Once a decision is made that adoption is the plan for the child, family finding should start, even if a placement order is still awaited. Guidance states that babies under six months old should be placed within three months and older children within six months of the decision.

Authority to place for adoption

Even when the agency has decided that adoption is in a child's best interests, it cannot place him for adoption without statutory authority to do so. The agency is authorised to place a child for adoption if either:

- the placement is a voluntary one with full parental consent (s19 ACA)
- a court makes a placement order (made with or without parental consent) (s21 ACA).

---

33   *P (A Child)* [2008] EWCA Civ 535 (Court of Appeal).

The consent route is appropriate where parents relinquish their child; a placement order is appropriate for children coming to adoption via care proceedings.

Approving potential adopters

There is a two-stage process for adoption approvals, except for some foster carers and previously approved adopters who can by-pass Stage One, the pre-assessment process, which lasts about two months. It focuses on initial training and preparation and, through prescribed checks and references, determines whether there is any reason to exclude the applicant as a potential adopter. Adopters must undergo medicals, provide at least three references and have full criminal record checks. Convictions or cautions for some offences (such as offences against children and using child pornography) constitute an automatic bar to becoming an adopter; other offences are a matter for the agency's judgment. Prospective adopters must also be given information, counselling and training about the task of adoption. The agency then decides whether to proceed to Stage Two. If not, the adopter can use the complaints procedure.

Stage Two is the assessment process itself, which should be completed in four months. A detailed report must be compiled.[34] The applicant sees and can comment on the report, except for the references and medical report. He must also be invited to a Panel meeting. The Panel's job, after considering all the material before it, is to recommend whether the applicant is suitable to adopt a child and it can advise about the age, sex and number of children for whom he is suitable. The agency decision maker must consider the Panel's recommendation.

If the agency considers a person not suitable to adopt, it must notify him of this view and the reasons for it. He then has 40 days to make representations to the agency or to apply for an independent review panel[35] to consider his case.

Once adopters are approved, their cases must be reviewed annually.

---

34   AAR 2005 r30(1) and Parts 1 and 3 of Schedule 4.
35   The independent review mechanism is rarely used: Ofsted reports that only ten cases were referred to the IRM nationwide between 1 April 2011 and 31 March 2012.

Matching

As was said in the European Court of Human Rights,[36] adoption is about 'giving a family to a child and not the child to a family.' Matching is the delicate process of trying to find for the child – or children, given that where possible siblings should be placed together – adopter(s) with the qualities and capacities to meet as many of their needs as possible. Guidance is emphatic that rigid policies about matching in terms of the age, status, racial or cultural background are not child-centred and are not acceptable.

Both children and approved adopters who are not being considered for a match locally three months after approval should be referred to the national Adoption Register to broaden the search.

Prospective adopters must receive appropriate information about the child, including a copy of the child's permanence report, to enable them to make an informed decision. Being open with adopters, including giving information about any challenging behaviours, is important: in one case[37] adopters successfully sued a local authority for failing to inform them of the severity of the child's behavioural difficulties, which caused the adoptive mother to suffer a psychiatric illness. They would not have gone ahead with the placement had they known the truth. However, adopters' preparation and training should make them aware that no child comes with guarantees; some behaviours only manifest themselves and some secrets are only disclosed once a child feels secure.

When a proposed match is selected, an adoption placement report is presented to Panel for recommendation, then on to the decision maker.

Fostering for adoption

Amendments to regulations[38] allow approved adopters to be given temporary approval as foster carers for a named child. This enables the child to be placed at an earlier stage with the family which may

---

36   *Fretté* v. *France* [2003] 2FLR 9 (ECtHR) at paragraph 42.
37   *A & B* v. *Essex County Council* [2003] 1FLR 615 (High Court).
38   reg 25A Care Planning, Placement and Case Review (England) Regulations 2010.

become his adoptive family, thus reducing the number of moves he experiences.[39]

Parental consent

> s52(5) ACA 'Consent' means consent given unconditionally and with full understanding of what is involved; but a person may consent to adoption without knowing the identity of the persons in whose favour the order will be made.

Conditional agreement ('I agree as long as I can have contact') or without full understanding (due to learning difficulties, mental health problems or emotional distress) is not consent at all, so the case proceeds as if there is no agreement.

The ACA requires the consent of each 'parent', but in ACA (unlike CA89) the word 'parent' only means a parent with PR. So a father without PR is not required to give consent or have it dispensed with. In adoption, unmarried couples have equal rights if they are adopters but not if they are the birth family.

Placement by consent

s19 ACA applies when the birth parents unconditionally agree to their child being placed for adoption. Although not limited to any particular situation, the classic scenario is the relinquishment at birth of an unplanned baby.

In one relinquishment case[40] the mother was clear from the outset that she wanted her baby adopted. The local authority quite unnecessarily started care proceedings, meaning they had to allege likely significant harm. There was absolutely no need for this – it was exactly the situation for which s19 ACA was intended.

---

39   For guidance on fostering for adoption, see Coram (June 2013) *Fostering for Adoption: Practice Guidance*. Available at www.coram.org.uk/resource/fostering-adoption-practice-guidance, accessed on 2 April 2014.

40   *Re C (A Child)* [2007] EWCA Civ 1206 (Court of Appeal).

Case Study: A relinquished baby

Mary is an unmarried student expecting a baby conceived on a one-night stand. She asks the adoption agency to place the baby for adoption at birth.

The agency immediately begins counselling and providing information to Mary, gathering all necessary information and it can even take the first steps in family finding.

BIRTH FATHER
Mary is the only person with PR for the baby, so only her consent is required to place him for adoption. Can the father just be ignored?

VARIATION 1 – MARY NAMES THE FATHER
The agency should contact him, counsel him, seek information from him, discover his views and find out whether he has any intention of applying for PR, residence or contact,[41] making sure he is aware of his rights and encouraging him to take legal advice.

VARIATION 2 – IN SPITE OF SENSITIVE SOCIAL WORK, MARY IS UNABLE OR UNWILLING TO NAME THE FATHER
There are two options: either the agency can apply for a placement order (not normally required in a consent case) or it can apply to court[42] for directions. In a similar case[43] Munby J directed that beyond asking the mother once more for the father's name, no further steps need be taken to give him notice of intention to place the child for adoption. Sadly this means that the child will know nothing about one half of his identity and heritage and have no chance of a relationship with his father or paternal family.

---

41   AAR05 r14.
42   Family Procedure Rules 2010 r14.21.
43   *Re L: X County Council* v. *C* [2007] EWHC 1771 (Fam) (High Court).

VARIATION 3 – MARY NAMES THE FATHER BUT OBJECTS TO HIM BEING CONTACTED

This raises complicated questions of competing rights. Mary has the right to privacy. But, depending on the circumstances, the father (not to mention his extended family) may have rights under Article 8 (family life) and Article 6 (fair trial). The child's rights to a family life and to knowledge of his identity are also engaged. Each case is different and depends on its own facts. Legal advice is essential and an application to court is highly advisable. It is clear that no promises can be made to Mary to keep her secret.

In a case[44] which mirrored Mary's (young unmarried mother, one-night stand, pregnancy kept secret and a clear wish for adoption) the lower court had ordered the local authority to investigate the possibility of a home for the child in both the mother's and father's families. The Court of Appeal went back to first principles and focused on the child's welfare which governed everything, including the enquiries the authority was bound to make. Arden LJ said:

> In many cases disclosure will be in the interests of the child, but it cannot be assumed that it will always be so…exceptional situations can arise in which relatives, or even a father, of a child remain in ignorance about the child at the time of its adoption.[45]

The authority and Guardian were directed not to take any steps to identify the father or inform him of the child's birth, nor to assess the mother's family as potential carers.

In earlier cases, distinctions were drawn between fathers who had established a family life with the mother and those who had not. The Court of Appeal in *Re H; Re G*[46] said that the question was where a particular father lay on the spectrum of unmarried fathers (from a rapist at one extreme to a fully involved father at the other). There were different conclusions in the two cases before the court. One father had previously lived with the mother, they had an older child together whom the father saw and supported financially: he had a right to a family life with the new baby and had to be informed of the birth. The

---

44   *C (A Child)* [2007] EWCA Civ 1206 (Court of Appeal).

45   *C (A Child)* at paragraphs 23–24.

46   *Re H; Re G (Adoption: Consultation of Unmarried Fathers)* [2001] 1FLR 646 (Court of Appeal).

other couple had never lived together and had lost touch: that father had no Article 8 rights and no right to be informed of the baby.

Each case is different and it is important to tease out the issues. Is there a reasonable justification for the refusal? Is there any evidence to support any allegations – for example if a mother claims her parents abused her as a child, are there any records to support that claim? Or if she alleges that the birth father is violent, has she ever reported this? On the other hand, is there any positive information to indicate that wider family members might be able to offer the child a home? Arden LJ cautioned: 'the court or adoption agency cannot simply act on what the mother says. It has to examine what she says critically. It is a question of judgment whether what the mother says needs to be checked or corroborated.'[47]

A cautionary tale appeared in a case[48] where the mother relinquished her baby for adoption at birth, alleging that the putative father had been violent and insisting that he should not be contacted. The baby was placed for adoption with experienced adopters and settled beautifully. Only when the adoption application was made did the court insist that the father be informed. He turned out to be 'unimpeachable' and engaged to be married to a nursery nurse. The mother admitted that her allegations of violence were untrue. The father wanted to care for the baby, who was by then settled and bonded with the adoptive family. The failure to tackle the issue earlier meant the court was faced with an impossible choice (in the end the baby stayed with the adopters).

A similar situation arose[49] when a baby was removed under an ICO, followed by a CO and placement order. The father had been 'cruelly deceived' and only began to suspect the truth around the time the child (by then already some three years old) was placed for adoption. A DNA test confirmed paternity and he applied unsuccessfully to be allowed to contest the adoption. While he was trying to appeal this refusal, unbeknown to him or his lawyers, the adoption order was made. The Court of Appeal was disturbed by the procedure and recognised his bitter heartache but the reality was that he had never even met the child, who had been settled for over two years with the adopters. Wall P said: 'How can we, how could any judge, take the risk of disturbing that?'

---

47   *C (A Child)* [2007] EWCA Civ 1206 (Court of Appeal) at paragraph 41.
48   *Re O (Adoption: Withholding Agreement)* [1999] 1FLR 451 Court of Appeal, a case under the old adoption law, but still a striking illustration of the dilemma.
49   *C (A Child)* [2013] EWCA Civ 431 (Court of Appeal).

Case Study: A relinquished baby (continued)

Mary gives birth to baby Charlie. She confirms she wants him to be adopted and consents to him being placed for adoption.

Consent to placement

Mary's consent is required at two stages: first consent to placement, then consent to the adoption itself.

Mary can consent to placement for adoption under s19 ACA. The adoption agency contacts CAFCASS, informing them in writing that Mary is prepared to consent, providing a copy of Charlie's birth certificate, Mary's name and address, a chronology of the agency's actions and confirmation that the legal position has been explained to Mary including providing written information. A CAFCASS officer witnesses Mary's consent on the prescribed consent form.[50]

Once consent is given, the local authority is authorised to place Charlie for adoption. He immediately becomes a 'looked after' child, even before he is actually placed.[51] Mary should be invited to be involved in choosing a family for Charlie (on an anonymised basis). Mary's consent can be to placement either with specified adopters or with any adopters identified by the agency.[52] The problem with consent for an identified placement is that it becomes invalid if the placement cannot proceed for whatever reason, so it is best to ensure that there is a contingency of consent to placement with other adopters chosen by the agency in that case.

Case Study: A relinquished baby (continued)

Ann and Andrew are selected as adopters for Charlie. Mary is happy and wants to get the whole process over as quickly as possible.

---

50   Forms prescribed by the Family Procedure Rules 2010.
51   s18(3) ACA.
52   s19(1)(a) and (b) ACA.

Advance consent to adoption

Consent to the order itself is usually given during the adoption proceedings, some time after the placement. However, for a parent in Mary's position there is the option under s20 ACA of giving advance consent to the adoption order itself at the same time as agreeing to placement or at any time thereafter. The consent can be limited to an adoption order in favour of the identified adopters or to adoption by any adopters chosen by the agency.[53] Mary can also declare that she does not wish to be informed of any adoption application being made, thus choosing to have no further involvement in the process, although she can later withdraw that statement if she changes her mind.[54]

Mary's consent to Charlie's adoption is not valid until he is at least six weeks old.[55] There is a prescribed form to record her consent to adoption which again must be witnessed by a CAFCASS officer. This form is sufficient to satisfy the court of Mary's consent when the time comes to make the adoption order.

The consent form Mary proposes to sign is of profound significance; she is agreeing in advance to lose all PR for and all legal relationship with Charlie for life. Clearly, the greatest care must be taken to ensure that Mary truly understands the implications of her actions.

Parental responsibility

As soon as the agency is authorised to place a child (whether through parental consent or a placement order), the agency acquires PR.[56] Parents do not lose PR unless and until the final adoption order is made. So when Mary consents to Charlie's placement, she and the agency share PR.

When a child is placed with prospective adopters, before they even apply for an adoption order they also acquire PR.[57] So PR for Charlie is now shared four ways. However, it is an unequal relationship as the agency can restrict the exercise of PR by the other parties. The agency should be clear from the outset exactly what role Mary will continue to

---

53 s20(2) ACA.
54 s20(4) ACA.
55 s52(3) ACA.
56 s25(2) ACA.
57 s25(3) ACA.

play in Charlie's life and how much autonomy Ann and Andrew have before the adoption order is made.

Once the agency is authorised to place Charlie, contact is no longer governed by CA89. Deciding who Charlie should have contact with is an exercise of PR, so effectively is decided by the agency, subject to any contact order made by the court under s26 ACA.

Withdrawal of consent

What if Mary changes her mind? She has the right to withdraw both her consent to the placement and her advance consent to the adoption order. However, the effect of her change of heart depends on its timing. Before Mary signs her consent she must understand that she cannot simply change her mind later and undo everything.

VARIATION 1 – MARY CHANGES HER MIND AND WITHDRAWS CONSENT BEFORE CHARLIE IS PLACED WITH ANN AND ANDREW

The agency is no longer authorised to place Charlie for adoption. Without consent, only a placement order[58] can authorise placement for adoption and the agency is unlikely to have grounds to apply. Even so, Mary cannot simply go to the foster home and take Charlie – only the authority can move him.[59] Unless it applies for a placement order, the authority must return Charlie to Mary within seven days of her withdrawal of consent.[60]

VARIATION 2 – CHARLIE IS ALREADY PLACED WITH ANN AND ANDREW BEFORE MARY CHANGES HER MIND BUT THEY HAVE NOT YET APPLIED TO COURT

The agency notifies Ann and Andrew of Mary's change of heart and they have 14 days to return him to the agency (seven days if he is under six weeks old) – failure to do so is an offence. The agency must then return Charlie to Mary (again unless the agency applies for a placement order).

---

58   See Chapter 16 for more information on placement orders.
59   s30(2) ACA.
60   s31(1) ACA.

VARIATION 3 – CHARLIE IS PLACED AND ANN AND ANDREW HAVE MADE THEIR COURT APPLICATION BEFORE MARY CHANGES HER MIND

Once the application is under way, unless Charlie is still under six weeks old,[61] it is too late for Mary simply to change her mind and have Charlie back.

> s52(4) ACA The withdrawal of any consent to the placement of a child for adoption, or of any consent given under s20, is ineffective if it is given after an application for an adoption order is made.

Ann and Andrew do not have to return Charlie unless the court says so.[62] Effectively the court goes on to decide the adoption application. If the withdrawal of consent is 'ineffective', logically the consent must still stand. Mary may not now oppose the adoption order being made unless she obtains court leave to do so,[63] which will only happen if the court is satisfied that there has been a change in circumstances since she gave her consent.

The consequences of Mary's advance consent are therefore far-reaching. Once the adoption application has been launched, possibly as little as ten weeks after Mary gave consent, her chances of resisting the adoption are extremely limited.

VARIATION 4 – DARREN CONTACTS THE ADOPTION AGENCY SAYING HE HAS JUST HEARD ABOUT CHARLIE'S BIRTH, HE IS CHARLIE'S FATHER AND WANTS TO CARE FOR HIM

Darren does not have PR. Unless and until he acquires it, he is not a 'parent' whose consent is required to Charlie's adoption. Mary is unlikely to sign a PR agreement so his only option is to apply to court for a PR order under s4 CA89, which is bound to take time.

If Charlie is already placed with Mary's consent before Darren acquires PR, under s52(10) ACA Darren is treated as having consented in the same terms as Mary, so he is bound by a decision Mary took before he even knew of Charlie's existence. It is hard to see how that

---

61   *A Local Authority* v. *GC* [2008] EWHC 2555 (Fam) (High Court).
62   s32(5) ACA.
63   s47(3) ACA.

is the unconditional consent given with full understanding usually required of parents in adoption.

If Darren objects to adoption, he is in the same position as Mary in the previous examples, so it depends at what stage in the process he tries to 'withdraw' his deemed consent. If the adoption application is already underway, he must show a change in circumstances to acquire court leave to oppose the adoption order.

Minimum placement period

In normal agency cases such as Charlie's, the child must be in placement for at least ten weeks before the adopters can apply to court.[64]

This minimum period is usually sufficient in straightforward cases, but where children have more complex needs, prospective adopters may require more time before they are ready to apply and the agency may need longer to be confident the placement is working. Even if the statutory minimum period has elapsed, the court cannot make an adoption order unless it is satisfied that the agency has had sufficient opportunity to see the child at home with the adopter(s).[65] Regulations[66] prescribe the frequency of social work visits and reviews.

VARIATION 5 – THE AGENCY BECOMES CONCERNED ABOUT CHARLIE'S PLACEMENT WITH ANN AND ANDREW. ALTHOUGH THE COUPLE WANT TO PROCEED, THE AGENCY DECIDES TO REMOVE CHARLIE

The agency can give the couple seven days' notice, following which they must return Charlie.[67] In such cases the High Court has made it clear[68] that Article 6 requires fair procedures to be followed, including giving the carers a chance to answer concerns raised. The carers' potential remedy would be to seek judicial review including an interim order to prevent removal.

---

64   s42(2) ACA.
65   s42(7) ACA.
66   AAR 36.4.
67   s35(2) ACA.
68   *DL and Another* v. *LB of Newham* [2011] EWHC 1127 (Admin) (High Court).

Adoption application

All court proceedings under ACA are governed by Part 14 of the Family Procedure Rules 2010 and associated Practice Directions.

The application is made by filing at court the prescribed form, the child's birth certificate, the applicants' marriage/civil partnership certificate (if any), a copy of any placement order and a fee. In a contested case, there must also be a Statement of Facts setting out the reasons for asking the court to dispense with parental consent.

Confidentiality

Adoptions are commonly arranged on a confidential basis, even where parents actively request adoption and certainly where parents are hostile or even dangerous. Adopters can be allocated a serial number[69] which is used in all court documents instead of their names.

If a placement is confidential make sure everyone involved – including office support staff – is acutely aware of the need to maintain confidentiality and files are clearly marked to highlight the issue. There are a thousand ways for information to slip out – a parent catching sight of a file's label, an unguarded comment, or documents being sent out by mistake, not to mention social media and the power of the internet.

In one case[70] the local authority promised adopters confidentiality yet their name was mentioned to the mother and grandmother and they were telephoned from the grandmother's home with no attempt to conceal their number. The adopters then suffered a campaign of harassment which they believed was from the birth family. The court said the local authority owed the adopters a duty of care and would have been liable for damages but for a lack of evidence about the harassment.

Never guarantee confidentiality – nothing is ever 100 per cent secure; all you can promise is that everyone will do their best, following the agency's clear procedures. If maintaining confidentiality is not practical – perhaps because the child might reveal information during contact – discuss this with the prospective adopters in advance so they can consider their position before committing themselves.

---

69   Family Procedure Rules r14.2.
70   *B and B* v. *A County Council* [2006] EWCA Civ 1388 (Court of Appeal).

Court

When the application is issued, the court appoints a CAFCASS officer, fixes a first directions hearing or issues directions and asks the adoption agency to provide a copy of the consent form and a report. The case timetable is fixed, including the date of the final hearing. The court must manage the case actively including, where appropriate, encouraging co-operation and narrowing the issues in dispute. Generally, reports filed in the proceedings are confidential and are not disclosed even to the parties except that individuals have the right to see anything written about them.

Agency report

The agency must file a comprehensive report, the required content of which is set out in Practice Direction 14C,[71] including information about:

A – the report's authors and procedural matters

B – the child and birth family

C – the prospective adopter(s)

D – the placement

E – recommendations.

CAFCASS

The CAFCASS officer is to safeguard the child's interests and to file a thorough report. As well as witnessing any consent, she must investigate all relevant circumstances and provide the court with any assistance it requires.

Contact

Before making an adoption order the court must look at existing or proposed contact arrangements, obtain the views of the parties and consider whether there should be any arrangement for contact post-adoption.[72]

---

71   Available at www.justice.gov.uk/courts/procedure-rules/family/practice_directions/pd_part_14c, accessed on 30 March 2014.
72   s46(6) ACA.

The court can make a s51A ACA order for contact alongside the adoption order if that is in the child's best interests. For more on contact in adoption cases, see Chapter 16.

The adoption order

Even where consent is clear and all parties agree, the court does not simply rubber-stamp the arrangement; it must carefully consider all the elements of s1 ACA and consider the reports filed before deciding whether an adoption order is appropriate.

Unless the parent has leave to oppose the adoption, the final hearing is usually straightforward. Nevertheless, birth parents are notified of the final hearing and have the right to attend. For this reason the court may consider it inappropriate for the adopters or child to attend[73] but in this case the court should arrange for a celebratory event for adopters and child. This takes place at least 14 days after the order (the time limit for lodging an appeal) and birth parents are not notified. This symbolic occasion affirms and celebrates the momentous decision that is adoption.

Points for practice

1. Never forget the unique and far-reaching characteristics of adoption and its human rights implications.

2. Take legal advice if a mother wants her baby placed for adoption without telling the father or her extended family.

3. Regularly refer to the basic principles set out in s1 ACA.

4. Ensure birth parents are in no doubt about the enormity of giving consent under s19 or s20 ACA.

5. Adoption involves a lot of paperwork. A very organised approach is needed to get it all done in time.

6. Never guarantee confidentiality, but ensure all possible measures are taken to try to preserve it.

---

73   Guidance issued by the President of the Family Division 3 October 2008.

Chapter 16

Placement Orders, Contested Cases and Contact

Non-consensual adoption

The Supreme Court decision in the seminal care case *Re B*[1] emphasised the draconian nature of non-consensual adoption, an option to be used as a last resort where nothing else will do. Henceforth we can expect greater scrutiny and more rigorous probing by the court of any plan for adoption against parental opposition.

Following *Re B*, in *Re B-S* the Court of Appeal criticised:

> ...the recurrent inadequacy of the analysis and reasoning put forward in support of the case for adoption, both in the materials put before the court by local authorities and guardians and also in too many judgments. This is nothing new. But it is time to call a halt.[2]

Where a care plan is adoption, clear justification and reasoning is required. The Court of Appeal insisted that local authorities and Guardians should file proper evidence with a 'balance sheet' style analysis of the arguments for and against each of the possible options and making fully reasoned recommendations: 'sloppy practice must stop.'[3]

---

1   *Re B* [2013] UKSC 33 (Supreme Court) – see Chapter 13.
2   *Re B-S* [2013] EWCA Civ 1146 (Court of Appeal) at paragraph 30.
3   *Re B-S* at paragraph 40.

Placement orders

> s21 Adoption and Children Act 2002 (ACA): A placement order is an order made by the court authorising a local authority to place a child for adoption with any prospective adopters who may be chosen by the authority.

In the absence of parental consent, obtaining a placement order is the only way an adoption agency can be authorised to place a child for adoption. Generally speaking, care orders (COs) and placement orders go together; indeed, there is a statutory duty[4] to apply for a placement order if adoption is the proposed care plan in care proceedings.

Consent to placement under s19 ACA is practically incompatible with care proceedings: it cannot be validly given during care proceedings,[5] and consent previously given is invalidated if a care order is made.[6] After a care order, although valid s19 consent can be given, the agency has the option of seeking a placement order[7] anyway and is often best advised to do so.

Every effort must be made to seek a placement order at the same time as the CO to avoid the delay of more proceedings later. Logically, the court must decide on the threshold criteria first and then consider the welfare stage, care plan and placement order application, but it can hear all the evidence and arguments in the same hearing and deliver one judgment covering both applications.

s21 ACA refers to the 'local authority', but the Court of Appeal confirmed that, in applying for a placement order, the authority acts as an adoption agency.[8] It cannot make the application until it is satisfied that the child ought to be placed for adoption,[9] but thanks to amended regulations this question goes direct to the decision maker, not to Panel.

In care cases where adoption becomes the care plan, within the 26-week timescale the authority must:

---

4   s22(2) ACA.
5   s19(3)(a) ACA.
6   s19(3)(b) ACA.
7   s22(3) ACA.
8   *Re P-B (Placement Order)* [2006] EWCA Civ 1016 (Court of Appeal).
9   s18(2) ACA.

- amass the evidence to establish the threshold criteria
- carry out all necessary assessments (including parents and extended family)
- reach reasoned recommendations on the appropriate order and care plan
- seek the agency's decision
- prepare and issue a placement order application.

This requires good organisation, a keen awareness of law and procedure and a constant eye on timescales.

Grounds

The link between placement orders and COs is clear from the grounds set out in s21(2) ACA. An order can only be made if:

- the child is subject to a CO (which might have been made minutes earlier)
- the threshold criteria are met even if there is no CO
- the child has no parents or guardians (a placement order is the only option as there is no-one to give s19 ACA consent).

Adoption must be in the child's best interests, so it must be the decided plan not just a possible option. In a case[10] where two children needed a therapeutic placement before anyone could know if they would ever be adoptable, it was premature for the court to make a placement order. But there is no need for an adoptive family to be identified at this stage; indeed, a placement order can be made for a child who is suitable for adoption, even if it may ultimately prove difficult or even impossible to find adopters.[11]

Welfare

The court's paramount consideration is the child's welfare throughout his life and it must consider the welfare checklist and other factors set out in s1 ACA.

---

10   *Re T (Children: Placement order)* [2008] EWCA Civ 248 (Court of Appeal).
11   *Re S-H (A Child)* [2008] EWCA Civ 493 (Court of Appeal).

Parental consent

For each person with parental responsibility (PR) the court must:

- be satisfied that s/he consents unconditionally and with full understanding to the child's placement for adoption, or
- dispense with his/her consent.

It is possible for one parent to consent and the other's consent to be dispensed with, or for both parents to have consent dispensed with but on different grounds.

Dispensing with consent

In reality, where parents object to adoption, the real contest (indeed, usually the only contest) is at the placement order stage, not the adoption itself where the parents are only allowed to contest if they have leave to do so. Furthermore, at the placement order stage, the child has not yet been placed, whereas by the adoption hearing the child is settled, leaving the parents with an uphill struggle even if, exceptionally, they are allowed to contest. The placement order is therefore the most crucial legal step in moving a child's case towards adoption.

The grounds for dispensing with parental consent are the same for placement orders and adoption orders. There are three possibilities:

- the parent/guardian cannot be found
- the parent/guardian is incapable of giving consent
- 'the welfare of the child requires the consent to be dispensed with.'[12]

CANNOT BE FOUND

The court expects that extensive efforts have been made to find parents before dispensing with their consent on this ground. If you are involved in such a case, list all the avenues pursued and seek directions as to whether anything further should be done.

---

12   s52(1)(a) and (b) ACA.

INCAPABLE OF GIVING CONSENT

This may be established through mental illness or learning disability sufficiently profound to prevent a parent from understanding the issues, or through physical incapacity (such as a coma). In such cases, her interests are represented by the Official Solicitor.

WELFARE

In practice, this is by far the most common ground for dispensation with consent.

In a leading case,[13] Wall LJ said that the language of the Act is straightforward: the court must consider whether the welfare of the child requires adoption. It is important to note that the word in the statute is 'requires', a strong word, meaning more than something which is optional, reasonable, desirable or simply convenient. It is also important to note that what is required is adoption, not just removal from home or even long-term placement elsewhere. As the Supreme Court emphasised in *Re B*, adoption is a last resort where nothing else will do. Proportionality demands nothing less, always remembering that adoption is the most drastic interference possible with family life.

s1(1) ACA is pivotal in the welfare decision; the child's welfare throughout his life is the paramount consideration, considering the welfare checklist with its recognition of the life-long effect of adoption.

How can parents oppose? Other than repeating their arguments against the CO (denying significant harm or responsibility for it) their arguments are likely to centre on the necessity for an adoption plan, for example arguing for:

- another chance at rehabilitation immediately or keeping the door open for another chance in the future
- family placement
- fostering to preserve the child's identity and contact, perhaps especially where there are other siblings who are not to be placed for adoption
- a less drastic order, such as special guardianship.

---

13   *Re P (A Child)* [2008] EWCA Civ 535 (Court of Appeal).

What if a parent simply cannot accept adoption as a matter of principle? One case[14] dealt with a mother's opposition to adoption partly on religious grounds – she was a Muslim and adoption is not recognised under Sharia law. Munby J held that a parent's religious belief can never be the deciding factor when considering a child's future. The mother's human right to freedom of religion (Article 9) was qualified by the child's right to a family life (Article 8), albeit in a substitute family. Her beliefs in themselves may be reasonable but her withholding of consent was not.

Placement order application

The procedure for a placement order is similar to an adoption application except that the local authority is the applicant and the child is an automatic respondent. The authority must file a statement of the facts relied on in any application to dispense with parental consent. If the application is made alongside care proceedings, the court gives directions to deal with both applications together.

Contact with placement orders

Before making a placement order, the court must consider and invite the parties to comment on any proposed contact arrangements.[15] On application by any of the parties or of its own accord, the court can make a contact order under s26 ACA alongside a placement order. Such contact orders can later be varied or revoked by the court and contact can be suspended for up to seven days in an emergency. However, generally agencies much prefer to be left with the discretion to arrange contact without being bound by a court order.

As a placement order comes before the child is placed – indeed, in some cases an adoptive family may never be found – contact under a placement order may differ from that envisaged under an eventual adoption. Arrangements need to be flexible enough to adapt as the situation develops, for example scaling down contact towards a goodbye visit prior to placement.

---

14 *Re S; Newcastle City Council v. Z* [2005] EWHC 1490 (Fam) (High Court), a case heard at the very end of the old legislation but with an eye to ACA.

15 s27(4) ACA.

Effect of a placement order

Once a placement order is made:

- the agency is authorised to place the child for adoption
- the agency obtains PR for the child, shared with the parent(s) and (upon placement) with the prospective adopters, but the agency decides how PR is exercised
- the CO is suspended (not discharged)
- Children Act 1989 (CA89) contact orders and provisions are superseded by ACA
- no-one other than the agency can remove the child from the placement.[16]

Duration of placement orders

A placement order is intended to be a step towards adoption, not a long-term order. It therefore lasts until either:

- an adoption order is made, when it is automatically discharged
- it is revoked
- the child turns 18 or marries under 18.

Revocation

Placement orders can be revoked under s24 ACA, applying the s1 ACA principles. If a placement order is revoked, any pre-existing CO revives. The local authority and the child have a right to apply for revocation but others (including parents) can only apply if:

- the child is not placed for adoption and
- they obtain court leave.

As placement orders are intended as a step towards adoption, revocation could be appropriate if it becomes clear that adoption is no longer viable or the right plan. One such case[17] centred on failure to thrive, but the child's weight actually declined in foster care and there was a very serious professional disagreement about the way forward. Even though

---

16   s34(1) ACA.
17   *Re S-H (A Child)* [2008] EWCA Civ 493 (Court of Appeal).

there was no realistic prospect of a return home, it was no longer clear that adoption was the right plan so the Court of Appeal granted the mother leave to apply to revoke the order.

To obtain leave the parent must first show a change of circumstances since the order was made. This is necessary but not sufficient – the court will also consider the child's welfare and the prospects of success of the substantive application.[18] The application for leave does not stop the agency placing the child with prospective adopters but if the agency knows an application is pending it would not be appropriate to do so without court leave.[19] Placing deliberately to frustrate a leave application could lead to judicial review. If leave is granted and the revocation application goes ahead, the child cannot be placed without court permission.

Changing names on placement

The interim period in which a child is placed for adoption but not yet adopted can be a delicate one. Adopters may want to start to call the child by their own surname, to claim the child as part of their family and to avoid compromising their confidentiality but the law is clear: while a child is placed for adoption, in the absence of written consent of parents with PR or court permission, no-one can 'cause the child to be known by a new surname'.[20] In a case where surname change is particularly important, court leave should be sought at the placement order hearing.

The ACA does not mention first names, but the High Court considered the issue in a case[21] involving two children whose first names were changed, one because the prospective adopters did not like the child's name, the other because the foster carers already had a child with the same name in placement. The court was very clear that a child has a right to the name s/he is registered with. Adopters have no right to change a child's name until the adoption order is made, and foster carers are never entitled to do so. Local authorities should make this plain

---

18   *Warwickshire County Council* v. *M* [2007] EWCA (Civ) 1084 (Court of Appeal).
19   *Re F (Placement Order: Revocation)* [2008] EWCA Civ 439 (Court of Appeal).
20   s28(2) and (3) ACA.
21   *Re D, L and LA (Care: Change of Forename)* [2003] 1FLR 339 (High Court), a case heard under the old legislation but the principles still apply.

to carers at the outset. If there is a good reason to change a name the authority should consult parents and approach the court if necessary.

Parental consent to adoption

The issue of parental consent, already considered when the placement order was made, has to be dealt with again on the application for the adoption order itself. The wording of s47 ACA is convoluted but, in essence, for an adoption order to be granted, parental consent must be given or dispensed with. The grounds for dispensing with consent to an adoption order are the same as for a placement order. Parents are only entitled to contest adoption applications if they have court leave and they can only be granted leave if there has been a change in circumstances since the placement order was made or consent was given.[22]

A change in circumstances is necessary but not sufficient – the court then goes on to evaluate the case to decide whether to give leave. Factors include the prospects of success in resisting adoption (not necessarily in securing the child's return) and the impact on the child of leave being granted or not. The child's welfare throughout his life is paramount.

What kind of changed circumstances justify allowing a parent a second bite of the cherry? Until the Court of Appeal case of Re B-S,[23] cases were very strongly in favour of adopters and the birth parents' chances by the time the case reached the final adoption hearing (when the child is, by definition, settled with a new family) were vanishingly small. The parents' status as parties to the final adoption hearing seemed almost illusory.

The Court of Appeal signalled a change in approach. It cast doubt on previous cases which suggested that leave would be given only in exceptionally rare cases and stressed that this provision is intended to be a meaningful remedy to the potential benefit of parents and children, not a hurdle which is practically insurmountable.

In deciding whether to give leave, the court must weigh up all the positives and negatives, considering the long term, the child's welfare throughout his life. Logically, the greater the change in circumstances and the stronger the parent's grounds for seeking leave, the stronger must be the welfare arguments to refuse it. The fact that the child is in

---

22   s47(5) ACA.
23   *Re B-S (Children)* [2013] EWCA Civ 1146 (Court of Appeal).

placement is not determinative, although the adverse effect of disturbing arrangements is a factor to consider. Potential disruption to the adopters (and thus the child) caused by a contested adoption is not a strong factor.

However, notwithstanding the Court of Appeal's comments, in the case itself the mother's appeal against refusal to grant leave was dismissed in spite of an 'astonishing' improvement in her circumstances. Time will tell whether further human rights challenges will follow. Until then, it remains difficult to envisage a case in which a parent will be given leave to oppose, still less successfully contest, an adoption application solely on the basis of changes to her own situation. However, things may be different if such changes are coupled with problems in the prospective adoptive placement. One mother was given leave to oppose an adoption because in addition to significant progress on her part, the prospective adopters had also separated and only the prospective adoptive father (whose new partner was expecting a baby) continued to pursue the adoption application.[24]

Adoption and contact

The classic legal model of adoption envisaged a clean break between the child and birth family, but today older children with memories of and attachments to their birth families are placed for adoption and we know more about children's need to understand their identity and origins. In consequence, adoptions have become increasingly 'open'. However, the term 'open adoption' has no legal definition and there is no common understanding about its use, which ranges from the mildest degree of information sharing to adoption with direct contact. To avoid misunderstanding, it is best simply to specify the arrangements for each case.

The child's needs for contact should be analysed before even searching for a family and it will of course have been considered at the placement order stage. Contact with people other than parents (especially siblings) must not be overlooked. An ideal placement may not exist, in which case some compromise has to be made between the child's conflicting needs for a permanent home and for ongoing contact.

---

24   *Re L (Leave to Oppose Making of Adoption Order)* [2013] EWCA Civ 1481 (Court of Appeal).

Before making an adoption order, the court must consider existing or proposed arrangements for contact and obtain the parties' views.[25] Contact arrangements should be separately considered for each child remembering that plans may be different among children in the same family, or different contact may be appropriate between the child and various members of the family. In practice, direct face-to-face contact remains rare in adoption, but some form of letterbox contact, such as an annual letter, perhaps with a photograph, at least for a few years, is quite common. However, each child's case should receive individual consideration rather than imposing a standard policy: there should be no sense of a formulaic response. The wishes and feelings of the child and the adopters are of course very important; they are the ones who will have to live with its consequences of any arrangement. We must always remember that, as most children are adopted under the age of five, we are considering a very long timescale and imposing an inflexible solution is unlikely to be appropriate in the long term.

The agency should be able to explain to the court:

- the purpose of contact
- the reasons for the type and frequency of contact proposed
- how long the arrangement is to continue, when and by whom it is to be reviewed
- what happens if contact is not taken up or if there are problems
- what happens if the child's needs change or he later wants more/less contact/none at all.

Contact orders

When an agency has placed or is authorised to place a child for adoption and when a court is making or has made an adoption order, contact is covered by s51A ACA[26] instead of s8 CA89. Orders for contact, including to a birth family member, can be made at the same time as the adoption order or any time afterwards. An application can be made by the adopters, the child or anyone else who has court leave. In deciding whether to give leave, the court must consider any risk of causing

---

25   s46(6)ACA.
26   s51A ACA introduced by s9 of the Children and Families Act 2014, in force from 22 April 2014.

disruption to the child, the applicant's connection with the child and the views of the child and the adopters. Such an order can be varied or revoked later. The possibility of orders made or varied post-adoption may arguably undermine the permanence and security of adoption.

Time will tell whether the amended law will lead to a change in the court's approach. Traditionally, courts are generally reluctant to make contact orders in adoption. If contact is agreed, the court prefers to trust the adopters to meet the child's needs as time goes on, rather than impose an order, and this is of course consistent with the 'no order principle'.

The Court of Appeal[27] is clear that the imposition of contact orders not agreed by the adopters is 'extremely unusual'. This principle applies to contact even at a 'seemingly innocuous' level. Thorpe LJ found[28] that ordering adopters to provide a single passport-sized photograph once a year paid 'scant regard to the interests and rights of the child whose welfare after all has to be paramount in the exercise of these discretionary decisions', going on to ask:

> Does it not amount to a violation of the rights of the child that without any benefit to her, without any need in her, she is the participant in a process which…may be impossible for her to understand in years to come as she acquires understanding of her past and of the sort of father that she has?[29]

One case[30] in which a contact order was made alongside an adoption order against the wishes of the adopter was unusual in that the adopter had been the child's foster carer since he was a baby and contact had been occurring once a month with the grandmother who also cared for the child's half-siblings. The judge was clearly torn but ultimately decided that to protect the child's best interests throughout his life, contact was necessary so he imposed an order. However, if he had had to choose between adoption and contact, he would have chosen adoption without hesitation; as it was, it was possible to have both. The highly

27 Wall LJ in *Re R (Adoption: Contact)* [2005] EWCA Civ 1128 (Court of Appeal), cited with approval in subsequent cases.
28 *C (Children)* [2012] EWCA Civ 1281 (Court of Appeal).
29 *Re C* at paragraph 6.
30 *MF v. LB of Brent & Ors* [2013] EWHC 1838 (Fam) (High Court).

unusual facts of the case mean that it is unlikely to unleash a flood of contact orders attached to contact orders.

Where contact is agreed but an order is not appropriate, the best solution is often to add a recital to the order.[31] A recital is not part of the order so is not directly enforceable, but it records on the face of the order that it is made on the understanding that an agreement is in place.

What if promised contact does not happen?

A court order is directly enforceable; an agreement for post-adoption contact is not. If adopters do not stick to an agreement for contact, an application for an order might be made later but court leave will be required first.

The Court of Appeal[32] has said that adopters should always give reasons for altering an agreement made at the time of adoption and the court can consider whether those reasons are adequate. In that case, adopters had reduced contact between their adopted seven-year-old and her 17-year-old sister from three meetings a year to one, with two-way indirect contact. This was because they felt the direct contact had an adverse effect on their child, and they worried about security as the sister retained links with the birth mother. The local authority viewed the stability of the placement as the priority. The 17-year-old wanted to apply to court to restore the original agreement but the court found the adopters' position was reasonable. If, however, they had completely gone back on their previous agreement, the application would have been allowed to proceed.

The message for practice is clear: adopters should never agree to – and should not be pressurised into agreeing to – any contact arrangement which they are not absolutely committed to keep. Contact must be a key part of the training and preparation of adopters and the significance of agreeing to any sort of contact must be clearly explained to them.

31   A recital was held to be more appropriate than an order in *N* v. *B & Ors* [2013] EWHC 820 (Fam) (High Court).

32   *Re R (Adoption: Contact)* [2006] 1 FLR 373 (Court of Appeal), a case heard at the very end of the old legislation but the same principles still apply.

Points for practice

1. Whenever possible, seek a placement order at the same time as a care order.

2. Prepare with your legal team your arguments to justify adoption and dispense with parental consent for the placement order; this, not the adoption, is the key stage at which to deal with parental opposition.

3. Carefully reason through plans for contact between the child and significant people both before and after an adoptive placement is found, remembering the very long-term nature of adoption.

4. Make sure adopters are truly committed before any contact is offered.

Appendix 1A

Children Act 1989 Key Sections by Number

Section	Subject
1(1)	welfare principle
1(2)	no delay principle
1(2)(A)	presumption of involvement of both parents in child's life
1(3)	welfare checklist
1(5)	no order principle
1(6)	parental involvement in child's life not to put child at risk of harm
2	parental responsibility (PR) – general
2(7)	ability of one person with PR to make decisions
3	PR – meaning
4	PR orders and agreements for unmarried fathers
4A	PR orders and agreements for step-parents
4ZA	PR for second female parent
5	guardianship for orphans
7	welfare reports to court
8	child arrangements orders (residence, contact), prohibited steps and specific issue orders
10	right to apply for s8 orders
11A–P	contact activity directions, monitoring, enforcement orders and compensation orders
14A–G	special guardianship orders
16	family assistance orders
17	children in need

Section	Subject
17(10)	definition of children in need
20	accommodating children voluntarily
22	general duties to looked after children
22A–G	placement of looked after children (order of precedence)
23A–E	duties to young people aged 16+
24A–D	after care provisions
25	secure accommodation
25A/26	independent reviewing officers
27	other agencies' duties to assist in providing services to children in need
31	threshold criteria for care/supervision orders
31(9) and (10)	definition of 'harm'
33	effect of a care order
35	effect of a supervision order
37	reports to court where court suspects significant harm
38	interim care and supervision orders
38(6)	assessments under interim orders
39	variation and discharge of care orders
43	child assessment orders
44	emergency protection orders (EPOs)
46	police protection
47	duty to investigate child protection referrals
48	warrants etc. to assist with executing EPOs
91(14)	court's power to prohibit further applications
Schedule 2 part 1	strategic duties and services for families
Schedule 2 part 2	looked after children

Children Act 1989 Key Sections by Subject

Subject	Section
Accommodation	20
After care provisions	24A-D
Assessments under interim orders	38(6)
Care proceedings – grounds	31
Care order – effect	33
Child arrangements order	8
Child assessment order	43
Child protection investigation	47
Child in need	17
Child in need – definition	17(10)
Child in need – services	Schedule 2 part 1
Contact – child in care	34
Contact – private law	8
Discharge/variation of care orders	39
Discharge/variation of s8 orders	8(2)
Duties to people aged 16+	23A–D
Emergency protection orders	44
Guardianship (orphans)	5
Harm	31(9) and (10)
Independent reviewing officers	26
Interim care/supervision orders	38
Looked after children – duties	22, schedule 2 part 2
Looked after children – placement	22A–G

Subject	Section
No delay principle	1(2)
No order principle	1(5)
Other agencies' duties to assist – child protection	47
Other agencies' duties to assist – child in need	27
Parental involvement in child's life not to put child at risk of harm	s1(6)
Police protection	46
PR – exercise by one person	2(7)
PR – general	2
PR – meaning	3
PR orders/agreements – fathers	4
PR orders/agreements – step-parents	4A
Presumption of involvement of both parents in child's life	s1(2)(A)
Preventing future applications	91(14)
Prohibited steps orders	8
Report to court – suspected significant harm	37
Report to court – welfare	7
Residence orders	8
Section 8 orders – right to apply	10
Secure accommodation	25
Special guardianship orders	14A–G
Specific issue orders	8
Supervision orders – effect	35
Threshold criteria	31
Warrants etc. to assist executing EPOs	48
Welfare checklist	1(3)
Welfare principle	1(1)

Appendix 2

Order for Residence, Special Guardianship and Adoption at a Glance

Residence	Special Guardianship	Adoption
Children Act 1989 (CA89)	CA89	Adoption and Children Act 2002 (ACA)
s8 CA89	s14A–G CA89	Whole Act
s1 CA89	s1 CA89	s1ACA
Child's welfare paramount	Child's welfare paramount	Child's welfare throughout his life paramount
s1(3) CA89 welfare checklist	s1(3) CA89 welfare checklist	s1(4) ACA welfare checklist
Parents automatic right to apply; some others have automatic right; others need leave	Parents cannot apply; some have automatic right, others need leave	Only adopters approved by an agency can apply
Court may request welfare report s7	Court must consider local authority report	Court must consider adoption agency report
Determines with whom child lives	Appoints special guardian (SG) who decides where child lives	Appoints adopters who decide where child lives
Confers PR shared equally	Confers PR – shared but can be exercised to the exclusion of others	Confers exclusive PR
Parent(s) retain PR shared equally	Parent(s) retain PR but SG can exercise exclusively	Parent(s) lose PR
Not a 'parent'	Not a 'parent'	Parent

Residence	Special Guardianship	Adoption
Family relationships do not change	Family relationships do not change	All relationships with birth family end; new relationships created with adoptive family
No change to inheritance	No change to inheritance	Inheritance dependent on relationships transfers from birth to adoptive family
No name change without consent of all with PR or court order	No name change without consent of all with PR or court order	Automatic right to change child's name
No removal from UK for over one month without consent of all with PR or court order	No removal from UK for over one month without consent of all with PR or court order	No limit on removal from UK
Order lasts to 18	Order lasts to 18	Lifelong
Can be revoked on application – parents have right to apply	Can be revoked on application but parents cannot apply without leave	Irrevocable
s8 order for contact can be made	s8 order for contact can be made	s51A ACA order for contact to be made
Local authority discretion to provide financial support including possible financial support	Local authority duty to assess support needs and devise package including possible financial support	Agency duty to assess support needs and devise package

Appendix 3

Contact Aide-memoire

Guiding principles

- The child's welfare is paramount (s1(1) CA89).
- The welfare checklist applies (s1(3) CA89). The child's wishes and feelings must be considered.
- Delay is likely to be harmful (s1(2) CA89).
- Contact must be safe.
- Everyone's right to family life must be respected (Article 8) and competing rights balanced.

Starting point
If the person concerned has a presumption of contact such as:

- statutory presumption of reasonable contact for parents of children in care (s34 CA89)
- principle that children should have contact with their parents

then proportionality requires the least restrictive arrangement consistent with the child's welfare. Consider the advantages and disadvantages of each option to find the best solution overall. Consider the child's needs in the round.

1. Informal arrangements
Can contact be left free and unrestricted? If not, to what level of detail must it be prescribed?

2. Direct contact
Can the child have face-to-face contact? Consider:

Staying contact

- frequency
- length of stay
- special arrangements for birthdays, Christmas/other festivals, school holidays, etc.

Visiting contact

- frequency
- length
- venue
- attending school concerts, sports days, etc.
- special arrangements for birthdays, Christmas/other festivals, school holidays, etc.

Conditions/safeguards

Are conditions needed to make contact work? What and why? For how long? Does it need review? Consider:

- who can attend (parent alone or new partners, extended family, etc.)
- contact handover arrangements
- venue (parent's home or a neutral venue)
- pre-conditions (e.g. parent not to be drunk on arrival)
- supervision:
  - why
  - by whom (social work professional/community centre/family member/trusted friend)
  - what level of supervision (close supervision or periodical monitoring).

3. Indirect contact
As well as or instead of direct contact, consider:

Type of contact

- telephone calls
- webcam video calls
- text messages
- letters
- emails
- cards
- social networking sites
- presents (how often? what value?)
- photographs or video messages
- progress/school reports.

Frequency

Times

Duration

Special arrangements for Christmas/other festivals, birthdays, school holidays, etc.

Conditions/safeguards
Are conditions needed to make contact work? What? Why? Consider:

- limitations on type of contact
- reciprocal or one-way
- monitoring/censoring content
- confidentiality of addresses/phone numbers/school details
- value and frequency of gifts.

4. For all contact
Consider:

- how contact fits in the child's life as a whole (taking a short- and long-term view);
- when and by whom arrangements should be reviewed
- what happens if there is a problem.

Appendix 4

Care and Accommodation at a Glance

In Care	Accommodated
s31 CA89	s20 CA89
Child subject to court order	No court involvement
Local authority has PR	Local authority has no PR
Parents retain PR	Parents retain full PR
Local authority can limit parents' exercise of PR when necessary in child's interests	Parents delegate aspects of PR to local authority
Lasts until 18 unless order discharged	Lasts as long as parents require
Parents cannot remove child from placement	Parents with PR can remove child from placement at any time without notice
s8 or special guardianship orders ended by care order	s8 or special guardianship orders remain in force
Contact regulated by s34	Contact regulated by s8
Child is 'looked after'	Child is 'looked after'

Appendix 5

Summary of Duties to 'Looked After' Children

Welfare
Safeguard and promote welfare (s22(3)(a) CA89).

Services
Use any services available to children living with their own parents (s22(3)(b) CA89).

Consultation
Ascertain the wishes and feelings of the child, parents, anyone else with PR and any other relevant person before making any decision about a looked after child (s22(4) CA89). Give these due consideration (s22(5) CA89).

Religion, culture, etc.
Give due consideration to the child's religious persuasion, racial origin and cultural and linguistic background in making any decision for a looked after child (s22(5)(c) CA89).

Placement
Provide accommodation for a looked after child by placing him with a parent or someone else with PR; if not possible, with a relative, friend or other connected person registered as a foster carer; if not possible, in the most appropriate placement.

If possible, place near home, avoid disrupting education, place with siblings and in accommodation suitable for any disabilities (s22C CA89). s98 of the Children and Families Act 2014 obliges local authorities to enable former relevant child to stay put with former foster carer to the age of 21. Financial support must be provided.

Care Planning, Placement and Case Review (England) Regulations 2010 apply.

Family and friends carers must be registered as foster carers following Fostering Services (England) Regulations 2011.

Secure accommodation

Child can only be placed in secure accommodation for more than 72 hours with a court order under s25 CA89.

Reviews

Appoint an Independent Reviewing Officer for each child.

Reviews to be conducted following Care Planning, Placement and Case Review (England) Regulations 2010. First review within 20 days, second within three months, thereafter every six months (minimum),

Contact

Arrange contact:

- for child in care – for anyone with a presumption of reasonable contact (s34(1) CA89) or a contact order (s34(2) or (3) CA89)
- for accommodated child – for anyone with a contact order (s8 CA89).

Promote contact between child and parents, anyone with PR and any relative, friend or other person connected to him unless not practicable or consistent with his welfare (Schedule 2 paragraph 15 CA89).

Arrange independent visitor for child who has infrequent/no visits (Schedule 2 paragraph 17 CA89).

Informing parents

Inform parents and others with PR of child's address unless child is in care and giving information would prejudice his welfare (Schedule 2 paragraphs 15(2) and (4) CA89).

Leaving care/accommodation

Advise, assist and befriend all looked after children to promote their welfare when they are no longer looked after (Schedule 2 paragraph 19A CA89).

16- and 17-year-olds

For 'eligible' children (16- and 17-year-olds looked after for at least 13 weeks after the age of 14 and continuing beyond the age of 16):

- assess needs for advice, assistance and support while being looked after and thereafter
- prepare and keep under review a pathway plan
- provide a personal adviser while he is looked after (Schedule 2 para 19B CA89).

For 'relevant' children (young people aged 16 or 17 who were 'eligible' but are no longer looked after):

- keep in touch
- appoint a personal adviser
- assess needs for advice, assistance and support
- prepare and keep under review a pathway plan
- safeguard and promote welfare including maintaining him, providing accommodation, and providing assistance for education, training or employment (s23B CA89).

18–21-year-olds (and beyond if still in education)

For former relevant children (i.e. over-18-year-olds who were previously 'relevant' or 'eligible'):

- try to keep in touch
- provide and keep under review a pathway plan
- provide a personal adviser

- assist with expenses for employment, education or training
- give other assistance for his welfare (s23C CA89).

Advice and assistance

For under-21-year-olds who were looked after at any time between 16 and 18:

- contact him as appropriate
- advise and befriend
- assist, including providing cash (in exceptional circumstances)
- contribute to expenses for employment, education or training.

Appendix 6

Emergency Protection Order Aide-memoire

1. Take legal advice

2. With your lawyers, analyse the grounds for emergency action

- Exactly what significant harm do you believe the child will suffer if action is not taken?
- How pressing is the risk – is it imminent?
- How serious is the risk – is the child in danger?
- Is there evidence to substantiate your belief?
- Is there any other way to manage the risk?
- Is it a true emergency? What would happen if there were a delay of one to three days (to allow care proceedings to start)?
- What are the implications of (a) taking or (b) not taking emergency action for the human rights of:
  - o the child (Article 2 – right to life; 3 – protection from torture, etc.; 8 – family life)
  - o the parents (Article 6 – fair trial; 8 – family life).

3. Consider notice to the parents

- Start with the presumption that they should be given notice.
- Is there a compelling case to proceed without notice?

- Exactly what do you believe will happen if you give notice?
- What is your evidence to justify that belief?

4. Application

- Seek legal representation.
- Present the court with detailed and precise evidence.
- Present the court with copies of any relevant documents (assessments, reports, letters, Case Conference minutes, etc.).
- Ensure the evidence is accurate, balanced and fair.
- Ensure the court is fully and fairly informed of the applicable law.
- Keep a full note of the hearing.
- Make any other necessary applications – exclusion requirement, warrant to enter and search premises, warrant to search for other children or warrant for police to assist.

5. Serving the order

- Serve the order as soon as possible.
- Give parents a copy of all documents presented to court.
- Give parents a note of the evidence and submissions presented to court.

6. Acting on the order

- Consider whether implementing the order is necessary and justified.
- Review the case daily.
- Arrange reasonable contact for the child and parents.

Appendix 7

Care and Supervision Orders at a Glance

Care order	Supervision order
Threshold criteria s31CA89 must be met	Threshold criteria s31CA89 must be met
Child's welfare is paramount s1(1) CA89	Child's welfare is paramount s1(1) CA89
Welfare checklist applies s1(3) CA89	Welfare checklist applies s1(3) CA89
Local authority has PR	Local authority does not have PR
Parents retain PR but local authority can limit their exercise of PR where necessary	Parents retain full PR
Local authority responsible for child's accommodation and maintenance	Local authority duty to advise, assist and befriend
Local authority decides placement	Parents decide where child lives
Parents cannot remove child from placement	Parents can move child where they like
Local authority can move the child from placement (including placement at home) without notice	Local authority cannot remove the child from home without fresh legal authority
Order lasts until child 18 unless discharged by court	Order lasts one year. Extension possible to maximum three years
Order continues unless ended by court	Order ends unless continued by court
Child is a 'looked after child'	Child is not looked after
s8 orders incompatible with care order	s8 orders can exist alongside supervision order
Contact regulated by s34 CA89	Contact regulated by s8 CA89
Can be discharged or replaced by a supervision order	Can be discharged. Cannot be replaced by a care order – fresh application needed

List of Statutes

311

List of Cases

Index